STUDIES ON THE
ANCIENT PALESTINIAN WORLD

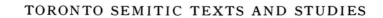

TORONTO SEMITIC TEXTS AND STUDIES

Studies on the Ancient Palestinian World

PRESENTED TO PROFESSOR F. V. WINNETT

on the occasion of his retirement

1 July 1971

EDITED BY

J. W. WEVERS AND

D. B. REDFORD

UNIVERSITY OF TORONTO PRESS

TORONTO SEMITIC TEXTS AND STUDIES

edited by J. W. Wevers and D. B. Redford

1

Essays on the Ancient Semitic World

2

Studies on the Ancient Palestinian World

© University of Toronto Press 1972

Printed in U.S.A. for
University of Toronto Press
Toronto and Buffalo

ISBN 0–8020–5254–1
Microfiche ISBN 0–8020–0033–9
LC 79–151397

Preface

The present volume of essays is offered as a tribute to our beloved friend and colleague Professor F. V. Winnett, upon his retirement. In keeping with Professor Winnett's province of scholarly endeavour the topics range over the wide fields of biblical exegesis and textual studies, and Palestinian archaeology. Disparate as these several disciplines may appear at first glance, there is an underlying unity here that links the essays in the common aim of elucidating and explicating the text of the Old Testament. As more than one scholar has recently noted, modern biblical research is coming more and more to involve 'the treatment of details which seem to be incidental or accidental. Narratives which contain names or specific forms of cultic actions, patterns of thought, or other concrete cultural features which can be checked by extra-Biblical sources can thus be controlled' (G. Mendenhall and G. E. Wright, *The Bible and the Ancient Near East* [New York, 1965], p. 41). The painstaking, detailed work envisaged by these guide-lines will involve specialists to a degree unknown before. Increasingly biblical scholars are feeling the need to provide a second string to their bows, and simple exegesis is finding such bizarre bed-fellows as anthropology, field archaeology, art history, linguistics, and economics.

The papers which follow well exemplify this current need to bring specialized skills to bear upon the interpretation of Scripture. In the area of field archaeology Professor James B. Pritchard writes on 'An Incense Burner from Tell es-Saʿidiyeh, Jordan Valley,' Professor William L. Reed contributes a study on 'The Archaeological History of Elealeh in Moab,' and Dr A. D. Tushingham publishes 'Three Byzantine Tombstones from Dhībân, Jordan.' These three papers, each from a scholar who has worked in the field with Professor Winnett, contain unpublished material of great interest, and are therefore welcome members of the collection. The text and versions of the Old Testament have attracted the attention of two of the contributors. Professor E. J. Revell continues his studies in Hebrew vocalization and pointing in a paper entitled 'The Placing of the Accent Signs in Biblical Texts with Palestinian Pointing.' Pursuant to his studies in the field of Septuagint, Professor John W. Wevers writes on 'The Textual Affinities of the Arabic Genesis of Bib. Nat. Arab. 9.' Professor R. J. Williams' contribution is in the field of Hebrew syntax, and deals specifically with 'Energic Verbal Forms in Hebrew.' In the broader area of biblical history and exegesis the papers range over four topics which are hotly debated in scholarly circles at present. Professor W. S. McCullough writes on 'Israel's Eschatology from Amos to Daniel,' Professor Robert C. Culley on 'Oral Tradition and Historicity,' Professor N. E. Wagner on 'Abraham and David?' and Professor D. B. Redford on 'The Taxation System of Solomon.' Professor A. K. Grayson edits a new text from Baghdad which sheds more light on the final days of Assyria. Professor Winnett's bibliography was prepared by his student, Mrs Ann Bembenek (née Rowley), M.A.

This work has been published with the help of grants from the Humanities Research Council, using funds provided by the Canada Council, and from the Publications Fund of the University of Toronto Press.

TORONTO   J.W.W.

June 1969   D.B.R.

Contents

Contributors

James B. Pritchard
University of Pennsylvania Museum, Philadelphia

William L. Reed
Department of Religion, Texas Christian University

A. D. Tushingham
Royal Ontario Museum, Toronto

E. J. Revell
*Department of Near Eastern Studies, Victoria College,
University of Toronto*

John W. Wevers
*Department of Near Eastern Studies, University College,
University of Toronto*

Ronald J. Williams
*Department of Near Eastern Studies, University College,
University of Toronto*

W. S. McCullough
*Department of Near Eastern Studies, University College,
University of Toronto*

Robert C. Culley
Faculty of Divinity, McGill University, Montreal

N. E. Wagner
Department of Near Eastern Studies, Waterloo Lutheran University

D. B. Redford
*Department of Near Eastern Studies, University College,
University of Toronto*

A. K. Grayson
Department of Near Eastern Studies, University College,
University of Toronto

Ann Bembenek
Graduate Student, University of Toronto

Sigla

STUDIES ON THE
ANCIENT PALESTINIAN WORLD

An Incense Burner
from Tell es-Saʿidiyeh,
Jordan Valley

JAMES B. PRITCHARD

Among the most important artefacts found during the 1966 season of excavations made by the University Museum of the University of Pennsylvania at Tell es-Saʿidiyeh, Jordan, is a small limestone incense burner,[1] now in the National Museum in Amman.[2] The object is important for the history of occupation at this site in the central Jordan Valley because of its association with a large, open-court building, almost square, measuring 21.95 by 22.05 metres, that stood on the acropolis of the tell. The incense burner was found on the floor of room 4, one of the seven rooms that surrounded a central courtyard; apparently it belonged to the last users of the complex.[3] The fixing of a date for the building in which this object was found is difficult because few other objects were found in it and connections which may have existed between the building and contemporary structures elsewhere on the tell have as yet not been established. Over its ruins had been built another rectangular building which, at the present stage of our study of the remains, seems to belong to the second century B.C. A sample of charcoal (P.1446) taken from the floor of the room in which the incense burner was found has been analysed by the Carbon-14 Laboratory of the University Museum and found to have a date of 343 ± 52 B.C. (5730-year half-life). The incense burner is also important as a unique example of a class of ob-

---

1 Field catalogue no. S1181/St.82S.14.
2 See preliminary reports by the writer on the season in RB, 73 (1967), 474–6, pl. 38b; *Expedition*, 11/1 (1968), 20–2; *Illustrated London News*, 2 July 1966, pp. 25–7.
3 The grid reference is 31-E-6/7; see *Expedition*, 11/1 (1968), 21 for a plan of the building.

jects found in southwestern Arabia, Palestine, Mesopotamia, and Cyprus. It combines the three features of geometric designs, graffiti, and an inscription, which, although they appear separately or in combinations of two of these elements elsewhere, are found together in only one other example.

DESCRIPTION

The Tell es-Saᶜidiyeh incense burner[4] was cut from a block of soft limestone which originally measured at least 7 cm. long, 6.7 cm. wide, and 7 cm. high. The sides were tapered toward the base, which measures 5.7 by 6 cm., and the stone between the four legs, one at each corner of the base, was cut away. A basin, about 1 cm. deep, was cut in the top, with sides slightly bevelled inward and with a rim around the perimeter slightly less than 1 cm. wide. The sides of the burner were polished by an abrasive which has left diagonal marks that are still visible on side D (see plate).

The sides were covered with pigment or paint. Sides D and F are red, and sides C and E black. The bottom (B) was painted with two bands, approximately 1.3 cm. wide. The one extending between sides C and E is black, conforming to the colour of the two sides; that connecting sides D and F is red, as are these sides. The longer band overlays the shorter. The colouring is abraded in places, but enough remains to indicate the original treatment of the stone surface.

The second stage in the decoration was the incising of the rim of the top, the sides, and the base with geometric designs cut with a sharp instrument through the coating of colour into the soft stone, so that the white of the incisions stands out against the red and black backgrounds.

The decoration around the rim of the top (A) consists of eight circles, each with a smaller one inside. These were crudely drawn, without a compass, but evenly placed, one at each corner and one at approximately the centre of each side. These concentric circles match in size and design the thirteen that appear on the four sides of the burner.

The decoration on the sides is divided into three registers or zones that continue around the four faces in continuous friezes. The upper register, averaging 2 cm. in width, is a reserved band bordered above and below with a zigzag line that provides a saw-tooth decoration as

---

4 See accompanying plate for photographs. The drawings were made by Sally Harris Todd.

a border. The teeth of the 'saw' are incised with diagonal incisions. Horizontal lines at the top and bottom serve to contain the upper register.

The second register consists of a narrow band of vertical lines contained by two horizontal lines, one at the top and one at the bottom, running around the four sides. The vertical lines are arranged in groups of from four to nine strokes forming panels separated by blank spaces. There seems to be no pattern in the alternation of the number of strokes in the individual panels.

The third and widest register is the most complex. On the opposing sides C and E the design consists of a series of lozenges, each with a pair of concentric circles in the centre. The space between the lozenges is hatched with diagonal lines. Four lozenges appear on side E, and five on side C. The third register on the other two sides (D and F) is decorated differently. On these sides, in the intervals between three 'column' decorations of vertical and horizontal hatching are two X-like designs hatched diagonally. At the meeting point of the two bars of the cross, or X, there is a pair of concentric circles matching those of the third register on the other two sides and those incised on the rim. The entire third register is contained by two horizontal lines that extend around the four sides.

The feet are incised with double zigzag lines, but the resulting triangles are not hatched as are those in the upper register. The zigzag design is bordered at the top by one horizontal line that runs around the incense burner, and two lines are incised at the bottom of each foot. From the arrangement of the design it is apparent that the lines incised on the four feet were cut after the stone between the legs had been cut away.

The crossed bands painted on the bottom (B) of the burner are incised with zigzag lines with smaller triangles or chevrons filled in. The band across the longer axis runs over that of the shorter. Each band is bordered by two lines.

The final stage in the decoration was the addition of the two crude drawings (D and F) and the inscription (C). It is obvious from the placing of the animal on side D, principally in the upper register but with feet extending through the second and into the third register of the carefully planned geometric design, that this graffito was an afterthought and not part of the original plan. The animal seems to have been intended for a horse, since the mane is represented by lines extending upward from the neck and a loop is attached to the head to indicate an ear. The four legs are shown by simple lines.

In the upper register of side F there appears a crude graffito of

A

B

C

D

E

F

CM.

A   B

C   D

E   F

CM.

what may have been intended as a composite figure. Its horizontal position was probably determined by the long and narrow shape of the space available in the upper register, which could not accommodate this type of figure drawn vertically. In the lower part of the figure one can see an attempt to represent a human body, with right arm raised and the left extended downward. The legs are not differentiated and no feet are represented. The upper part of the figure appears to be the head of an animal, or possibly of a bird, since the six lines extending from the head suggest feathers.[5] Yet another possible interpretation is that the head is that of a snake. But, despite the uncertainty over the head, it seems reasonably clear that the figure is a composite creature, perhaps intended to serve an apotropaic function.

The inscription was incised into the reserved space of the upper register of side C with a broader instrument than that used in the cutting of the geometric designs and one more comparable to that used for cutting the figure in the upper register of side F. The letters are cut to a uniform depth, except for the enigmatic stroke to the right of the vertical of the second letter (from the right).

Our first reading of *lyknw* for the inscription[6] presented a major problem. Although all the letters (except the *y*, with the lightly incised mark to the right of the downstroke) could be found in Hebrew and Phoenician inscriptions extending from the eighth through the fifth centuries, no convincing parallels could be found in any one inscription or in inscriptions from any one general period. Professor Frank M. Cross, Jr., has suggested that the script is lapidary Aramaic and as such is to be read *lzkwr*, 'Belonging to Zakkūr.'[7] This reading has the advantage that all the letters fit nicely into the period of the late sixth to the fourth centuries and the name Zakkūr is well attested.[8] Forms comparable to our *l*, *k*, *w*, *r*, are to be found in the Saqqarah stela,[9] which is dated to 482 B.C. Also analogous is the script of the Teima stela,[10] which has in line 13 a clear form of our *z*.

5 See E. Porada, *Corpus of Ancient Near Eastern Seals in North American Collections* (Washington, 1948), nos. 608 and 609, middle Assyrian cylinders of the twelfth to tenth century B.C.

6 See footnote 2.

7 Letter of 30 January 1969.

8 See M. Noth, *Die Israelitischen Personennamen* (Stuttgart, 1928), p. 187, for use of *zkr* in names; and H. Donner and W. Röllig, *Kanaanäische und aramäische Inschriften* (Wiesbaden, 1962–4), vol. 2, pp. 205–6, for listing of names.

9 M. Lidzbarski, *Handbuch der nordsemitischen Epigraphik* (Weimar, 1898), pl. 28:1, p. 448.

10 CIS, II, 113.

The Assuan stela[11] has good examples of our *r* and *w*. For the *w* there is also the Tobiah inscriptions at ꜥAraq el-Amir;[12] the form of this letter is identical with that on the Tell es-Saꜥidiyeh burner.[13]

The identification of this distinctive, small limestone cube with a basin and four legs as an incense burner was first made on the evidence from examples found in South Arabia. Two examples in the University Museum collections are inscribed with the names of materials known to have been burned as incense. The first of these[14] is inscribed with the four words *qlm*, *ḏrw*, *rnd*, and *ḥḏk*. The second[15] bears the inscription *rnd*, *ḏrw*, *lbny* and *qsṭ*. It has long been recognized that these are words for kinds of incense[16] and describe the materials used in the burners. Further epigraphic evidence for associating this object with the burning of incense appears in an Aramaic inscription on a burner found at Lachish containing the word *lbntʾ*, 'incense' or 'frankincense.'[17] Corroborative evidence is available from tests made by Dr H. J. Plenderleith, of the British Museum, on traces of a greasy, dark-brown substance found in the basins of three cuboid limestone burners found at Hureidha in the Hadhramaut.[18] He verified that the material was resin and observed that it gave off a fragrant odour on being heated. In the light of the inscriptional evidence as well as of the examination of actual residue found in ex-

---

11 CRAIBL, 1903, pl. opp. p. 270.

12 E. Littmann, *Greek and Latin Inscriptions*, sec. A, 1 (Publications of the Princeton University Archaeological Expedition to Syria, in 1904–05, div. III; Leyden, 1914), pp. 1–4.

13 For these references I am indebted to Professor Cross, who has also kindly made the following comments on the forms of the letters to support a date for our inscription within the limits of the late sixth to early fifth century, 525–475 B.C., or ca. 500 B.C. in round numbers: '*Kaf* is early; I know no form like this later than 482 B.C. (the Saqârah Stele); *waw* is the form of the late sixth to fourth centuries (latest, the Tobiah form, fourth century); *nun* is impossible – the form is too short by far; *reš* is fairly early with slanting, long left tick. *Zayin*: the mark to the right of downstroke above the tail is a slip or scratch. The form is perfect for late sixth and fifth. *Lamed* fits the earlier sequence but is dangerous to use.'

14 30–47–31, RES 4249; see ANEP, 581, for bibliography, and R. L. Bowen, Jr., and F. P. Albright, *Archaeological Discoveries in South Arabia* (Baltimore, 1958), p. 151, pl. 96.

15 30–47–32, RES 4255; see ANEP, 579, for bibliography, and Bowen and Albright, *Archaeological Discoveries*, p. 151, pl. 96.

16 See N. Rhodokanakis, AOT, 470; W. F. Albright, BASOR, 132 (1953), 46.

17 O. Tufnell, *Lachish* III (London, 1953), pl. 68:1; Albright, BASOR, 132, 46–7.

18 G. Caton Thompson, *The Tombs and Moon Temple of Hureidha (Hadhramaut)* (London, 1940), pp. 49–50.

amples of this class of objects there can be little doubt about their purpose and use as incense burners.

EXAMPLES FROM SOUTH ARABIA

No less than twenty-seven examples of limestone incense burners are known to have come from southwestern Arabia. Some bear South Arabic inscriptions, as those in the University Museum[19] and two in the Peabody Museum, Harvard.[20]

Five examples have been excavated by G. Caton Thompson at Hureidha.[21] She dates this series from the c or post-c phase of the Moon Temple to the Seleucid period.[22] All these are cuboid, with perpendicular sides,[23] and range in height from 5.2 to 14 cm. None bears an inscription, but all but one are incised with a limited repertoire of cross-hatching and vertical incisions. All are reported to have been reddened with haematite staining on the sides.

Richard L. Bowen, Jr., has published drawings of two squat, cuboid burners from Beihan, decorated with cross-hatching over the entire sides, and assigns them to the first century B.C.[24]

From the Timna᷎ Cemetery Ray L. Cleveland has published full descriptions and photographs of ten incense burners.[25] With the exception of one clay example (TC 1915) all are of stone and roughly cuboid in shape. In height they range from 5 to 11.5 cm. Three bear fragmentary inscriptions.[26] In addition to the more usual decoration of zigzag lines around the sides to form a row of triangles and a criss-cross hatching, eight of the ten examples exhibit the unique design of recessed panels, as if in imitation of architectural features. In the most elaborate example, TC 2011, both a secondary and a tertiary recess appear in the panels. Four legs, generally square, are set at the corners of each burner, except for two examples[27] which are legless.

19 In addition to the two examples mentioned above, there is an uninscribed example, 30-47-43, which belongs to the same collection.
20 Nos. 36-5-60/2492, Jamme 384, and 35-18-60/2417, Jamme 385; both are described and drawn in Bowen and Albright, *Archaeological Discoveries*, pp. 150–1, pl. 96; see for inscriptions A. Jamme, *Bi. Or.*, 10 (1953), 94–5.
21 *The Tombs and Moon Temple of Hureidha*, pp. 49–50, pls. 16:1–5, 17:1–5.
22 Later than 300 B.C., on the basis of parallels with a Gezer example from a cave-tomb (*ibid.*, p. 153).
23 With one exception, A 3.27.
24 Bowen and Albright, *Archaeological Discoveries*, p. 153, pl. 96, bottom.
25 Ray L. Cleveland, *An Ancient South Arabian Necropolis* (Baltimore, 1965), pp. 118–20, pls. 90–2.
26 TC 536 & 537, TC 1751, and TC 1862.
27 TC 1708 and TC 1915.

On three of the burners remnants of a 'rusty' stain are reported. One limestone burner (TC 1955) had been covered with a hard lime plaster before the application of the dark rusty colour and the incising of the decoration.

In his survey of the antiquities of the Aden Protectorates, G. Lankester Harding found a fragment of a limestone burner at Mashgha in Wadi Idm, a site which may date, according to Harding, at least in part from the seventh or even the eighth century B.C.[28] At Makainan he found three stone burners, two of which were decorated with incised vertical lines;[29] and a plain, limestone example apparently was found at Adiat es-Sultan.[30]

The features which the South Arabian examples of the cuboid incense burner share with that from Tell es-Saʿidiyeh must now be considered. Common features include the use of soft limestone, the block of stone standing on four feet, the depression in the top (although it is frequently deeper in the South Arabian examples), and the presence of colouring on the sides and occasionally elsewhere. Zigzag and vertical lines as elements of decoration are shared by both the South Arabian examples and the burner from the Jordan Valley. It is noteworthy, however, that in the twenty-seven examples from South Arabia there is no use of the concentric circles and there are no lozenges, no diagonal hatching, and no graffiti of animals or other figures. Nor is there any recorded example of decoration on the base or rim.

INCENSE BURNERS FROM PALESTINE

At Tell Jemmeh (Gerar) Flinders Petrie discovered thirteen incense burners in levels 203 to 195.[31] Two were fairly well preserved on four sides,[32] and the remainder were recognizable fragments. All bear designs, apparently incised in the surface of the limestone. The height of the three examples which could be measured ranges from 6 to 8 cm. With but one exception,[33] these burners are decorated with geometric or conventional designs, including cross-hatching, zigzag

28 G. L. Harding, *Archaeology in the Aden Protectorates* (London, 1964), pl. 33:62; see p. 12 for discussion of date.

29 *Ibid.*, pl. 35:41, 42, 43.

30 *Ibid.*, pl. 19:51, where the burner is shown with the pottery from that site.

31 Flinders Petrie, *Gerar* (London, 1928), pls. 40, 41, 42:5, 6; the fragment on pl. 41:13 is from level 181 and Petrie questions the date on pp. 18–19.

32 *Ibid.*, pl. 40:1–4 and 5–8.

33 *Ibid.*, pl. 14:15.

lines, triangles, chevrons, concentric circles in rows to form a guil-loche, spirals, vertical and horizontal lines, panels, and circles with dot. In addition, examples have within well-planned panels natural-istic representations of palm trees,[34] camels or some other humped quadruped,[35] a composite creature with four legs and a bird's head,[36] pairs of oryxes and ibexes,[37] dog, hare, human figures and animals with bird's feet.[38] Most elaborate of all the scenes is a panel in two stages[39] which appears to imitate a mural painting in which there are divisions of rooms. K. Galling suggests that the scene is so crudely executed that the artist must have had a foreign exemplar.[40] What is clearly evident here, however, is that the graffiti of naturalistic fig-ures were planned at the time the geometric decoration was made and were not an afterthought as were those in the Tell es-Saᶜidiyeh example.

Opinions for the dating of the Tell Jemmeh burner have varied. Petrie placed the range roughly between 700 and 500 B.C. or later.[41] K. Galling, in his review of the publication, assigns them to about 625 B.C.;[42] K. M. Kenyon dates them to 'probably' the seventh to sixth centuries B.C.;[43] W. F. Albright lowers the date to the sixth to fourth centuries B.C.[44] One clue as to the sequence of this important series of burners may be seen from the levels in which they were found. As Petrie pointed out, the earliest[45] were carefully engraved with geometric designs. The naturalistic designs of figures follow, and the end of the series is represented by geometric decoration in very rough form.[46]

At Gezer, R. A. S. Macalister found six examples of the burner in his 'Hellenistic' stratum, four bearing both naturalistic and geomet-ric decorations,[47] one with geometric designs,[48] and one undecorated except for a horizontal line on one side.[49] Within a border of hatch-ing and hatched triangles on one burner is a scene of action in which a man struggles with a much larger animal, behind which is an eight-

34 *Ibid.*, pl. 40:1.
35 *Ibid.*, pl. 40:2–3.
36 *Ibid.*, pl. 40:4.
37 *Ibid.*, pl. 40:5–8.
38 *Ibid.*, pl. 41:10.
39 *Ibid.*, pl. 41:10.
40 ZDPV, 52 (1929), 248.
41 *Gerar*, pp. 18–19.
42 ZDPV, 52 (1929), 248.
43 J. W. Crowfoot *et al.*, *Samaria-Sebaste* III (London, 1957), p. 466.
44 BASOR, 98 (1945), 28.
45 *Gerar*, pl. 41:12, 18, 19.
46 *Gerar*, p. 19.
47 R. A. S. Macalister, *Gezer* II (London, 1912), figs. 524:2, 525, 526:1, 2.
48 *Gezer* II, p. 444.
49 *Gezer* II, p. 444.

pointed star. On one of the two broken sides a man is shown, apparently stabbing an animal in the back; and on the other side appear a stag and its hind.[50] On another burner are two horned animals, one licking the tail of the other,[51] within a border of hatched triangles at the top and of spirals at the bottom. Macalister reports that the top is decorated with scratched frets and spirals, and that one of the broken sides has an animal with long ears and the other a man in a short-sleeved tunic, driving an animal whose tufted tail alone is left.[52] The third well-decorated piece[53] has two animals with long ears, within a border of hatched triangles at the top and spirals at the bottom; on another face is a fragmentary scene of an animal falling victim to a man with a spear. The rim of the depression in the top is decorated with criss-crossed triangles and a spiral in the corner that is preserved. A fourth example is decorated with triangles, a zone of vertical lines, and a crude drawing of a small animal on the face of a leg.[54]

The similarity between the Gezer examples and those from Tell Jemmeh is clearly established by the borders of hatched triangles and spirals shared by both groups. The naturalistic scenes, as well as the scenes of action, are well placed within prepared panels. This similarity is enough to place the two series within the same time span.[55] It is noteworthy that the Gezer examples display dramatic action and motion in contrast to the static impression one gets from the Tell Jemmeh burners.

Although more than two hundred limestone altars or stands were found at Lachish, only one is shown as having had feet and a shape comparable to our example.[56] It is a cuboid stand, 16.5 cm. high, and has sides each measuring 11 to 12 cm. in width. A lightly scratched inscription appears on one side below two zigzag lines with a reserved space between them. An Aramaic inscription, beginning *lbnṭ*, 'incense,' is dated to the fifth to fourth century by A. Dupont-Sommer.[57] Other decoration consists of vertical lines on two sides

50 *Gezer* II, fig. 524:2.

51 *Gezer* II, fig. 525.

52 *Gezer* II, p. 445.

53 *Gezer* II, fig. 526:1, 2.

54 *Gezer* II, fig. 526:2a.

55 See W. F. Albright, who dates both groups to the sixth to fourth centuries (BASOR, 98, 28).

56 *Lachish* III, pl. 68:1, p. 383.

57 *Lachish* III, p. 358; W. F. Albright, who reads the remainder differently, agrees on the reading of the first word and in general on the dating of the object to the fourth and possibly to the late fifth century (BASOR, 132, 46).

below the register bordered with zigzag lines (and a ladder design on one side) and a palm tree with an unidentifiable object beside it.

Two limestone burners are published in drawings by J. L. Starkey and Lankester Harding in the report on the cemetery at Tell el-Farᶜa (S). On one[58] two animals drawn in a style like that of the Tell Jemmeh examples are preserved. Both appear in panels bordered at the bottom by hatched triangles. The second[59] shows three men, each armed with two spears resting on the shoulder, in a panel bordered at the top with hatched triangles and at the sides and bottom with a line of spirals, like those employed in the borders of a Tell Jemmeh example.

Among the finds at Samaria are two limestone incense burners. One[60] is without decoration and was reported to have been found with Hellenistic pottery. The other[61] is painted red and decorated on the four sides. The upper zone is remarkably similar to that on the Tell es-Saᶜidiyeh example. Between a zigzag line above and one below, hatched diagonally, and forming saw-tooth designs, is a row of incised dots. Below the upper zone is a narrow zone of dots, spaced closer than those above. The lower half of the object bears on the three sides shown what seem to be representations of a wild boar with a belt decorated by a zigzag line around its body and a small circle on its rump. On side *a* the animal is shown with mouth wide open; on side *b*, there are two boars, one following the other; and on side *c* the one appears as on side *a*, but with his mouth closed. Above the boar on side *a* there is a sun-disk with rays or a many-pointed star. Since the animals fit neatly into the panels there seems to be no question but that the reserved space had been left for them.

Small incense altars, about 8 cm. square, dating from the fifth to fourth centuries, are reported from Makmish.[62] According to N. Avigad, 'one of them has incised decorations showing geometric patterns and crude animal figures resembling the altar from Gezer'[63] and another has figures like Maltese crosses and a lattice pattern in red paint.[64] One example incised with triangles and scalloped design

---

58 *Beth-Pelet* II (London, 1932), pl. 88:14.
59 *Beth-Pelet* II, pl. 93:662.
60 *Samaria-Sabaste* III, fig. 119:2; p. 466.
61 G. A. Reisner, *Harvard Excavations at Samaria, 1908–1910* (Cambridge, 1924), II, pl. 80a–c; I, p. 333.
62 N. Avigad, IEJ, 10 (1960), 95.
63 *Gezer* II, fig. 525.
64 IEJ, 10, 95.

was found in stratum 3a (Hellenistic) at Ashdod.[65] Mention should also be made of a burner found at the Egyptian site of Tell er-Retabeh, but clearly in the Palestinian tradition.[66] The decoration is limited to geometric designs in bands of zigzag lines and hatching.

In lower Transjordan three burners have appeared at Petra, one of stone and two of clay,[67] four at Tell el-Kheleifeh,[68] and two stone examples with simple line decoration at Khirbet Tannur.[69] The poor workmanship exhibited in the cutting or forming (as in the case of the clay models) and in the crudely executed designs of these Transjordan examples clearly brands them as degenerate types of the Palestinian and Arabian examples.

COMPARISONS BETWEEN SOUTH ARABIAN AND PALESTINIAN BURNERS

It is immediately apparent when one compares the incense burners found in South Arabia with those found in Palestine that there is a marked difference in styles of decoration. Instead of the repertoire of geometric motifs limited to triangles and a criss-cross design found on the South Arabian examples, there appears on the Palestinian burners a much greater variety of decoration. Triangles and cross-hatching do appear, but in addition there are spirals, guilloches, lozenges, circles, figures like Maltese crosses, and half-circles or scallops. Whereas reserved panels are left for neatly cut inscriptions on the South Arabian burners, when they appear on the Palestinian examples they are often filled with either naturalistic drawings or scenes of action, as in the Gezer pieces.

The major contrast between the two regions is in the complete absence of naturalistic drawings on the South Arabian burners and the general use of pictures of animals, trees, and men on the sides of the Palestinian examples. The repertoire of representations includes palm trees, the dog, hare, the goat (?), oryx, ibex, birds, the boar (?), camels (?), composite creatures, men in combat, and men armed with spears.

65 M. Dothan and D. N. Freedman, *Ashdod* I (Jerusalem, 1967), pp. 26–7, fig. 9:8, pl. 9:14.
66 W. M. F. Petrie, *Hyksos and Israelite Cities* (London, 1906), pl. 36C:13.
67 Crystal M. Bennett, *Archaeology*, 15 (1962), 239, top, and also in N. Glueck, *Deities and Dolphins* (New York, 1965), pl. 193d.
68 *Deities and Dolphins*, pl. 193e.
69 *Ibid.*, pl. 193b, c.

EXAMPLES FROM OTHER AREAS

In 1942 Liselotte Ziegler published a study of clay burners, similar in size and form to the limestone examples, found at the sites of Uruk, Babylon, Ashur.[70] Of the forty examples from Uruk the largest group consisted of those decorated with panels of diagonal crosses. One of the fifteen examples of this type of decoration has a cross almost identical with those on sides D and F of our burner.[71] The saw-tooth motif of the upper zone of our example is also found incised on the clay burners from Uruk.[72] Another element found in the decoration of the Uruk burners is the lozenge or rhomboid with circle and dot in the centre.[73] All the designs on these examples from Mesopotamia are geometric, with the one exception of a side decorated with a reed.[74] Ziegler dates both the Babylon and Uruk examples to the Neo-Babylonian period.[75] In 1962 Sir Leonard Woolley published a selection of fifteen clay incense burners made from a large group of specimens from Ur, most of which belonged to the Neo-Babylonian period, saying that 'most of the rest were found in the upper levels of the site and are not likely to be much older.'[76] To be associated with this group, in that they were made of clay, but from a later date, are the two burners at the Arabian site of Thaj, which lies in eastern Arabia near the Persian Gulf.[77]

It should also be mentioned that yet another area, Cyprus, has provided examples of the limestone incense burner. The similarity to our example is, however, limited: the double saw-tooth decoration is found on only one side of an example from Tamassos[78] and

70 'Tonkästchen aus Uruk, Babylon und Assur,' ZA, 13/47 (1942), 224–40.
71 *Ibid.*, fig. 23; see also a similar example from Ashur in fig. 52.
72 *Ibid.*, fig. 33c.
73 *Ibid.*, fig. 36.
74 *Ibid.*, fig. 3.
75 W. F. Albright, BASOR, 132, 46, agrees that none of her material comes from before the sixth century, although a dubious specimen from Ashur may require pushing back to the late seventh century.
76 *Ur Excavations*, vol. IX, *The Neo-Babylonian and Persian Periods* (London, 1962), p. 103, pl. 36.
77 H. R. P. and V. P. Dickson, *Iraq*, 10 (1948), 1ff., pl. II, 1 (top) and P. J. Parr, BASOR, 176 (1964), 21, 1:11, 12, for drawings of two examples now in the British Museum.
78 M. Ohnefalsch-Richter, *Kypros, the Bible and Homer* (London, 1893), p. 477, pl. 199:5; see also pl. 133:8, for an example from Athiaenou, which has long legs and is decorated with graffiti of a human, an animal figure, and two trees below a border which is faintly incised with the double saw-tooth design.

the base and one leg of another on which there is the remnant of both a vertical and a horizontal band decorated with the double saw-tooth design.[79]

CONCLUSIONS

After this survey of analogous material in other regions, what can be said about the affinities of various features of our burner to those found elsewhere? Except for the general form and the use of colour and bands of triangles to decorate the sides of the Tell es-Saʿidiyeh incense burner, it has very little in common with those found in South Arabia. The basins cut in the top of the latter are generally much deeper and naturalistic representations are unknown. Our burner does have certain geometric patterns in common with the Tell Jemmeh decorations, such as chevrons,[80] circles,[81] and lozenges or rhomboids.[82] But the use of large panels for drawings of flora and fauna distinguishes this group from the type to which the Tell es-Saʿidiyeh example belongs. Similarly, our example has little in common with those from Gezer, either in geometric motifs or in the style of portraying animals or humans. The free and clean style of the horse in side D of the Tell es-Saʿidiyeh burner has its closest analogy in the flowing lines of the two animals depicted on the sides of the fragmentary piece found at Tell el-Farʿa (S).[83] A striking similarity appears in the double saw-tooth decoration of the upper zone of the burner from Samaria.[84] Here the 'teeth' of the saw are also decorated with diagonal lines as they are in the upper zone of our example.

The closest similarities to the geometric motifs in the broadest and most distinctive zone of the Tell es-Saʿidiyeh burner are, however, to be found impressed on the clay burner of the Neo-Babylonian period found at Uruk. There one sees not only the diagonal cross with a circle in the centre within a square panel,[85] but the saw-tooth design in the upper zone[86] and the lozenge with circle and dot in the cen-

79 E. Gjerstad and J. Lindros, *Swedish Cyprus Expedition* (Stockholm, 1935), vol. II, pl. 160:21.
80 *Gerar*, pl. 41:11, 12, 14.
81 *Gerar*, pl. 41:14.
82 *Gerar*, pl. 41:11, 12, although they are much smaller there.
83 *Beth-Pelet* II, pl. 88:14.
84 *Harvard Excavations at Samaria, 1908–10*, II, pl. 80a–c.
85 L. Ziegler, ZA, 13/47, fig. 23, and fourteen other examples.
86 *Ibid.*, fig. 33c.

tre.[87] From these indicators it would seem likely that the inspiration for the geometric decoration on our burner – as possibly also that for the Samaria example cited above – came from Babylonia. The feature of the crossed bands on the bottom remains, as far as we know, unique.

The two graffiti on the sides, carved subsequently, are most probably Palestinian, to judge from the widespread use of naturalistic designs on burners found in that region. The inscription in letters which belong to this region is additional evidence for asserting that the piece, while bearing evidence of influence from outside, was at least at some stage of its fabrication and use indigenous to the region in which it was discovered.

87 *Ibid.*, fig. 36.

The Archaeological History of Elealeh in Moab

WILLIAM L. REED

Considerable evidence has been gathered during the last forty years regarding the ancient history of the land of Moab, that fertile region located east of the Dead Sea. Surface exploration was the first method employed to identify and describe some of the numerous tells that are located in Moabite territory. This was followed by several archaeological expeditions to such Moabite cities as Dibon (modern Dhībân), Medeba, Mount Nebo, and Heshbôn (modern Hesbôn). In 1962 it was the privilege of the writer to organize an expedition which completed a series of four soundings at the site of Elealeh (modern el-ʿAl), and since that time he has continued an investigation of the evidence pertaining to the history of the site.[1] Although the picture with reference to Moab in general, and Elealeh in particular, is by no means a complete one, some important features of the archaeological history have emerged.

Ancient literary records preserve the memory of the identification

---

1 The present report is intended in part as a means of honouring Fred V. Winnett and of calling attention to his contributions to the field of Moabite studies. During his first term as director of the American School of Oriental Research in Jerusalem, Winnett directed the first season of excavations at Dibon in 1950–1. Prior to this and in subsequent years he explored many of the other Moabite sites. The present writer has been privileged to be associated with Winnett in several phases of this work, first as a Fellow of the Jerusalem School in 1937–8 when some surface explorations in Moab were conducted under the sponsorship of the school. In 1951–2 the writer directed a second campaign at Dibon in behalf of the school and with the guidance provided by Winnett's reports of the first campaign. In 1962 Winnett was the senior staff member at a series of soundings completed at Elealeh by the writer which were made possible by a grant from the American Philosophical Society.

of Elealeh with the modern village of el-ʿAl. The site is located in the
fertile plateau north of the river Arnon, approximately eight miles
north of Medeba, about one and one-half miles northeast of Heshbôn, and seven miles northeast of the traditional site of Mount
Nebo.[2] From the modern highway at the east it can be seen as a conspicuous tell whose summit rises 3,048 feet above sea level and about
80 feet above the surrounding plateau.

Although there is some uncertainty as to the meaning of the name,
it is probable that the present name preserves the ancient one. The
city is mentioned five times in the Old Testament (Num. 32:3, 37;
Isa. 15:4 and 16:9; Jer. 48:34), in each instance being listed with its
neighbour to the southwest, Heshbôn. The present Arabic name,
ʾel-ʿAl, as was noted by C. R. Conder, means 'the lofty place' and is
an appropriate designation because of its elevation and conspicuous
position.[3] The ancient Hebrew name was recorded as *ʾel ʿālēh* except
in Numbers 32:37 where it is written with a final aleph rather than
he (*ʾel ʿālēʾ*). The first two letters of the ancient name may represent
the equivalent of the Arabic article *ʾel*, 'the,' and the last letter represents an old nominal ending based on the verb *ʿālâh* ('to go up'). In
this case, both the ancient and modern names would mean 'the lofty
place,' or 'the promontory.' The alternative to this explanation is
that the ancient name is composed of the name for God (*ʾEl*) and the
verb *ʾālâh*. Thus the city name may have meant something like
'Whither God ascends,' but in the absence of early records concerning the worship of El at the site, it is probable that the name had a
geographical rather than a religious connotation.

According to the traditions of the Old Testament, Elealeh was located in an attractive grazing area for cattle in northern Moab which
was acquired for a period by the Reubenites. Mentioned with Elealeh
in Numbers 32:37–38 are Heshbon, Kiriathaim, Nebo, Baalmeon,
and Sibmah. The reference contains a curious note to the effect that
the names of the cities were to be changed, saying 'they gave other
names to the cities which they built.' Although the date of this reference is much later than the thirteenth century B.C. to which it refers,
it may contain an authentic tradition that the Reubenites, when they
rebuilt the Moabite cities that were captured, changed the names of

2 Brief reports of evidence from Elealeh have been published by the writer as follows: 'The Material Remains of the Ancient Moabites,' *Year Book of the American Philosophical Society, 1964*, pp. 585–9; 'The History of Elealeh (*ʾel-ʿAl*)
   in Moab,' *The College of the Bible Quarterly*, 42/1 (1965), 12–16.
3 *The Survey of Eastern Palestine*, vol. 1 (London, 1889), pp. 16f.; cf. Nelson
   Glueck, 'Explorations in Eastern Palestine, Part 1,' AASOR, 14 (1934), 6.

those that embodied terms for pagan deities.[4] There is no indication whether the older Moabite names, or the new, are the ones recorded in this text. What is usually considered a later tradition preserved in Joshua 13:15ff. makes no reference to Elealeh, which was doubtless included by implication only in the phrase 'all the tableland by Medeba; with Heshbon, and all its cities that are in the tableland.'

The two references to Elealeh in an oracle concerning Moab (see Isaiah 15–16) include it with other Moabite cities that were threatened with destruction. Because of certain similarities between this oracle and the one concerning Moab, contained in Jeremiah 48, the occasion for the oracles is not clear, whether having reference to an invasion from Assyria in the eighth century B.C. or to one from Arabia in the sixth century B.C. in the time of Nabonidus, last of the Babylonian kings. In any case, both oracles are valuable for the geographical information they contain with reference to Elealeh. Listed with several other cities located nearby, it is implied in these oracles that Elealeh was the scene of the activity of military Moabites, a region of abundance characterized by fruitful fields, vineyards, and winepresses, as well as by streets, house-tops, city squares, and religious shrines referred to as high places.

Although the Mesha stela attests for Moab in the ninth century B.C. a comparable condition of fertility and urban culture, it makes no reference to Elealeh, possibly because the territory of Mesha did not extend that far north. However, the northern border of Moab is not certain in view of the fact that some of the Moabite cities mentioned by Mesha have not yet been identified, but the possible references to Nebo and Medeba in lines 8, 14, and 30 would place Mesha's activity in the vicinity of Elealeh.[5]

Several notes regarding the archaeological history of Elealeh may be gleaned from the reports of early explorers and geographers. Edward Robinson identified Elealeh with el-ʾAl, locating it about 'half an hour northeast' of Heshbôn.[6] He also called attention to the fact that it was known to Eusebius in the *Onomasticon* and to Jerome. He mentions too the possibility that the place may have been referred to by Khŭlil Ibn Shâhîn as marking the northern limit of the province of Kerak, under the name of el-ʿAly. The reason for the uncertainty is that Elealeh may be too far north for the province of Kerak, and there is another site, located south of the river Arnon,

4 A. H. McNeile, *The Book of Numbers* (Cambridge, 1911), pp. 174f.
5 A. H. Van Zyl, *The Moabites* (Leiden, 1960), pp. 52, 190, 192, 194.
6 Edward Robinson, *Biblical Researches in Palestine*, 2nd ed., vol. 1 (London, 1856), p. 551.

bearing the modern name of Khirbet el-ʿAl, which is sometimes referred to in connection with the pilgrim tours to Mecca that followed this route. Carlo Guarmani, however, refers to the identification of Elealeh with el-ʿAl observed in 1864 during the course of his trip into the northern Najd for the purpose of purchasing Arabian horses; he referred to it as being located near the main pilgrim route from Damascus to Medina that passed to the east of Elealeh.[7]

Some of the data supplied by Conder as a result of his visit there in 1881 have special importance because a few of the structural remains have since disappeared.[8] Among them were a good specimen of a rock-cut winepress which was observed near the road, and on the summit at least two pillars, one of which Conder thought might be a *menhir*, as well as the remains of two buildings, the larger measuring 23 feet in width from north to south and about 35 feet in length. Although Conder's published floor plan indicates no apse, it is possible that his suggestion is correct that an early Christian chapel of the fourth or fifth centuries once existed on the eastern summit where only a few tesserae may still be found.

The identification of el-ʿAl with Elealeh was accepted by George Adam Smith, who observed that the site continued to be an important one until the time of the Crusaders when an expedition reached Elealeh in 1183, although the results are not indicated.[9] Doubtless the extensive mediaeval Arabic building remains which exist where our soundings were conducted are a memorial from the Crusader period.

A question may be raised as to whether or not Elealeh was located on the King's Highway (see Num. 20:17 and 21:22 and Deut. 2:27). The general features of Moabite terrain make it likely that such was the case and that Elealeh served as one of the stations that achieved importance by supplying provisions to caravans moving from Damascus to Aqabah. No information regarding the King's Highway has been preserved for the Persian period, but during the Roman period a highway was built by Trajan following his defeat of the Nabataeans. It is likely that Trajan's Road, beside which may still be seen an occasional Roman milestone, followed the general course of the King's Highway. At present the main automobile roads lie four or five miles east of Elealeh, but the road from Medeba to the Jordan Valley passes at the western base of the tell. Probably in ancient

7 Carlo Guarmani, *Northern Najd* (London, 1938), p. 69.
8 Conder, *Survey*, pp. 16–19.
9 *The Historical Geography of the Holy Land* (London, 1894), p. 619.

times this was also the case, although the changing political and military conditions in Moab may have caused caravans to change their routes at different times. The prominence of Heshbôn in the traditions about Sihon king of the Amorites suggests that Heshbôn was located on the King's Highway; the proximity of this city to Elealeh might be evidence for locating both sites on the ancient caravan route.[10]

Geographical considerations and literary references to Elealeh can now be supplemented by the results of the soundings conducted there.[11] It was not possible to determine the extent of the ancient occupation of the tell, which extends about 300 metres from north to south and about 200 metres from east to west. The choice of an area for soundings was determined in part by the fact that the slopes are located in privately owned fields under cultivation (figure 1), and the eastern summit is covered by a modern cemetery. Since neither of these areas could be excavated without considerable expense and negotiation, it was decided to explore the western half of the summit. The top of the tell covers an area of about 10,000 square metres, but the line of ancient walls visible in some places on the slopes suggests that in certain periods the city occupied a much larger area than the summit.

During the course of the investigations on the summit four soundings were made in a line extending approximately 65 metres north to south. Sounding 1 was located at the southwest corner of the summit,

10 For references to Heshbôn and the King's Highway, see Num. 21:22, 26–30, 34; the biblical atlases consulted by the writer usually do not attempt to trace the line of the highway north of Heshbôn. An exception is the *Westminster Historical Atlas to the Bible*, edited by G. E. Wright and F. V. Filson (rev. ed.; Philadelphia, 1956), pl. vi; this map places Elealeh at the point where the King's Highway divides with one branch leading to the Jordan Valley and the other in the direction of Damascus. F. M. Abel identifies Elealeh with el-cAl and notes that it was a large village about one mile from Heshbôn located on the main road leading to Philadelphia; see his *Géographie de la Palestine* (Paris, 1933), vol. I, p. 186.

11 The soundings were completed under the direction of the writer during the period from 24 May to 2 June, 1962. A labour force of thirty men and boys from el-cAl was employed. The staff included Dr Fred V. Winnett, senior supervisor; Mr Gustav Materna, surveyor; Mr Mohammad Darwish, representative of the Jordan Department of Antiquities, supervisor; Annetta P. Reed, recorder; and Russell M. Reed, student assistant. Technical assistance was provided by the late Dr Awni Dajani, director of the Jordan Department of Antiquities, and by Sheikh Abdl Hadhi Hussein Manasseh of el-cAl; assistance with photography and restoration of pottery was provided by Mr Farid Markos and Mr Mahmud Mustafa of the Jordan Archaeological Museum.

FIGURE 1 General view of Elealeh from the west. The modern walls at the base of the tell, at the south, and extending across the summit are constructed of field-stones, and they contain also some stones from ancient buildings. The stone wall directly below the summit extends about twelve metres from north to south and stands six courses high. It was observed by early explorers and thought by some to be the remains of an Early Bronze Age city or tower wall, but no archaeological evidence of the date has been discovered. The line of the ancient road at the base of the tell is visible at the west of the modern wall; the road connects Medeba and Heshbôn with the Jordan Valley.

FIGURE 2 General view of soundings 2, 3, and 4 from the south, with Dr Fred V. Winnett inspecting sounding 3. The rough foundation wall in the foreground in sounding 4 is typical of the walls that were also excavated in the other soundings. Beyond the tell at the north are some of the fertile grain fields which extend around the tell at the east and south.

FIGURE 3 Storage jar (AL 224a) found in sounding 3, about 1.05 cm. below the surface (see also figure 8). The ware is dark grey, medium coarse; four handles; indentations include 'piecrust' rim, thumb-mark pattern, triangular and rectangular indentations, and wavy line decoration. Exact parallels are not known; some features of the decoration and the ware are characteristic of the early Arabic period.

FIGURE 4 Storage jar with Arabic inscription (AL 223) found in sounding 1, about 3.15 metres down from the top of the south wall. The ware is pinkish, medium well-fired; one fragmentary handle, sharply profiled rim, wavy line decoration.

TOP: FIGURE 5 Painted sherds from sounding 3. The ware is medium coarse, poorly fired, decorated with black, brown, or dark red paint; found in debris 10 to 150 cm. below surface of adjacent walls; mediaeval Arab type.

FIGURE 6 Miscellaneous sherds from sounding 1. Darkened sherds are fragments of cooking-pots; found in debris 110 to 215 cm. below surface of adjacent walls; Iron II type.

where there are the stone walls of a room measuring about 5 by 12 metres. The surface remains at this point suggest that the room was one of several which adjoined a courtyard, the whole area now filled with debris.

In sounding 1, and the others that followed, a plot was marked out adjacent to one wall so as to leave balks in which stratification could be observed. Sounding 1 covered a rectangular area measuring 5 by 6 metres. Sounding 2, located about 45 metres north and nearer the centre of the tell, covered an area measuring 2 by 2.5 metres. When bedrock was reached in this sounding at about 3.5 metres below the surface, it was possible to open sounding 3 located 10 metres farther north and near the edge of the summit. In an effort to secure further evidence concerning the stratification and the dates of the walls which appeared in each of these areas, sounding 4, measuring 4.5 by 5 metres, was made at a point 5 metres southwest of sounding 2 (figures 2 and 7).

Bedrock was reached in soundings 2 and 4, the ones nearest the centre of the tell, at 3.5 and 4.4 metres respectively. Although sounding 1 was continued to a point about 5.5 metres and sounding 3 to a point about 3.3 metres below the surface, bedrock was not reached in these areas. These measurements make it obvious that the tell is not entirely artificial, as formerly thought, but was originally a hill on which the city was built; the accumulated levels become thicker as one moves from the centre of the tell to its slopes.

The pattern in each sounding was similar in that there were found two sets of house walls at different levels and with different orientation, suggesting two periods of occupation in this part of the tell. Although the upper walls may be ones that were reused from the Iron Age, the latest pottery associated with them shows them to have been last used during the early and mediaeval Arabic periods. The upper walls, the tops of which are visible on the surface, doubtless formed a part of a large caravanserai last occupied during the period of the Crusades. The lower walls consist mostly of rough-hewn stones and larger boulders, against which there was debris containing pottery that is predominantly from the Iron I and Iron II periods. It is probable that this area of the tell was occupied as early as the twelfth century B.C. and that subsequent rebuilding removed all traces of structures that may have existed here between the end of Iron II and the early Arabic period.

One of the purposes of the soundings, in addition to attempting to determine the stratification at Elealeh, was to ascertain the usefulness of soundings at such a Moabite site. Because of the extensive

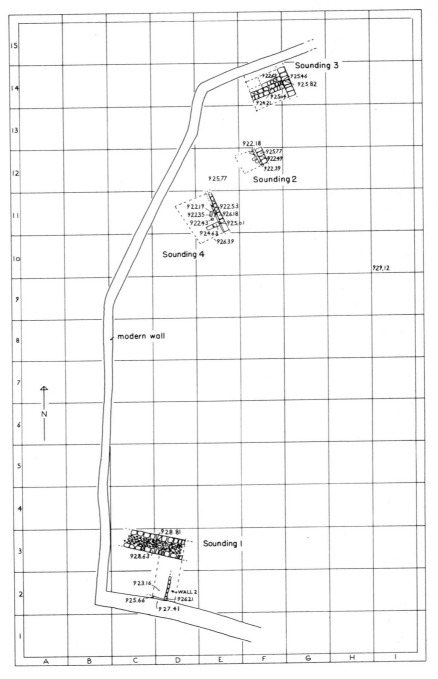

Sounding 3
922.62
925.46
925.82
925.04
924.21

922.18
925.77
922.49
922.39
Sounding 2

925.77

922.19   922.53
922.35   926.18
922.43   925.01
924.63
926.39

Sounding 4

929.12

modern wall

N

928.81
928.63
Sounding 1

923.16
WALL 2
925.66   926.21
927.41

0   5   10 M.

use of large stones in the ancient buildings, and their accumulation in the debris adjacent to the foundations, it was difficult to distinguish different levels of debris, and in no case was it possible to detect a foundation trench, as can often be done at a mud-brick site (such as Jericho – Tell es-Sultan). Although the main features of the occupation, as indicated by the presence of building remains and floor levels reported above, were revealed by the soundings, the fine points of stratification can be determined only by extensive excavations covering large areas.

As a general indication of the importance of ceramic vessels to the ancient inhabitants, it may be reported that 86 baskets of sherds were found in the four soundings as follows: 17 in sounding 1, 28 in sounding 2, 23 in sounding 3, 18 in sounding 4. Surprising success was experienced in restoring a number of the large storage jars that were found in each of the soundings. Although it is clear that much of the pottery resembles pottery from Palestinian sites, there are some types that are not well known and may be characteristic of Moabite pottery (figures 3, 5, 6, 8). Closest affinities are with the pottery from Dibon,[12] but no exact parallels are known for one type of storage jar (figure 8, no. 225), or the 'piecrust' decorated type (figure 3; figure 8, nos. 224, 224a).

A study of the material shows that not a single sherd of the distinctive Nabataean egg-shell ware was found. Although it may some day appear elsewhere on the mound, the absence of any trace of Nabataean occupation in the soundings tends to confirm the thesis of Nelson Glueck, made on the basis of surface exploration, that Nabataean occupation extended north of Petra to a line drawn from the north end of the Dead Sea through Medeba to the desert, thus excluding Elealeh.[13]

12 See Fred V. Winnett and William L. Reed, 'The Excavations at Dibon (Dhîbân) in Moab,' AASOR, 36–37 (1964), discussions of pottery.
13 Nelson Glueck, *The Other Side of the Jordan* (New Haven, 1940); he states that 'the northern limit of Nabataean Transjordan may be fixed by the sudden and complete cessation of Nabataean pottery on an east-west line which may be drawn approximately from the north end of the Dead Sea through Madeba to the desert. It is amazing that north of this approximate line no Nabataean pottery is found, except in a few isolated places. This can be understood, we believe, only through the realization that the northern part of the Nabataean kingdom in Syria was reached not through northern Transjordan but through the Wadi

FIGURE 7 Plan of soundings 1, 2, 3, and 4. The soundings are located where the tops of buried stone walls are visible on the surface; the numbers indicate the elevations above sea level; a modern cemetery is located directly east of soundings 2 and 3.

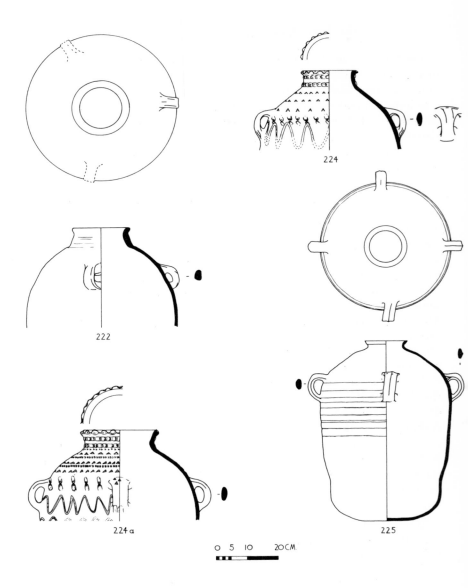

0 5 10   20 CM

FIGURE 8 Drawings of storage jars.

No. 222   Three handles; coarse, heavy grey ware; north side, 90 cm. below surface; mediaeval Arab type; sounding 3.

No. 224   Two handles; coarse, heavy grey ware; similar in decoration to no. 224a; 105 cm. below surface; sounding 2.

No. 224a   See figure 3.

No. 225   Four handles; medium fine, dark grey ware; grits; horizontal parallel indentations; imperfectly fired on rim, shoulder, and rounded base; 280 cm. below surface; some features similar to Iron II; sounding 3.

Sherds found in the debris of each sounding indicate that some part of the tell must have been occupied in the Early and Middle Bronze, Iron I and Iron II, Roman, Byzantine, and Arabic periods, although it is not yet possible to associate structural remains with each of them.[14] The source of the Byzantine and Roman pottery in the debris became clear when fragments of mosaic floors and large underground chambers dating to those periods were pointed out by the villagers at several points on the east slopes of the mound. Large-scale excavations would no doubt uncover structures dating to each of the archaeological periods mentioned above.

Mention may be made of a brief Arabic 'blessing' text found in sounding I, about 3.15 metres down from the top of the south wall (figure 4). The text was inscribed on the shoulder of a large jar prior to firing. The depth at which it was found suggests that the occupation during the early and mediaeval Arabic periods must have covered several centuries. No exact parallels are known to the writer, although examples of early Arabic texts on ceramic vessels have been discovered at Abū Gôsh in western Palestine, at Siyagha, the memorial of Mount Nebo, located about seven miles southwest of Elealeh, and at Khirbet el-Mefjer, north of Jericho.[15] A possible reading of our text is: 'Blessing from Allah; exalted may he be.' It is curious that one word of the inscription ('exalted') may appear also in both the ancient and modern names of the city, although this is by no means certain. Several letters at the end of the inscription are not clear, and it may be that instead of a verb the name of a person is to be read. Dates varying from the eighth to the tenth century A.D. have been proposed for such texts.

Sirhan' (p. 175). Contrasted with this view is that held by Harding who thinks that during the period of King Obadas I, 'the whole of East Jordan must have been under Nabataean rule'; see G. Lankester Harding, *The Antiquities of Jordan* (London, 1959), p. 122.

14 In accordance with an agreement with the Jordan Department of Antiquities the following materials were placed in the Museum in Amman: a copy of the register, a complete set of photographs and drawings, seven ceramic vessels that were restored completely or in part, the Arabic jar inscription, one Arabic coin, miscellaneous metal objects including iron nails, bronze rings, a camel bell, etc., and a representative selection of sherds. A copy of the register, a complete set of photographs and drawings, field notes, and a representative collection of sherds are located at Texas Christian University, Fort Worth, Texas.

15 R. de Vaux and A. M. Steve, *Fouilles à Qaryet el-ᶜEnab Abū Gôsh* (Palestine, 1950), pp. 144–6 and fig. 33, nos. 1, 4; Sylvester J. Saller, *The Memorial of Moses on Mount Nebo* (Jerusalem, 1941), pt. I, p. 276 and pt. II, pl. 123, inscription XXXVI; D. C. Baramki, 'The Pottery from Kh. el-Mefjer,' QDAP, 10/I (1940), 72, 78; figs. 9, 40; pl. XVIII, 7.

Fifteen ancient cisterns once used for the storage of rain-water were detected, although none was excavated and doubtless more lie buried beneath the debris. Their number and presence suggest that there has been no major change in the amount of rainfall within the historical period; the ancient Moabites, like the modern inhabitants, must have depended for their water supply upon rainfall and the conservation of water in cisterns.[16]

The presence of an unusually large number of huge storage jars, especially in the Arabic and Iron Age periods, suggests that the early literary references to the site as being located in a rich agricultural area are correct. The evidence from the soundings seems to indicate that Elealeh was located on or very near the King's Highway, and it is likely that the storage jars were required for commercial purposes. Their presence may illustrate some of the Old Testament allusions to the city (see above), including the memory that it was located in a region where cattle were raised, where there were vineyards, wine-presses, fruit, and grain, entitling the district to be called a fruitful land. The reliability of the literary allusions which imply the fertility of this Moabite plateau, so near the desert of Arabia, was demonstrated during our visits to the region over a period of several months. It was observed that the pattern of rainfall is such that often, even when there is a drought in Jerusalem, the pastures and grain fields of Elealeh have received enough rain to make them the 'bread-basket' of the area. Such a territory would fit admirably the setting for the original home of Ruth, ancestress of David, whose family provided a refuge when famine existed in Bethlehem.

From this report it will be clear that the archaeological history of Elealeh cannot yet be presented in every detail, and that only as large-scale excavations may be possible at the site will new chapters be added to the history. However, the general features have become clear, and they add a new dimension to modern understanding of the ancient land of Moab.

16 Winnett and Reed, *The Excavations at Dibon*, pt. II, pp. 46f.; pl. 99.

Three Byzantine Tombstones from Dhībân, Jordan

A. D. TUSHINGHAM

Professor Winnett, as historian and philologist, has always been interested in inscriptions. His contributions to scholarship in this field are amply attested in the bibliography of his works included in this volume. It is not surprising, then, that one of the reasons leading him to initiate excavations at the ancient Moabite city of Dibon (present Dhībân) in the autumn of 1950 was the hope that further fragments of the famous Moabite stone (discovered in 1868) and, perhaps, other early inscriptions would come to light.[1] This expectation, held also by his successors on this important site, has been largely frustrated although a chance discovery revealed the existence of another Moabite stela, probably earlier than that of King Mesha,[2] and two inscriptions of the Roman period have added substantially to our knowledge of the site in the later period.[3]

There is ample evidence to indicate that Dhībân shared in the general prosperity of the Byzantine period but, surprisingly, few Christian tombstones have been reported. This paucity becomes more obvious when one realizes that diligent search and careful recording have produced 426 inscriptions, mostly on tombstones, from that area of ancient Moab lying between the Wâdī al-Ḥasā (biblical river Zered) and the Wâdī al-Mūjib (biblical Arnon).[4]

1 Fred V. Winnett and William L. Reed, 'The Excavations at Dibon (Dhībân) in Moab,' AASOR, 36–37 (1964), 11.
2 Roland E. Murphy, 'A Fragment of an Early Moabite Inscription from Dibon,' BASOR, 125 (1952), 20ff.; Winnett and Reed, 'Excavations at Dibon,' 23.
3 Winnett and Reed, 'Excavations at Dibon,' 63f.; A. D. Tushingham, 'An Inscription of the Roman Imperial Period from Dhībân,' BASOR, 138 (1955), 29ff.
4 Reginetta Canova, Iscrizioni e Monumenti Protocristiani del Paese di Moab (Rome, 1954); hereafter 'Canova.'

During Dr Winnett's season at Dhībân in 1950–1, a tombstone was found in the village (where it had probably been built into a house wall) and brought to the excavators. It is this stone which initiated the present study.[5] It became apparent that there were similarities between it and a fragment, registered in the 1951–2 season, and published by Dr Reed.[6] Finally, F. J. Bliss reported a third tombstone from Dhībân[7] for which he provided a transcription and a partial reading, but no photograph or description. To the author's knowledge, these are the only tombstones reported from the Dhībân region.

TOMBSTONE I (figure 1)

This stela, apparently of soft local limestone, measures roughly 1.03 metres high by 0.50 metre wide. Its thickness is not known but is probably no more than 0.10 meter. The top is roughly rounded and the base squared. The rectangular, inscribed panel appears to be slightly inset and is surmounted by a *crux quadrata* inscribed within a circle. The stone was broken across, obviously recently, for the two pieces fit smoothly together. Wear and spalling of the surface here and there have obscured parts of the text, particularly in the fourth line. Below this, although there is room on the panel for additional writing, the face is blank.

The text is read as follows:[8]

STĒLĒ STE / PHANOU TH / EONOU ĖTOU / A
Stela of Stephanos (son of) Theonas, one year old.

The script is of the square or angular type which appears to date from the second half of the fifth century.[9] The first sigma has a very short lower horizontal stroke, while the upper horizontal appears to continue across as the upper bar of the tau. The sigma-tau of 'Steph-

---

5 The description of the stela and the reading of the inscription are based entirely on a photograph kindly provided by Dr Winnett in 1968. It has not been possible to study the stone directly, nor are squeezes available.

6 Winnett and Reed, 'Excavations at Dibon,' 64 (with drawing of text) and pl. 83.1; Dr Reed has generously provided the photograph from which the present plate was made.

7 F. J. Bliss, 'Inscriptions collected in Moab' (with notes by A. S. Murray), PEQ, 1895, 372. Our figure 2 is a photograph of the drawing there reproduced.

8 Uncertain letters are marked by a superscript dot; parentheses enclose suggested readings; a diagonal line indicates the end of a line of text.

9 Canova, pp. cx f. and column 2 of table II, opp. p. cxii.

Figure 1

Figure 2

Figure 3

anou' may be ligatured, possibly at top and bottom.[10] The assumed patronymic following the name of the deceased is uncertain. The first letter may be an epsilon but is more probably a square thēta. The name Theonas is known from the Moabite region.[11]

On the basis of the other two inscriptions (see below), we would have expected the patronymic to be followed by ETŌN or ETĒ and a numeral indicating the age of the deceased at the time of death. The single letter in the fourth line is most easily read as an ēta, i.e. 8, but the preceding word ends quite definitely in omicron-upsilon, a genitive singular. For this reason, the numeral is read as alpha, with the assumption of damage and a purely fortuitous vertical stroke to the left which gives the appearance of ēta. If our interpretation is correct, we may supply the letters epsilon and tau before the omicron-upsilon at the end of the third line.[12]

TOMBSTONE 2 (figure 2)

Because only a drawing of the text of this tombstone was published, it is not possible to say anything of the form of the stone, its decoration, or its dimensions.

The text is read as follows:

STĒLĒ / . . EAṄÒỲ /ALESOỲ /ETŌN E
Stela of (?) . . eanos (son of) Alesos, 5 years old.

There can be little doubt that the first word is to be read STĒLĒ as in inscription 1. Further, the inscription is again in the square or angular character. This fact raises considerable doubt on the correctness of the transliteration of line 2. The tiny round omicron is obviously in the margin and should be disregarded. The apparent juxtaposition of a round and a square epsilon is also inexplicable. The patronymic[13] of the third line is clear enough, especially if the diagonal stroke de-

10 The reading STEPHANOU is not absolutely certain. The three faint vertical strokes at the beginning of the second line most probably represent a square phi, particularly as the middle line appears to project slightly above and below the others. These three strokes may, however, be read as a mu, in which case it is possible that the last letters of line 1 are to be read as GE(R), and the whole name as 'GERMANOU' (see Canova, inscriptions no. 61 from Kerak and nos. 392 and 401 from Maḥaiy). As, however, there is no trace of a rho at the end of the first line, it is probably easier to interpret as we have above.

11 Canova, inscription no. 90.

12 It is true that the visible marks resemble part of a kappa or an upsilon in reverse, but such appearance may be a result of accident or of lighting only.

13 The name occurs in inscriptions nos. 334 and 336 of Canova.

scending from the line above is considered part of a final upsilon. The fourth line apparently gives, as the original publisher saw, the age of the deceased at his death.

TOMBSTONE 3 (figure 3)

Dr Reed gives the measurements of this fragment as: maximum height, 56 cm.; maximum width, 27 cm.; maximum thickness, 9 cm. In spite of its broken condition, it is clear that it resembles in many respects stone 1. At the top appears a portion of a *crux quadrata* inscribed in a circle. We may estimate, on the basis of the preserved arc of the circle, that this stela was originally about the same size as no. 1. The break at the bottom suggests that the inscription was contained within a prepared panel, but left an unfilled space below the fourth line. The lettering appears to be larger than that on stone 1, and the margins may have been wider.

The text is read as follows:

(S)TĒL(Ē) / (A)ḊAMÍ(OU) / (A)LEISE(OU) / (E)TŌN L
Stela of Adamios (son of) Aleiseos, 30 years old.

There can be little doubt of the reading of the first line. The word STĒLĒ appears to be roughly centred beneath the cross symbol, allowing no room for the beginning of the name of the deceased on the first line. Of the name, only the two letters AM seem reasonably clear, but there is room at the beginning and end of the line for at least one more letter. Our reconstruction of the name,[14] however, is purely hypothetical. The patronymic, on the third line, could be a variant spelling of the Alesos met in stone 2 above. The final epsilon could be taken as the first letter of the word ETŌN, completed on the next line, but there seems to be room for another epsilon at the beginning of this line. It should be noted, finally, that this inscription combines square and rounded letters.

The readings here proposed for the proper names in the three inscriptions may be, at least in part, hypothetical but it is clear that the formula in all is the same. All three begin with the word STĒLĒ. All apparently give the name of the deceased and a patronymic, both in the genitive case. Two certainly give the age of the deceased at death; the other may do so. The two for which evidence is available have a *crux quadrata* at the top and empty space below the fourth

14 The name appears in Canova, inscription no. 295.

line. None give the date of death, or any information about the deceased.

Without denying that certain of these features are to be found in the gravestones of the Kerak region,[15] differences definitely exist. By far the most common grave formula in the Kerak district is ENTHADE KEITAI, the Greek equivalent of *hic iacet*, followed in most cases by ZĒSAS (or ZĒSASA) 'having lived' so many years (expressed usually with the accusative ETĒ but sometimes the genitive ETŌN) and by TELEUTĒSAS (or TELEUTĒSASA), 'having died,' followed by the date. This formula does not occur on the three stones known from Dhībân, although the age at death is given.

The conclusion to be drawn – if these three gravestones are to be considered typical – is that in the Dhībân area, just as in southern Palestine[16] and the Kerak district,[17] there were local peculiarities which are probably the result of divergent tastes and traditions. As all the tombstones appear to be Christian, whether or not the personal names reflect a Greco-Roman or Semitic background, such divergences may reflect the practices of different dioceses or, perhaps, of major monastic establishments.

15 The *crux quadrata* and the related Maltese cross are illustrated in Canova, inscriptions nos. 33, 34, 39, 93, 115, 202, 210, 300, etc. The word STĒLĒ is found on inscriptions nos. 27, 34, 91, 93, 102, 115, 129, 151, 212; it also occurs on a tombstone from Feinân (classical Phaino, biblical Punon) south of the Wâdī al-Ḥasā (see A. Alt in ZDPV, 1935, 66, fig. 3) and is apparently common in parts of Egypt (see H. LeClercq, 'Stèle' in *Dictionnaire d'archéologie chrétienne et de liturgie*, vol. 15, pt. 2 [Paris, 1953], p. 1673; see also *Dict.*, vol. 4, pt. 2 [1921], pp. 2493, 2514, 2548).

16 G. E. Kirk, 'Early Christian Gravestone-Formulae of Southern Palestine,' PEQ, 1939, 181–6.

17 Canova, pp. lxxviii ff.

The Placing of
the Accent Signs in
Biblical Texts
with Palestinian Pointing

E. J. REVELL

I INTRODUCTION

I

It is currently the common opinion among scholars that Palestinian accent signs are not used to mark the position of the main word stress, as is true of many Tiberian signs. However, it is difficult to believe, when reading the texts, that the placing of these signs is entirely haphazard. The purpose of this paper is to investigate this feature to see whether any motivation for the placing of the accent signs can be discerned.

2

The six texts chosen for study are ideal for our purposes. They all use the same set of accent signs, and therefore form a homogeneous group in which it is likely that any conventions regarding the placing of the signs would be used consistently.[1] In addition, they are not pointed with vowel signs, so it is not possible that a vowel sign could have displaced an accent sign from its conventional position. All texts are from the Taylor-Schechter collection of the Cambridge University Library. Only one, TS MISC. 2:71, has been published before. The others, TS MISC. 1:112, MISC. 2:31, NS 45:42+50, NS *58:2, and NS 173:1, are described in the appendix.[2]

---

1 A considerable variety of accent signs occurs in Palestinian texts. Apart from this group, no more than three texts are found with the same set of signs.
2 The asterisk on TS NS *58:2 indicates a false number. See note 32. TS MISC. 2:71 is published in M. Dietrich, *Neue palästinisch punktierte Bibelfragmente* (Leiden,

3

The accent signs used in these texts are shown in table I.[3] The disjunctive accents are shown consistently, and with a few variations from the accentuation of the received tradition as represented by the third edition of *Biblia Hebraica* (BHK). As is usual in Palestinian manuscripts, no sign is used corresponding to BHK silluq, and the same sign is used where BHK has atnaḥ and segolta, zarqa and legarmeh, pashta and yetib, and geresh and gershayim. The same is true of zaqef and zaqef gadol, except in TS NS 45:42+, where two dots are added to the Palestinian sign (producing the Tiberian form) in seven out of eight cases where BHK has zaqef gadol. The dots could have been made by the Palestinian or a Tiberian hand.[4] Conjunctive accent signs are not usually used. However, in MISC. 2:31 telisha qeṭana is apparently marked,[5] and in NS 45:42+ a post-positive dot is occasionally used as a general conjunctive sign.[6]

T A B L E   I
SIGNS CORRESPONDING TO THE TIBERIAN ACCENTS

Atnaḥ	—	Tifḥa	—	Geresh	´
Segolta	—	Zarqa	|—	Legarmeh	|—
Zaqef	⊥	Pašṭa	⁖	Pazer	ᵛ
Rebia	⸗	Tebir	—	Telisha	⊥

1968; hereafter 'Dietrich'), as ms Cb 7. I am very grateful to the Library Syndicate of the Cambridge University Library for allowing me to use the other texts. The information given is taken, in all cases, from a study of original texts. It occasionally disagrees with published transcriptions.

3   Not all accents are found in all texts. Signs corresponding to Tiberian accents are lacking as follows: telisha gedola, MISC. I:112, MISC. 2:31, NS *58:2, NS 173:1; pazer MISC. I:112, NS 45:42+, NS *58:2, NS 173:1; zarqa and segolta, MISC. I:112, NS *58:2, NS 173:1; legarmeh, MISC. I:112, NS *58:2; zaqef gadol, NS 173:1; geresh, MISC. I:112.

4   TS MISC. 2:25 is another ms of a type in which zaqef gadol is not normally distinguished, but in which this distinction is made, either by the original accenting hand, or by the later addition of the two-dot Tiberian zaqef sign to a prepositive non-Tiberian zaqef sign. See my paper read at the Fifth World Congress of Jewish Studies.

5   Jer. 3:16. The sign is a prepositive circle, which is not used elsewhere to mark this accent. The Tiberian sign appears on the same word. It is, however, possible that both signs are Tiberian, and one is a correction of the other.

6   Judg. 4:1, 4 and 5:5. For the sign see, for example, P. Kahle, *Masoreten des Westens* II (Stuttgart, 1930), ms H.

II   THE PLACING OF THE ACCENT SIGNS

1

A survey of the texts studied here quickly shows that, although certain accent signs are always prepositive or post-positive (see table I), the majority are not tied to a particular position on the written word (such as the middle). It would seem, then, that if the signs are placed according to some convention, it must be connected (as in BHK) with the structure of the word. Accordingly, in the following survey, the position of the accent signs is catalogued according to word structure, both morphological and phonological. In the latter sphere, syllabic structure and stress position as represented in BHK are taken into consideration.

2

In many situations, accent signs are placed in a non-BHK position with reasonable consistency. For example:

(i) The 2 ms. suffix *-əkɔ*.[7] The accent is never placed on the last syllable of a word containing this suffix, but is generally placed on the syllable before the kaf, *-Cə́kɔ* (12 cases). Where the base to which the suffix is bound ends in two different consonants, the accent is placed on the last syllable of the base, *-CV́CCəkɔ* (2 cases).[8] Where the base is a feminine singular form noun, the accent is placed once according to the usual pattern for this suffix, *-Cɔtə́kɔ*; twice following the usual pattern for feminine nouns, *-Cɔ́təkɔ* (see (ii) below); and once anomalously.[9] In contrast to this clear divergence from BHK, in words containing other bound forms of this pronoun, *-kɔ* (following a vowel), *-ɔk* and *-ɛkɔ* (pausal), and *-ɛykɔ* (on plural nouns, etc.), the accent sign is usually placed, as in BHK, on the syllable preceding the kaf (18 cases). Exceptions are: *ˤɔ́lɛykɔ* (MISC. 2:71, Ezek. 28:7, 29:3, typical placing for *ˤɔl-* see II.5.iv) and *ɔ́šahə̆rɛkkɔ* (NS 173:1, Isa. 26:9, anomalous).

(ii) Feminine singular form nouns with pronominal suffixes. In this situation the accent sign is usually placed on the feminine marker,

---

7   Hebrew forms are given in transliterations of the BHK form (note ɔ qameṣ, *a* pataḥ, *e* ṣere, *ɛ* segol, *ə* shewa, *ă* etc. ḥatefs) or schematically (c any consonant, v any vowel). The position of the Palestinian accent sign is marked by an acute accent over this form. Note that this does not imply that the vowels of the Palestinian form were the same as those of BHK. Note also that when suffixes are transliterated the vowels preceding the actual pronominal morph are given for clarity.

8   *bəsɔ́ˤdəkɔ, tipˀə́rtəkɔ*, NS 45:42+, Judg. 4:9, 5:4.

9   *ubitəbunɔtə́kɔ, ḥɔkmɔ́təkɔ, birəkullɔ́təkɔ, bəḥɔ́kmɔtəkɔ*, MISC. 2:71, Ezek. 28:4, 4, 5, 5.

-*ǿt-* (19 cases). It is placed on the bound pronoun only six times, of which two (2 ms. -*ékɔ*,[10] see above) are special cases. The others are: 2 ms. -*ǿkɔ*, once (see above); 2 fs. -*ék*, twice;[11] and 3 fpl. -*ɔn* once.[12]

(iii) The noun *yiśrɔʾel*. The accent sign is usually placed on the penultimate syllable, *yiśrɔʾel* (22 cases). In the three remaining cases it coincides with the BHK stress position.

(iv) First or second person perfect forms with waw 'consecutive.' The texts contain nine of these forms stressed in BHK on the last syllable. In one, the Palestinian accent sign occupies the same position. In the remaining eight, it is placed on the penultimate syllable [13]

3

Other cases of consistent placing of the accent sign in a non-BHK position could be adduced, but in most situations there are two possibilities for the placing of the sign: the BHK position, or one non-BHK position. Occasionally further non-BHK positions are found, but these form a very small proportion of the whole. Examples are:

(i) The 3 mpl. suffix -*eyhɛm*. The accent sign is placed on the final syllable of a word containing this suffix (as in BHK) in 6 cases; on the penultimate in 8; elsewhere, once.

(ii) The 2 fs. suffix -*ɔ/ayik*. The accent is placed on the penultimate syllable of a word containing this suffix (as in BHK) in 10 cases, on the antepenultimate in 13.

(iii) Feminine singular form nouns. In the absolute forms of these nouns, the accent is placed on the final syllable (as in BHK) in 32 cases; on the penultimate in 28 cases; elsewhere, once.

(iv) Masculine plural form nouns. In the absolute forms of these nouns, the accent is placed on the final syllable (as in BHK) 50 times; on the penultimate 22 times; elsewhere, twice.

4

As these examples show, the general tendency is to place the accent closer to the beginning of the word than in BHK. This is most marked in words which have (in BHK) a stressed, open, final syllable (compare 3.iii with 3.iv above). Of these, the tendency is more marked in words where the penultimate syllable is open and has a 'full' vowel, and in longer words. Table II analyses the position of the accent signs

---

10 *hɔkmɔtékɔ, mɔsukkɔtékɔ*, MISC. 2:71, Ezek. 28:7, 13. Cf. *zulɔtekɔ*, NS 173:1, Isa. 26:13.

11 *rɔmɔték, libbɔték*, MISC. 2:71, Ezek. 16:25, 30. Cf. *rɔʿǿtek, kɔlimmɔ́tek, ibid.*, Ezek. 16:23, 52, and other forms.

12 *lɔqadmɔtɔ́n, cf. lɔqadmɔ́tɔn*, both MISC. 2:71, Ezek. 16:55.

13 *wɔhikrattíy*, MISC. 2:71, Ezek. 30:15. Cf. *wɔhiśbáttiy, ibid.*, Ezek. 30:10, and similar forms, *ibid.*, Ezek. 16:53, 28:22, etc.

in a group of words according to these criteria, showing the position
as (1) on the final syllable or (2) on the penultimate.[14]

TABLE 11

	1	2
Total words ending -cv (161 in all)	47%	53%
Of these (a) forms ending -vcv (67)	41%	59%
others (94)	50%	50%
(b) words of two syllables (41)	68%	32%
words of three syllables (76)	42%	58%
words of four or more syllables (44)	34%	66%

5

This tendency towards penultimate accent position is, however, by
no means consistent. The following shows the position of the accent
sign in groups of words of similar syllabic structure as (1) on the final
syllable or (2) on the pentultimate:

	(1)	(2)
(i) Feminine singular form nouns	32	28
Nouns ending in (BHK) -eh or -ɛh	11	3
(ii) Nouns ending in (BHK) -iy 'gentilic'	–	7
Nouns from 'final weak' roots ending -iy[15]	5	–
(iii) 'Strong' verb forms ending -cv	24	30
'Weak' verb forms ending -ɔh, -ɛh, -eh	14	1

Compare also
(iv) Prepositions with 'light' suffixes:
    ɔl-   accent sign is on the suffix in 6, on the base in 4.
    ᶜl-   accent sign is on the suffix in 1, on the base in 8.
(v) The above examples merely show cases which do not follow the
general tendency. The placing of accent signs on 'segolate' nouns
shows an opposite tendency. The sign is placed on the penultimate
syllable (as in BHK) in 36 cases, and on the final syllable in 30 cases.
6

Whereas in most situations some of the accent signs do not appear in
the BHK stress position, in a number of cases the signs are consistently placed in this position. Examples are given in the preceding
paragraph. As a further illustration, words with a two-syllable pro-

---

14 Forms included are: words with pronominal suffix -iy or -ow; verb forms, perfect
   3 fs. or 3 mpl., imperfect or imperative; 2 fs. or 3 mpl. feminine singular form
   nouns, which have, in BHK, stressed open final syllables.
15 ṣɔbíy MISC. 2:31, Jer. 3:19; períy MISC. 2:71, Ezek. 17:23; nɛhíy/nɔhíy, NS *58:2,
   Jer. 9:17, 18; libɔkíy, NS 173:1, Isa. 22:12.

nominal suffix with (BHK) penultimate stress can be cited. These are:
3 ms. *-ehuw, -ɛnnuw*; 3 fs. *-ɛnnɔh*; 2 ms. *-ɛkɔ, -ɛykɔ, -ɛkkɔ*; 3 fpl.
-hennɔh; 1 cpl. *-ɔnuw, -enuw, -eynuw*. The accent sign is placed on the
penultimate syllable, as in BHK, in 32 cases; on the antepenultimate
in 4 cases; elsewhere, once.

III   CONCLUSIONS

1

It has always been agreed that the position of some of the Palestinian
accent signs is determined as prepositive or post-positive. It is quite
clear from the information given above that the placing of the remainder is not haphazard either. They are placed, with rare exceptions, on one of the last three syllables of a word. Cases of uniform
accent position in words of identical or similar structure are too many
to be ascribed to chance. The information in II.4–5 above shows that
the placing of the sign is influenced both by the syllabic form and by
the morphemic structure of the word. It is highly probable, then,
that the factor which determined the position of the accent signs was
stress.

2

Current scholarly opinion holds that the Palestinian accent signs do
not mark the stress syllable. This opinion originated with Kahle, and
was based on the fact that the Palestinian accent position did not
always coincide with that of BHK.[16] Later scholars have repeated it
without further argument. The observation is perfectly correct, but
failure to mark BHK stress position is not the same as failure to mark
any stress position at all. It is surprising that scholars who were concerned to point out the differences between the vowel systems of BHK
and Palestinian Hebrew did not explore the possibility of there being
similar differences between their stress systems.

3

Scholars who hold that the Palestinian accent signs do not mark
stress position explain the fact that so many of them do appear on
the BHK stress syllable as the result of Tiberian influence.[17] This assumption is an integral part of the theory that Palestinian pointed
texts show a unilinear development from a 'Palestinian' use of their
signs to a 'Tiberian' use (i.e. that of BHK). The following features of

---

16 See H. Bauer and P. Leander, *Historische Grammatik der hebräischen Sprache*
(Hildesheim, 1965), no. 9r, p. 140.
17 See Dietrich, p. 110.

the form and use of the accent signs show, in my opinion, that this theory is untenable.[18]

(i) Of the signs used in Palestinian mss for disjunctive accents, only that for pashṭa appears in a single form. It is impossible to arrange the mss so that the signs for the other accents show a unilinear development, culminating in each case in the sign form closest to the Tiberian.[19]

(ii) The signs for most accents are consistently prepositive, postpositive, or impositive. However, the signs for segolta, rebia, geresh, and legarmeh occur in two of these positions, and that for telisha in all three. It is impossible to arrange the mss so as to show consistent progress towards the BHK position.[20]

(iii) In most mss silluq is marked only occasionally, if at all. The only one which uses a corresponding sign with anything approaching the consistency of its use in BHK is Bod. Heb. d29, f. 17–20,[21] which is not close to BHK in any other respects.

(iv) If the number of significant accent signs[22] appearing in the BHK stress position is expressed as a percentage of the total number in each ms, the expected progression from small figures for mss whose vowel and disjunctive accent systems are not close to those of BHK, to large figures where they are close, does not appear.[23]

(v) Thus, although various items from the differing features of the Palestinian mss can be grouped and seen as the result of chronological development, it is impossible to show that all such groups reflect a single line of development culminating in a close approach to BHK.[24] Any such set of items is quite as likely to reflect differences of tradi-

18 For the same conclusion derived from the use of the vowel signs, see my *Hebrew Texts with Palestinian Vocalization* (Near and Middle East Series, no. 7; Toronto, 1970), sect. v.14ff., and 18.

19 E.g. Dietrich's mss Cb 7, 9, 10, and 11 each mark a different accent as does BHK (atnaḥ, rebia, geresh, zaqef).

20 E.g. in TS NS 246:22. (A. Díez Macho, *Studia Papyrologica*, VI (1967), 15–25), the only ms with a post-positive segolta, geresh is prepositive. (On the placing of geresh, see Dietrich, p. 110.)

21 Dietrich, ms Ob 1.

22 I.e. signs which are neither prepositive or post-positive, nor on monosyllables, and so could indicate stress position.

23 E.g. J.T.S. MS 594, box B, env. 12 (P. Kahle, *The Cairo Geniza* [Oxford, 1959], appendix III), which uses Tiberian signs for atnaḥ, zarqa (Lam. 1:12?), geresh (Eccles, 11:6, Lam. 1:2, 4), and pataḥ, shows a figure of 62 per cent; TS 16:383 +NS 281:2 (Dietrich, ms Cb 10, and A. Díez-Macho, *Sefarad*, 23 (1963), 236–251), using Tiberian geresh, 73 per cent; and TS NS 249:10 (Dietrich, ms Cb 11), using Tiberian zaqef, 78 per cent. This criterion thus places these mss in the opposite order to that suggested by Dietrich (see p. 88*).

24 The development towards BHK suggested by Dietrich and others is no doubt at least partially correct (when not applied equally to all mss). Other possible de-

tion as chronological development, and some sets must have arisen in this way.[25]

4

Since Palestinian mss showing features close to BHK do not always show a high proportion of accent signs placed in the BHK stress position (see note 24), there is no basis for the claim that such high proportions are the result of Tiberian influence on a tradition in which the accent signs had no conventional position. The information given above shows that the placing of the accent signs was not haphazard. Furthermore, if accent position and stress position are equated, as the evidence surely warrants, the information collected here shows some illuminating complements and parallels to the information provided by the study of the vowel signs.

(i) In non-biblical Palestinian texts, there is usually no vowel sign written after the kaf of the 2 ms. pronominal suffix. As ben Ḥayyim has shown, the final vowel was lost through the influence of Aramaic.[26] The information in II.2.i above shows that the same influence is at work in the biblical pronunciation, and has caused the retraction of the stress, but not yet (as we know from texts with vowel signs) the loss of the final vowel. Thus the biblical pronunciation follows the same development as the non-biblical, but follows it more slowly, a conclusion already arrived at from the study of the vowel signs.[27]

velopments in the use of the vowel signs are suggested in my *Hebrew Texts with Palestinian Vocalization* (see note 18), sect. v.28. For the accent signs, developments possibly occurred in the number of distinct signs used for disjunctive accents, the same for conjunctive accents, and the extent to which significant accent signs are placed on the BHK stress syllable. This last item shows significant groupings when correlated with conjunctive (but not disjunctive) systems. Broadly speaking, in one-conjunctive systems, 50–56 per cent of the accents are placed on the BHK stress syllable; in two-conjunctive, 64–76 per cent; and in systems with more conjunctives, 82–90 per cent. Systems with no conjunctives show figures of 47–78 per cent, suggesting (if this feature does reflect chronological development) that in some cases the absence of conjunctive signs marks a 'simplified' and not a 'primitive' system (as with our group of texts, where these signs are not normally used, but were known – see 1.3 above).

25 The placing of accent signs will probably show differences of tradition similar to those found in the use of the vowel signs. For example, -ɔh 'directional' is not stressed in the texts discussed here (MISC. 1:112, Num. 4:43; MISC. 2:71, Ezek. 16:29, 17:20, 29:5; NS 45:42+, Judg. 3:23, 25) but is stressed in, for example, TS A19:11 (unpublished), Dan. 8:4, 7, and TS NS 249:6 + (see my article in *Textus* VII, no. 6.3), 1 Chron. 4:41, 5:9.

26 See Z. Ben Ḥayyim, *Studies in the Traditions of the Hebrew Language* (Madrid, 1954), pp. 51ff.

27 See my 'Studies in the Palestinian Vocalization of Hebrew,' in *Essays in the Ancient Semitic World*, edited by J. W. Wevers and D. B. Redford (Toronto, 1970), pp. 51–100, 1.42.

(ii) The strong tendency to stress the final syllable of 'segolate' forms (see II.5.v above) must be a parallel case of Aramaic influence. Others could be added.

(iii) There can be no doubt, considering the normal vocalization of these two types of structure in Palestinian biblical texts, that the stress patterns shown here result from a development which began with a situation similar to that shown by BHK. This repeats another conclusion drawn from the study of the vowel signs: the Palestinian pointing depicts a stage of the language which has developed further from their common origin than has that represented in BHK.[28]

(iv) The failure to distinguish waw 'consecutive' perfect forms (see II.2.iv) supports this conclusion. An early feature of the language is here almost completely lost, a trend which has already started in BHK.

(v) The other features noted here as divergent from BHK can also be taken as resulting from developments subsequent to the stage of the language represented by BHK.[29] They do not, of course, require this explanation, but it seems to me to raise fewer problems than the other possibilities.

5

It seems certain, then, that, in these texts, the Palestinian accent signs do mark stress position. The fact that, in most situations, the stress position is not stable, but varies between BHK and non-BHK positions, also parallels the state of affairs indicated by the use of the vowel signs in most Palestinian texts. An older pattern (here the BHK stress pattern) is in the process of change. In some situations, the change is virtually complete, and stress patterns are almost uniformly 'Palestinian,' but in others no change has taken place. In most situations, however, change is in progress, so that either of two stress positions is used. Thus it can be concluded here, as it was from the study of the use of the vowel signs, that the Palestinian pointing was produced by a group who were less successful in guarding their traditional pronunciation from change than were the massoretes of the ben Asher school.

---

28 See *ibid.*, 1.31ff.

29 The general tendency to retract the stress can be compared with the penultimate stressing general in Samaritan Hebrew; see Z. Ben Ḥayyim, *The Literary and Oral Traditions of Hebrew and Aramaic among the Samaritans*, vol. III, pt. 1 (Jerusalem, 1961), p. 26. This dialect has followed a different development from either BHK or Palestinian biblical Hebrew, and retains some ancient features, but is considered by Ben Ḥayyim to represent a later stage of the language than the Tiberian (see *ibid.*, p. VII).

APPENDIX: THE MANUSCRIPTS

TS MISC. 1:112   Part of two folios of parchment, now about 210 by 225 mm., somewhat damaged. The text is written in two columns of about 185 by 80 mm., with 33 or 34 lines per column. The script is a small, neat, formal Palestinian type, similar to that of TS MISC. 1:44.[30] The ink is olive-brown, badly faded in parts, for which reason fol. 1 was mostly retraced in black ink. The Palestinian accent signs were added in a dark grey ink. They appear to be almost completely confined to fol. 1, and are very difficult to read because of fading and partial obliteration by the retracing of the text. Folio 1 contains Numbers 3:48 to 4:45.

TS MISC. 2:31   Two fragments of a sheet of parchment, now ca. 240 by 185 mm., badly deteriorated, and with many tears and holes. The text is written in three columns of about 205 by 65 mm., with 36 or 37 lines per column. The script is a fairly free, rather clumsy Palestinian type in dark brown ink. Some parts of the text seem to have been retraced in a similar ink. The Palestinian accent signs, and also Tiberian vowels and accents, were added in an ink similar to that of the script. The Tiberian signs correspond fairly closely to BHK usage, but show deviations, such as the interchange of pataḥ/qameṣ and ṣere/segol. Owing to deterioration of the materials, the text on the verso is mostly illegible, and few Palestinian signs can be seen. The fragment contains Jer. 2:37 to 5:6.

TS MISC. 2:71   Discovered by Dr Manfried Dietrich, and described and partially published in his *Neue palästinisch punktierte Bibelfragmente* (Leiden, 1968) as ms Cb 7. Dr Dietrich is uncertain about the forms of the signs used for zarqa and segolta (see pp. 56f.). In my opinion, he has correctly given the single case of zarqa (Ezek. 17:19, as table 1 above), but I do not agree with his suggestion that segolta is marked with two dots (:) as I think the dots to which he refers were not made by the Palestinian hand (they are probably part of a Tiberian segolta sign). In Ezek. 28:25, as Dietrich notes, the atnaḥ sign is clearly used where BHK has segolta. The same sign is visible in Ezek. 17:16 (under the final *h* of *yhwh*, displaced by the lamed in the line below), and in Ezek. 17:19 (under the ꜣ of *ꜣny*). It is usual in Palestinian

30 Dietrich, ms Cb 4.

mss for the same sign to be used where BHK has both atnaḥ and segolta. The atnaḥ sign is used in both positions in other mss of the group described here (MISC. 2:31, Jer. 3:25; NS 45:42+, Judg. 2:12, 3:15, 4:18), in JTS MS 594. B.12, see note 23 (Lam. 1:12, under the *d* of *drk*, clear in the photograph, but overlooked in the transcription), and also in some Tiberian mss (e.g. TS 28:16, Ezek. 23:10, 22, and cf. Dietrich, p. 26).

TS NS 45:42+50   Two folios of parchment, about 230 by 220 mm., slightly damaged. The text of fols. 1 and 2r is written in three columns of about 200 by 65 mm., that of fol. 2v (the song of Debora) in two columns about 200 by 100 mm., with 33 to 36 lines per column. The script is a fairly formal square Palestinian type in dark brown ink. Some parts were retraced in black, partially obliterating the pointing, particularly on the lower half of fol. 2r. The Palestinian accent signs were added in an ink varying from dark brown to red brown. Subsequently Tiberian pointing was added in a similar, but generally paler ink. The pointing shows considerable divergence from BHK: e.g. qameṣ and segol and rare,[31] and are frequently replaced by pataḥ and ṣere. Occasionally accent signs are written in a position different from that of BHK. A later hand, with ink of the same colour, has, to some extent, harmonized this pointing with that of BHK. This fragment contains Judg. 2:2 to 5:26.

TS NS *58:2[32]   Three fragments of a leaf of parchment, originally about 255 by 230 mm., now badly torn and deteriorated. The text is written in three columns about 210 by 65 mm., with 35 to 37 lines per column. The script is a fairly free, rather clumsy Palestinian square type in dark brown ink. The Palestinian accent signs were added in an ink somewhat paler than that of the script. Tiberian vowel and accent signs were added in a somewhat darker ink. These show some deviation from the BHK system especially in interchange of segol and ṣere. Interchange of pataḥ and qameṣ occurs more rarely. Occasional accent signs differ in position from those of BHK. A later hand, with similar ink, has

---

31 It is possible that they were not used at all by the first Tiberian hand, but this seems unlikely.

32 When I first found this text, I provisionally assigned this number to it, and in fact obtained a photograph of it under this number. When the fragments in the box were prepared for binding, however, this text evidently became separated from its folder, and was given a new number, which I have not so far been able to trace.

harmonized some features of this pointing with the BHK tradition, particularly deviations in accent position. The legible part of the text covers Jer. 8:10 to 11:6. This fragment is very similar to TS MISC. 2:31 in script and layout, and it is possible (but I think unlikely) that they belong to the same ms.

TS NS 173:1 A fragment of a leaf of parchment, now 115 by 150 mm., with tears and holes. The text was written in three columns about 65 mm. wide. Part of recto col. 1 and 2 (verso col. 2 and 3) is preserved. The script is a fairly free, rather clumsy Palestinian square type in a dark brown ink. Some parts, particularly on the recto, have been retraced in a similar ink. The Palestinian accent signs were added in an ink similar to that of the script. Tiberian pointing was added in a generally paler ink. This shows some deviations from BHK in the interchange of ṣere/segol and (rarely) pataḥ/qameṣ, and also occasionally in the accent system. A later hand, in similar ink, has harmonized some of these features with the BHK system. The fragment contains Isa. 22:9 to 23:4 and 25:5 to 26:16. The fragment is similar in script, and (presumed) layout to TS NS *58:2, and might have belonged to the same ms.

The Textual Affinities
of the Arabic Genesis of
Bib. Nat. Arab 9

JOHN W. WEVERS

It is particularly appropriate in view of Professor Winnett's long interest in early Arabic studies to dedicate this renewed investigation
of the Arabic Genesis to him at the moment of his retirement from
teaching and to pay tribute thereby to a great but unassuming and
warm-hearted scholar with whom I have for two decades been privileged to work in close association.

In the process of collating the LXX subversions of Genesis for the
Göttingen LXX the unsatisfactory state of Arabic texts became immediately apparent. The Cambridge LXX[1] judiciously omitted the
Arabic evidence from its apparatus throughout, and one can readily
understand the editors' decision.

There are at least four old Arabic versions extant for the book of
Genesis which need mention. The texts of the London and Paris
Polyglots[2] represent the text of Saadia Gaon, a Jewish translation
from the Hebrew, but at times strongly influenced by the Islamic environment in which it was produced. This can be illustrated by the
peculiar attempts at identifying the nations in the 'Table of Nations'
of chapter 10, a list which even includes Mecca and al-Medinah.
Lagarde's edition of the Leiden ms, Warner Arab. 377, represents
this same text.[3]

Lagarde also edited as part II of the same volume another Arabic

1 *The Old Testament in Greek*, vol. I, *The Octateuch*, pt. I, *Genesis*, edited by
   A. E. Brooke and N. McLean (Cambridge, 1906).
2 The text of the London Polyglot is a copy of the Paris one.
3 P. de Lagarde, *Materialien zur Kritik und Geschichte des Pentateuchs*
   (Leipzig, 1867).

biblical text from Leiden, the Qarshuni ms Scaliger Arab. 230, which is a Catena text of Genesis with numerous patristic citations particularly from Ephrem the Syrian, Chrysostom, Jacob of Edessa, and Jacob of Serug. The lemmata include less than two-thirds of the text of Genesis and represent a popular translation of Paul of Tella's Syro-hexaplar. This text is well known from at least four mss which were hand-copied for Göttingen by the late W. Reimpell in 1911.[4] This copy was used by Rahlfs in his Genesis edition[5] as evidence for the Syro-hexaplar wherever the Syriac text was not extant. Its evidence is of doubtful value, however, since it is not only a translation of a translation, but it is at the same time a relatively free rendering of it. It should, I believe, not be cited critically, and its readings will in the main be disregarded in the critical edition.

Rhodes,[6] in a study of eighteen Egyptian Arabic Pentateuch mss, noted two distinct Christian versions in use in Egypt, one translated from the Coptic (presumably the Bohairic) for use by the Coptic or Jacobite church, and the other, in use by the Melkite community, which was made directly from the Greek. It is this latter version, represented by six mss,[7] that is of particular interest for the LXX scholar, and which is here to be subjected to textual analysis.

The first section of the paper deals briefly with the character of the version as reflected in the numerous unique readings it has. The main section presents the evidence for textual influences in the Arabic as it relates to the textual families or groups tentatively identified for Genesis. The paper concludes with a brief interpretation of the evidence.

In citing the evidence a certain order will be followed.[8] The hexa-

---

4   I am grateful to Dr Robert Hanhart, the director of the Göttingen Institute, for making this unique copy available to me.

5   A. Rahlfs, *Septuaginta Soc. Sc. Gott. auct. ed.* I. *Genesis* (Stuttgart, 1926).

6   J. F. Rhodes, *The Arabic Versions of the Pentateuch in the Church of Egypt* (Leipzig, 1921). Rhodes argues convincingly that the Melkite Arabic version was earlier (possibly eighth century) than the Jacobite one. For older literature cf. G. Graf, *Die chr.-arabische Literatur bis zur fränkischen Zeit* (1905), ch. 1; H. Goussen, *Die chr.-arabische Literatur des Mozarabes* (1909); P. Kahle, *Die arabischen Bibelübersetzungen* (1904).

7   The mss are Bibl. Nat., Paris, Arab 9, 10, 11, 16 and Bodl. Libr. Pocock 219 and Marsh 440. Of these the best written is the thirteenth-century Paris ms, Arab 9, which was the full Pentateuch but without *tafsir*. It is this text which has been used as a basis for the above study. I am grateful to the Bibliothèque nationale for providing me with a microfilm of this important ms.

8   The Göttingen Institute is responsible for the collation of all mss, and the editor for papyri, versions, and patristic evidence. The citations for the Old Latin are based on the Beuron critical text of B. Fischer, *VETUS LATINA: Die Reste der altlateinischen Bibel, nach Petrus Sabatier neu gesammelt und herausg. von der*

plaric evidence will be cited first, followed by the Catena group; then follow the families in alphabetical order, followed by the codd mixt, the uncials, the papyri, the Greek Fathers, the Versions, the Latin Fathers, and finally Arab. Only when a particular group's relationship is being investigated will that group head the list.

I

Arab is a relatively free rendering of its *Vorlage*, and more than four hundred unique readings have been recorded. There would be little point to listing these, and I shall give only a few examples to illustrate some of the characteristics of the translation.

A large number of unique readings show change in word order. These are mainly in the interests of good Arabic style.

1:10 tr τα συστηματα των
     υδατων/εκαλεσε
2:21 tr εκστασιν/επι τ. αδαμ

3:13 tr τουτο/εποιησας
42:28 tr προς αλληλους/λεγοντες

Of greater significance is the tendency of Arab to a shorter text; in fact, the version at times compresses the repetitiousness of its *Vorlage* into a more compact statement.

Erzabti Beuron (Freiburg, 1951–4). The following text families have been isolated for the Göttingen edition:
O: G–15–17–29–58–72–82–135–376–400–426–707. oI: 64–381–618–708; O' = O + oI. C: 14–16–25–77–128–131–414–422–500–551–646–739. cI: 57–73–78–413–550. cII: 18(to 47:15)–52–54(from 22:21)–79–313–408–569–615–761. C' = C + cI; C = C⁀ + cII; C'⁀ = C + cI + cII. b: 18(from 47:15)–19–108–118–314–537–Bˢ(to 46:28). d: 44–106–107–125–370(from 25:5)–610. f: 53–56–129–246–664. n: 75–458. s: 30–85–127–130–343–344–730(from 26:13). t: 46–74–76(to 42:1)–84–134–370(to 25:5). y: 71–121–318–346–392–424–527–619. z: 31–120–122–407–630. Uncials: A B D F L M. Codd mixt: 54(to 22:21) 55 59 76(from 42:1) 319 508–509 707ᴵᴵ 707ᴵᴵᴵ.

For convenience the following abbreviations will be used: for b: 19' = 19 + Bˢ, 118' = 118 + 314; for d: 106' = 106 + 125, 44' = 44 + 106, 107' = 107 + 610; for f: 53' = 53 + 664, 56' = 56 + 246; for s: 30' = 30 + 730, 343' = 343 + 130, 344' = 344 + 127; for t: 74' = 74 + 134, 76' = 76 + 370; for y: 71' = 71 + 619, 318' = 318 + 346, 346' = 346 + 527, 392' = 392 + 527, 424' = 424 + 527; for z: 31' = 31 + 122, 120' = 120 + 407; for O: 15' = 15 + 82, 17' = 17 + 400, 72' = 72 + 707, 135' = 135 + 376, 376' = 376 + 426; for oI: 64' = 64 + 708, 381' = 381 + 618; for C: 14' = 14 + 16, 77' = 77 + 131, 128' = 128 + 646, 414' = 414 + 422, 422' = 422 + 500, 500' = 500 + 739, 551' = 551 + 414; for cI: 57' = 57 + 413, 73' = 73 + 78, 413' = 413 + 550; for cII: 52' = 52 + 79, 408' = 408 + 569, 615' = 615 + 761; for Codd mixt: 59' = 59 + 707ᴵᴵ, Co = Bo + Sa. Other abbreviations are those common to the volumes in the Göttingen Septuagint.

13:9 om διαχωρισθητι απ εμου
15:2 om εγω–(v. 3)εδωκας
24:48 om και 2°–αβρααμ
34:3 δινας–ιακωβ] *ei*

41:30 om και 2°–fin
43:14 δωη–ανθρωπου] *erit*
  vobiscum
44:8 om προς–χανααν

However, the opposite tendency to amplify and thereby become more explicit is also seen.

18:8 αυτοις] *abraham ad ostium*
  tabernaculi
27:35 αυτω] *pater suus*

36:9 αι γενεσεις] *nomina filiorum*
41:8 αυτο] *interpretationem eius*
47:21 αυτω] *pharaoh*

The ms is rather carelessly copied as the substantial number of instances of parablepsis indicates. Some of these are added in the margin, probably by the original copyist.

10:31 αυτων 1° ⌢ 3°
15:21 και 1° ⌢ 2°
16:8 και 2° ⌢ 3°

19:30 αυτου 2° ⌢ 4°
25:21 αυτου 2° ⌢ 3°:txt

Other instances of carelessness may be cited as well.

9:23 σημ] *et ham*
20:2 μου 2°] *eius*

36:10 om ησαυ 3°
36:14 θυγατρος bis scr.

Instances of Hebrew influence through Saadia Gaon's translation are quite numerous, and are not overly surprising in an Egyptian version. I cite only a few.

25:30 εδωμ] *rufus* Saad Arab
31:47 βουνος μαρτος] *in hebraico*
  gilead Saad Arab
46:15 μεσοποταμια της συριας]
  fadan aram Saad Arab

46:20 εγενοντο] *nati sunt* Saad
  Arab
46:20 om εγενοντο 2°–fin (sub ÷
  in M-Syh) Saad Arab

II TEXTUAL AFFINITIES OF THE VORLAGE OF ARAB

1 *Affinities with the d group*

10:12 om ανα μεσον 2° 44-125
  La¹ Arab
12:18 om μοι 1° d⁻⁴⁴ 135 Arab
12:19 μου] σου d LaᴹArab

13:7 om ανα μεσον 2° 44-125 458
  Laᴱ
17:10 υμων 1°] σου d 54 Arm
  Eth⁻ᴾ GregIllyb Aug Ruf Arab

18:24 om παντα τον τοπον
d Arab
29:17 οι–ασθενεις] η δε λεια ην
ασθενης d Arab

37:6 om τουτον d 121 Arm Arab
40:2 om αυτου d⁻⁴⁴⁻¹²⁵ Phil La^S
Boh Arab

2   Affinities with the t group

2:15 fin] + αυτου t 319 343-344′ᵐᵍ
135 M La Eth Boh^L Arab
7:14 γενος 1°] + αυτων t 82
Syh(sub ast.) Sa¹⁹ Arab ⁹

25:6 αυτου 1°] του αβρααμ t 911
962 Boh Arab
35:17 om γαρ t Arab

3   Affinities with the b group

11:31 ηλθεν]–θον b 44 343 911
Arm Eth Arab
11:31 κατωκησεν] ωκησαν b Arm
Eth Arab
13:10 om πασα b Boh Ambr Arab
16:11 κς] ο θς b La^E Arab
17:10 om εις τας γενεας αυτων
b La Eth^C Arab
20:9 ημιν] μοι b Arab
20:9 ημαρτομεν]–τον b 107-610
Chr Arab
21:17 om σου b 17′ 392 55 Eth^P
La^E Sa Arab
22:2 ειπω] δειξω 19′ 54 Sa Ruf
MisMoz Arab
24:17 ειπεν] + αυτη b Eth La^I
Boh Arab
24:25 om και 2° b 125 318 14′-
77′-500′ 962 Boh Arab

24:45 διανοια (+μου)] + και ιδου
b 17 527 Boh(om και) Arab
25:34 πρωτοτοκια] + αυτου b
Arm^codd La^X Boh^W Arab
27:4 οπως] και b Arm La¹⁰⁰ Arab
29:4 om εσμεν b⁻ᴮ 319 17′ 55 Boh
Arab
29:23 om αυτην 1° b⁻¹⁹ Arm
Eth^PR Arab
30:4 om αυτω 1° b 52-408′-761
Boh Arab
30:17 tr τω ιακωβ/υιον πεμπτον
b Boh Arab
30:29 α]την δουλειαν ην b Co Arab
32:16 δεκα 1°] εικοσι b La^S Arab
32:17 εδωκεν] + αυτα b Sa²⁰ Boh
Arab
37:15 om λεγων b 17-135 961
Phil La^S Sa³(vid.) Arab

---

9 Abbreviations used for Sa are as follows. Full bibliographical information may
be found in the lists of A. Vaschalde and W. Till in RB, 1919–22 and BJRL, 43
(1959). 1 and 2, von Lemm; 3, Lefort; 4, Erman; 5, Till, *Saad. Fragm.*;
6, Schleifer; 7, Shier; 8, Gilmore and Renouf; 9, Winstedt; 10, Munier, *Recueil*;
11, Crum, *Short texts*; 12, Crum, *Cat JRL*; 13, Kahle; 14, Munier, *Sur deux
passages*; 15, Brooke; 16, Ceugney; 17, Wessely, *Texte I*; 18, Wessely, *Texte IV*;
19, Maspero; 20, Ciasca; 21, Till, *Kopt. Perg.*; 22, Crum, *Cat BM*.
    For the six mss collated for Eth, cf. J. O. Boyd, *The Octateuch in Ethiopic* acc.
to the Text of the Paris Codex, with the Variants of Five Other Manuscripts,
Bibl. Abess. III (Leiden, 1909).

41:8 om παντες 1° *b* 17-135 16
527 Boh Arab
44:2 εγενηθη] εγενετο *b* Eth Arab
44:24 fin] + ημων *b* 458 59 Arm
Boh Arab
45:7 υμων 3°] υμιν *b* 135 54 Boh
Arab

45:16 και 2°] πασα *b* 318 F Eth
Arab
46:26 ἐξ] πεντε 19' Arab
47:9 om ημερας *b* Eth Boh Arab
49:22 ηυξημενος 2°] + μου *b* B
La^E Sa Arab

4   Affinities with the n group

13:7 om των κτηνων 1° *n* 82 Sa
Arab
13:14 om νυν *n* 422* Arm Eth
Ruf Jub-lat Arab
24:43 εγω/ειπω *n* 314-537 Eth^P
Arab

27:19 φαγε] + απο *n* DialTA;
+ εκ Chr; + de Boh Arab
43:17 om ιωσηφ 2° *n* 761 71 Arab
43:26 om εις τον οικον *n* 82 Arab
46:4 om και 1° *n* Chr Arm La^s

a   Affinities attested only by 75

12:11 om αβραμ 2° 75 14 Chr
Arm Arab
20:6 om του μη αμαρτειν σε εις
εμε 75 Arab
21:1 om και 2°–fin 75 664^txt 346
Arab
21:9 om ος εγενετο τω αβρααμ
75 664^txt Eth Arab

21:26 om αυτω 75 761 44 Eth^PRa
Arab
28:8 χανααν] των χανανεων 75
Arm La^E Boh^L Arab
39:6 om αυτος 75 D Chr Arm Eth
Boh Arab

b   Affinities attested only by 458

6:16 της κιβωτου] αυτης 458
Sa Pal Arab
8:3 om το υδωρ 458 56* Arab
8:12 om ετι 1° 458 Boh Arab
12:18 om μοι 2° 458 127 Arm^txt
La^I Arab
13:7 om ανα μεσον 2° 458 44-125
La^E Arab
13:7 om των κτηνων 458 Chr Arab
16:3 om η γυνη αβραμ 458 125
Eth Arab
19:2 om και 2° 458 82* Arm Arab
27:21 om δε 458 Boh^W Arab
34:3 την παρθενον] αυτην 458
Arab

35:11 om εθνη 458 Boh^W Arab
37:11 fin] + τουτο 458 Boh Arab
40:22 om αυτοις 458 Arm^txt Arab
41:2 om ωσπερ 458 Arab
41:11 om ειδομεν 2° 458 Arab
41:12 om μεθ ημων 458 Arab
42:2 om και 1° 458 129* Arab
43:15 om ταυτα 458 962 Chr
Arm Sa^21 Arab
43:19 om του οικου 458 618^txt
Arm Arab
44:22 κυριω] + ημων 458 59 Syh
Boh Arab
44:30 om δε 458 Arm Eth Arab
48:17 om ιωσηφ 2° 458 Arab

5 Affinities with the f group

3:1 om των επι 56-664˙ Chr
JohCass Or-lat Arab

8:3 εικαδι] + ημερα 53-664^mg 319
72-82-376-400 Aug^var Arab

9:21 οινου] + αυτου 56-129-664
458 Ambr Aug Arab

10:32 κατα 2°] pr και 56'-129
Aug LibGeneal Arab

11:17 εβδομηκοντα] τριακοντα
664˙ Arab

11:25 εικοσι εννεα] ιθ̄ 53' (cf.
δεκα pro εικοσι in 319 82-376)
Arab

14:17 αυτω] αβραμ f^-56' La^I Sa^20
Boh Arab

15:18 κ̄ς̄] ο θ̄ς̄ f^-56 527 Arab

16:2 κ̄ς̄] ο θ̄ς̄ f Aug Arab

16:14 ιδου] pr και 53' 57 Arm
Arab

18:11 ημερων] εν τ. ημεραις
αυτων f Chr La^I Boh Arab

21:11 περι] + ισμαηλ 129-246
Boh Arab

22:23 om και βαθουηλ 664˙ Arab

24:51 λαβων] + αυτην 53' Aug^var
Arab

24:55 om δε 246 Arab

26:24 ειπεν] + αυτω f 59 Eth
La^E Boh Arab

26:32 om ουχ 53-664^c·pr·m·
Arm^codd Arab

27:7 φαγων] φαγω και 53'-56^txt
458 Arm Boh Aug Arab

29:14 αυτω λαβαν] λαβαν προς
ιακωβ 53' Eth Arab

29:22 τοπου] + εκεινου f^-56˙ La^s
Boh Arab

30:30 κ̄ς̄] ο θ̄ς̄ f^-53' 509 Co Arab

31:42 μοι] μετ εμου 53' 500 Chr
Arm Arab

32:13 ειπας] + μοι f^-56˙ Eth La^s
Boh Arab

34:7 εποιησεν] + συχεμ f A Eth
La^s Co Arab

35:9 ετι] οντι 53-56^mg 74 Boh
Arab

36:6 om κ. οσα περιεποιησατο
53' 509 Eth Arab

37:10 αρα] pr τεκνον f^-56˙ Arab

41:40 θρονον] + μου f^-56˙ Boh
Arab

42:5 αγοραζειν] + σιτον f^-56˙ Sa
Arab

42:38 om η αν πορευησθε 53' Chr
Jub Arab

43:18 om ιδοντες–ιωσηφ 53' 610
Arab

44:9 κονδυ] + απο 53' Arm Arab

44:20 om τω κ̄ω̄ 53' 125 25 Arab

44:30 εισπορευωμαι] – ρευσομεθα
53'(664–σωμ-) Arm Eth Sa
Arab

44:32 πατερα] + μου 53' Arm
Syh Boh Arab

44:33 fin] + αυτου f^-56c· Arm Syh
La^s Eth Boh Arab

46:5 αποσκευην] + αυτων 53' 527
59 Boh Arab

49:1 ειπεν B] + αυτοις f 707 75
59 Eth La^s Sa Arab

6   Affinities with the s group

20:4 tr αγνοουν ... /δικαιον s
57-78-550 346 730 Chr Arab
48:1 ιωσηφ] + λεγοντες 30-343-
344^{mg}-730 646 71 Boh Arab

49:22 ηυξημενος 1°] + μου 30-
343-730-(85-344')^{mg} M^{mg} La^E
Arab

7   Hexaplaric relations

a   Affinities with o

7:14 γενος 1°] + αυτων Syh(sub
ast)-82 t Sa^{19} Arab

7:14 γενος 3°] + αυτου Syh(sub
ast)-17'-376 Arab

9:24 οινου] + αυτου Syh(sub ast)-
17'-82-135 319 Arm

10:19 γομορρας] + και 17'-135
911(vid.) Arm La^o Eth Arab

18:28 om πασαν 72' Arab

19:16 fin] + κ. εξηγαγον αυτον κ.
εθηκαν αυτον απεξω της πολεως (c.var.) 15-72'-135-426-oI
73-57'^{mg} 246 343-(344')^{mg} 527
M^{mg} Boh Arab

20:3 εισηλθεν] ηλθεν O' Arm Syh
Eus Arab

20:10 εποιησας] + μοι Syh(sub
ast)–O'-376 Arm Tht Arab

22:13 κερατων] + αυτου O'-135-426
Pal Boh Hi Arab

22:21 πρωτοτοκον] + αυτου O'
La^o Arm Co Arab

23:3 fin] + αυτην 15-17'-135-
426-oI Arab

24:55 μητηρ] + αυτης O 509 Boh
Arab

24:67 οικον] + σαρρας O' (72'
σαρας) 413^{mg} 130^{mg}-344'^{mg}(sub
ast) 71-527-392 55 319 630 Co
Arab

25:24 ημεραι] + αυτης O' Boh
Ruf Ps-Phil Arab

29:13 εφιλησεν] + αυτον O'-58-82-
^{618} 75 509 Boh Arab

30:12 tr τω ιακωβ /υιον δευτερον
O 56' Arm Arab

31:50 fin] + ορων θεος μαρτυς
μεταξυ εμου και μεταξυ σου κ.
ειπε λαβαν τω ιακωβ ιδου ο
σωρος ουτος κ. ιδου η στηλη ην
εστησα μεταξυ εμου κ. μεταξυ
σου μαρτυς ο σωρος κ. μαρτυς
η στηλη (c.var.) O' 318-527 31
Arm Boh^W Arab

31:53 ημων] + (o)θ͞σ πατρων
(aut πατρος) αυτων (nostrorum
Arab) O-17'-58(G sub ast.vid.)
Syh Arm Arab

32:8 tr τ. βοας ... /τα προβατα
O-58 911 Syh Eth La^S Boh Arab

32:24 διεβη] διεβιβασεν αυτους
O'-58-400 Arm Arab

35:8 om ιακωβ O-376-426 25 318 L
961 962 Arm Eth^{CRa} La^X Sa
Arab

35:16 om επηξε—γαδερ G-426
Arm Arab

35:20 fin] + (v.21) κ. απηρεν ι͞η͞λ
κ. επηξε τ. σκηνην αυτου επ-
εκεινα τ. πυργου γαδερ O' 246

30-127-730-(344-343)sub ast.
46 346 31 Arab

36:40 om εν 2°–fin 17'-72-135
Arab

41:5 init] pr και (+*rursum* Arm
Boh Arab) υπνωσε(ν) O⁻¹⁷ 527
Arm Eth^CR Boh^LM Arab

41:35 tr ερχομενων ... /καλων
O⁻⁷²⁻³⁷⁶ 319 130 527 707^II D
Arm Arab

42:4 απεστειλεν] + ιακωβ O⁻⁵⁸
319 130 527 59 76 707^II D
Arm(pr ast) Arab

43:5 om λεγων O⁻⁸²⁻⁴²⁶⁻⁷⁰⁷ Eth
Arab

43:22 αργυριον] + ημων O⁻⁸²(426
c.pr.m.) 408 130 619 Syh Sa²¹
Arab

43:24 init] pr κ. εισηγαγεν ο
ανηρ τους ανδρας εις τον οικον
ιωσηφ Syh(sub ast)-15-29-72'-
376-F^bmg Arm Arab(om
τ. οικον)

44:22 πατερα 2°] + αυτου
Syh(sub ast)-O 46 Arm Boh
Arab

45:12 tr βενιαμιν/του αδελφου
μου O⁻⁷²' 54 Syh Arab

46:22 οκτω] τεσσαρες 15-29-426
Eth^CR Ps-Phil Vulg Arab

47:23 tr και την γην υμων/σημε-
ρον O Arm Boh Arab

49:29 init] pr και ενετειλατο
αυτους O⁻⁸² Arm Arab^mg(+*pater
eorum*)

b Instances of hexaplaric readings
present in Arab with wider ms support

3:22 ειπεν] + κ̅ς̅ M^mg(sub ast)
17'-135 C^⁷⁻¹⁸⁻⁶⁴⁶ 53-246-664^c
346-424 31 319 509 A Chr Genn
La^A Co Arab

7:14 γενος 4°] + αυτου Syh(sub
ast)-17' C^⁷⁻¹²⁸ s 346 319 730
Arab

13:18 πλατος b 129 y⁻³⁴⁶' 31' A
55 59 961 La^I] + αυτης rell
(pr ast. Arm)

16:4 κυρια] + αυτης Syh(sub
ast)-Arm(pr ast)-O⁻¹⁷'⁻⁷²⁻¹³⁵ C^⁷
319 911 Or Eth La^M Sa¹⁸ Bo
Arab

20:3 ειπεν] + αυτω Syh(sub
ast)-376 57^mg-73^mg-78-550 53-
664^c 75 130^mg t 71'-121-392'-318
z 54 55 59 La^I Co Eth Arab

27:41 διανοια 58 C^⁷⁻⁷⁶¹ s 424 509
911] + αυτου rell(pr ast Arm)

32:8 εις] pr (ast G 344^mg) τας

καμηλους O' 343-344^mg-730 46
509 M^mg Arm Eth^C Syh Arab

34:8 ψυχη] + (ast 344) αυτου
15-17'-135'-oI C^⁷⁻¹²⁸ n 30-344^mg-
730 318' 630 55^c Co La^S Arab

35:8 ρεβεκκας 118'-537 129 120'-
122 59' 509 A L 911 961 962
Bo^L Eth^-C] + (ast G) και
εταφη Chr rell

35:18 πατηρ] + (ast G) αυτου
O'⁻¹³⁵ 458 130 121-392 A Chr
Co Eth La^O Arab

35:29 εκλιπων 72-381' 128 125
53' 458 130 121-527 z⁻⁶³⁰ 509 A
961] + (ast G) ισαακ rell

36:18 fin] + (ast G) θυγατρος ανα
γυναικος ησαυ O' C' 53-56*-
664^mg 30-730 t⁻⁴⁶ 318'-392'-619
31-630 55 319 707^II D Arm Bo
Syh Arab

45:3 αδελφοι 58 128 118'-537

129^I 344^{txt} 71'-346 z A F* M]
+ (Ast Syh) αυτου rell
46:4 χειρας] + (Ast Syh) αυτου
O 128 $b^{-118-537}$ d 458 y^{-121} z 55 59
A M Bo La^I Arab
46:7 θυγατερες] + (ast Syh)
αυτου O^{-72} 14'-77'-500' 346' 31
Arm Eth Syh Arab^{mg}

47:11 πατερα 58-64' C'$^{-25-128-408-}$
$^{413-761}$ 56* 71'-121-318 z^{-31} 55 A
B M] + (ast Syh) αυτου Chr
rell
48:19 ηθελησεν] + (ast M 85) ο
πατηρ αυτου O^{-82} 646 s^{-130} M^{mg}
Sa^{20} (ed) Arab

8   Affinities with the C group

8:15 om λεγων C$^{⊃-500-646}$-78 134
730 Chr Eth^{-FH} Arab
10:20 εν 2°] pr και cII$^{-18-313}$ Eth
Arab
14:20 εδωκεν] + αβραμ C$^{⊃}$ 346
319^c 730 Arab
19:1 τω προσωπω] επι προσωπον C$^{⊃}$ Arm Bo Arab
22:2 om και 3° C$^{⊃}$ 370 Bo Arab

26:4 om παιαν C$^{⊃-25-128}$ 424 Arab
28:13 tr τ. πατρος σου/και ο
θεος ισαακ C$^{⊃}$ M Genn Eth
Arab
32:21 δωροις] + τουτοις C$^{⊃}$ 730
Bo Eth La^s Arab
33:17 om εκει C$^{⊃-16-128}$ 82 730 392*
319 Chr Sa^{20} (ed) Bo Arab

9   Affinities with the A related groups (y and z)

4:13 αιτια] αμαρτια 120' 72 Chr
Tht Or Eth Bo Ruf Arab
12:14 γυναικα] + αυτου 121-424-
619 31' A Co Eth Arab
17:20 σου] + και 424-619 z 15'-
72'-376 Hi Arab
17:26 εν] + δε 424-619 z Eth Arab
18:2 ιδων] + αυτοις 424'-619 31
Cyr Co Ambr Arab
19:33 om την νυκτην εκεινην 527
120' 59 319 D Chr Eth^{CG} Arab
20:15 om μου 121-619 31' 319 Bo
Arab
24:4 εγενομην] εγεννηθην 346'
D Chr Eth Arab
24:15 διανοια] + αυτου 424-619
z^{-630} 59 Arm Bo Arab
24:39 πορευσεται η γυνη] βου-
ληται η γυνη πορευθηναι 121-

619 31' 961 (vid.) Co Eth Arab
24:42 om συ 392' Arm Bo Arab
24:63 οφθαλμοις] + αυτου 619
z^{-630} Arm Bo Arab
25:25 υιος] + αυτης 527 509 Bo
Eth^{-P} Bo Arab
26:30 αυτοις] + ισαακ 527 Arab
27:14 δε] + ιακωβ 527 Arab
32:13 fin] + αυτης 346'-392 128
319 Co Arab
32:33 μηρου 1°] + ιακωβ A Arab
42:4 fin] + εν τη οδω 346'-
392(-ων) 31-630 128 76 319
509 707^{II} Bo^{VW} Sa Arab
45:19 γυναιξι] + υμων 346' 31 76
319 Bo La^s Arab
47:20 om αυτων 121 Arab
47:28 αι] pr πασαι 619 25 La^E
Arab

10   *Affinities with the Egyptian versions, i.e. Co' (and Pal?)*

a   Instances of unique agreement with Eth

2:2 om ων εποιησε Eth⁻ᴴ Arab

3:1 ειπεν] + *vobis* Eth Arab

3:11 tr τ. φωνην σου/ηκουσα Eth
Arab

4:22 om και αυτη Eth Arab

5:28 οκτω] *duo* Eth⁻ᴳ Arab MT

5:31 πεντηκοντα] *septuaginta*
EthᶠᴳᴴArab

5:31 τρια] *septem* Eth⁻ᴾ Arab

9:10 om παντων Eth Arab

9:12 διαθηκης] + *mei* Eth⁻ᴾ Arab

9:13 διαθηκης] + *mei* Eth Arab

9:16 διαθηκην] + *meum* Eth Arab

9:17 διαθηκης] + *mei* Ethᶜᴳ Arab

13:4 του θυσιαστηριου ου εποι-
ησεν εκει] *ubi fecerat altare* Eth
Arab

13:16 om και 2° Eth Arab

15:14 ω εαν δουλευσωσι] *qui
affligent eos* Eth Arab

16:6 σαραν] + *uxorem suam* Eth
Arab

17:8 om σοι και Eth Arab

17:23 om αυτω Ethᴾ Arab

19:37, 38 ουτος] pr *et* Eth Arab

21:8 om ο υιος αυτου Eth Arab

22:3 παιδας] + *eius* Eth Arab

22:20 om ιδον Eth Arab

22:20 om και αυτη Eth Arab

24:53 τω αδελφω] *patri* Eth Arab

24:54 om οι ανδρες Eth Arab

24:65 ειπεν] + *ei* Eth Arab

25:22 αυτη] *utero suo* Eth Arab

27:9 om εκειθεν Eth Arab

27:18 δε] + *ei* Eth Arab

28:13 ειπεν] + *ei* Eth Arab

30:15 ειπεν] + *ei* Ethᴾᴿ Arab

30:23 om ραχηλ Eth Arab

30:23 om μου Ethᴾᴿ Arab

30:26 om ινα απελθω Eth Arab

30:38 om τα προβατα 1° Ethᴾᴿ·
Arab

31:41 om εγω ειμι Eth Arab

31:48 om μαρτυρει 1°–αυτη Eth
Arab

31:50 ταις θυγατρασι] *eas* Eth
Arab

32:20 τω πρωτω και] *iterum*
Ethᶜ Arab

33:3 αυτος] *iacob* Ethᴾ Arab

34:13 om κ. ελαλησας αυτοις
Ethᶜᴴ Arab

34:31 ειπαν] + *ei* Eth Arab

35:20 αυτης] + *et* Eth Arab

36:12 τω ελιφας] *ei* Ethᶜ Arab

38:6 γυναικα] + *filio suo* Eth
Arab

38:18 ειπεν 2°] + *ei* Eth Arab

39:17 ημας] *me* Ethᴾ Arab

42:11 init] pr *et* Eth Arab

42:27 om και ην Eth Arab

43:16 om αυτοις και Ethᶜᴿᵃ Arab

43:16 om τον 1°–ομοιμητριον
Ethᴿᵃ Arab

43:25 δωρα] + *eorum* Eth Arab

43:28 ειπαν] + *ei* Eth Arab

44:10 ειπεν] + *eis* Eth Arab

47:25 ευρομεν] pr *et* Eth Arab

b   Instances of agreement with Eth, though not unique

1:24 om και 2° Ethᴾ 129 Sev Arab

2:17 φαγητε]–ης Ethᶜ Chr Arab

2:17 αποθανεισθε]–νη Ethᶜ Chr
Hi Aug Vulg Arab

3:19 init] pr και Eth 130 Cyp Hi
   Aug JohCass Arab
7:3 om πασαν Eth Ps-Phil Arab
9:6 εκχυθησεται] + το αιμα αυτου Eth 426 Arm Hi Arab
10:20 κατα] pr και Eth 318 Arab
10:20 εν 2°] pr και Eth cII⁻¹⁸⁻³¹³
   Arab
10:32 απο] pr et Eth Arm Arab
11:6 om παντα Eth 73 Arab
13:8 om ανθρωποι Eth Chr
   Ambrᵛᵃʳ Arab
13:9 tr αριστερα 1° ... /δεξια 1°
   Eth⁻ᶜ Chr Ambrᵛᵃʳ Ruf Arab
13:9 tr αριστερα 2° ... /δεξια 2°
   Eth⁻ᶜᴾ Chr Ambrᵛᵃʳ Ruf Arab
16:3 om η γυνη αβραμ Eth 125
   458 Arab
16:13 συ] pr et dixit Eth Arm
   Arab
17:10 και 2°] + inter Eth Arm
   Arab
18:24 om εαν ωσιν εν αυτη Eth
   Eus Arab
19:29 om πασας Ethᴾᴿ Chr Laᴵ
   Arabᵗˣᵗ
21:9 om ος εγενετο τω αβρααμ
   Eth 664ᵗˣᵗ 75 Arab
21:15 om μιας Ethᴾ Laᴱ Arab
21:26 om αυτω Ethᴾᴿᵃ 761 44 75
   Arab
22:5 αυτου 2°] ωδε Eth Chr
   Arm(pr υμεις) Arab
22:13 om οφθαλμοις αυτου Eth
   Ambr Arab
24:4 εγενομην] εγεννηθην Eth
   346′ D Chr Arab
24:35 tr προβατα ... /μοσχους
   Eth Arm Arab
24:37 tr γυναικα/τω υιω μου
   Eth⁻ᴿ 72′ 79-422 Arab

24:40 μετα] εμπροσθεν Eth 77
   Arab
27:14 om η μητηρ αυτου Eth⁻ᴾᴿ*
   Chr Arm Arab
27:25 ειπεν] + ei Eth La¹⁰⁰ Arab
27:45 om κ. την οργην Eth Or-lat
   Arab
28:16 om οτι Eth B Arm Arab
29:3 om εις τον τοπον αυτου Eth
   17′ Arab
29:32 ρουβην] rūbīl Eth Pesh
   Arabᴸ Arab. Jos hab ρουβηλος
   passim. Etiam in 30:14; 35:22,
   23; 37:21, 22, 29; 42:22, 37;
   48:5; 46:8, 9 et 49:3 (+Syh).
30:19 om ετι Eth⁻ᶜ 376 Arab
30:23 αφειλεν] + απ εμου Eth
   Cyr Arm Arab
30:28 om προς με Ethᴾ Laᴱ Arab
30:38 om ας ελεπισεν Eth⁻ᴾᴿ
   381′ Arab
31:29 om λεγων Eth Armᵗˣᵗ Arab
31:32 om η γυνη αυτου Eth 125
   Arab
31:37 om παντων Eth 376 Arab
31:52 om εγω Eth 135 Laˢ Arab
34:5 αυτων 3°] αυτων Ethᴾ 106
   246 84 Arab
34:24 om αυτων Eth 72 Arab
35:12 δεδωκα] dabo Eth Arm Arab
36:13 ζαρε] + και Eth ᶜ 72 Arab
36:20 λωταν] + και Eth ᶜ 646
   Arab
36:20 σωβαλ] + και Eth ᶜ 646
   Arab
36:27 om και ιωυκαμ Eth ᶜ Syh
   Arab
36:43 ουτος] pr et Eth Arm Arab
38:17 εαν δως] da mihi Eth Jud
   Arab
39:14 ημιν 2°] μοι Eth 135 Arab

39:20 εις τον τοπον] οπου Eth
    Chr Arab
42:10 ειπαν] + προς αυτον Eth
    58 Arab
42:11 εσμεν] + και Eth 246 Arm
    Arab
43:30 ιωσηφ] + et Eth Arm Arab
43:30 om γαρ Eth 619 Arm Arab

44:31 om δε Eth Chr Arm Arab
44:32 εκδεδεκται] εκδεξαμην Eth[P]
    72' Arab
47:24 om αυτοις Eth Arm Arab
49:16 om εν Eth Phil La[o] Vulg
    Arab
49:17 om και 1° Eth[-PR] La[o] Arab
50:7 και 3° ⌒ 4° Eth 551 59 Arab

c   Affinities with Eth and Sa

8:11 om καρπος Eth-Sa[19] Arab
9:13 της γης] pr inter Eth-Sa
    Arab
12:20 om περι αβραμ Eth-Sa
    Arab
18:9 om αποκριθεις Eth-Sa
    DialTA Quodv Arab
22:17 πληθυνω] + σε Eth-Sa 55
    Chr DialTA Hebr 6[14] Arab
27:4 om εγω Eth-Sa Ps-Phil Arab

30:16 ειπεν] + αυτω Eth-Sa
    44-106 246 La[8] Arab
31:44 και 3°] + inter Eth-Sa Arm
    Arab
31:48, 49 και 2°] + inter Eth-Sa
    Arm Arab
39:12 om αυτον Eth-Sa Arm Syh
    Arab
41:33 σκεψαι] + tibi Eth-Sa Arab

d   Affinities with Sa

6:16 της κιβωτου] αυτης Sa 458
    Pal Arab
7:2 προς σε] tecum Sa-Arab
7:4 απο] super Sa-Arab
7:14 και 2° ⌒ 3° Sa[9] 911 Arab
13:5 fin] + multa Sa-Arab
15:10 om αυτω Sa 408' Arab
18:10 εξει–σου] εσται τη σαρρα
    υιος Sa[20] Tht Chr LibGeneal
    Arab

19:17 ειπαν] + ei Sa-Arab
21:27 εδωκεν] + eos Sa-Arab
22:17 πληθυνω (σε)] + et multi-
    plicabo Sa-Arab
22:17 fin] + suorum Sa Arm Arab
29:2 ποιμνια 2°] προβατα Sa 75
    344[mg] 55 Arm Arab
46:25 om πασαι Sa-Arab
48:19 λαον] + magnum Sa-Arab
50:21 fin] + αυτων Sa 58 Arab

e   Unique agreements with Boh

14:20 fin] + quae erant ei Boh-
    Arab
19:13 αυτην] hanc urbem Boh-
    Arab
19:14 κ̄ς̄] deus Boh-Arab
19:20 om εκει σωθησομαι ου
    μικρα εστιν Boh-Arab

19:22 του σε εισελθειν] salvaberis
    Boh-Arab
20:16 διδραχμα] + argenti Boh-
    Arab
20:16 παντα] semper Boh-Arab
21:21 τη ερημω] monte Boh-Arab
21:30 om παρ εμου Boh-Arab

23:13 ειπεν] + *abraham* Boh-Arab

23:17 εστη] *erat* Boh-Arab

24:31 om δευρο Boh-Arab

24:32 και 4°] + *dedit* Boh-Arab

24:33 ειπαν] + *ei* Boh-Arab

24:46 αφ εαυτης] επι τον βραχιονα αυτης Boh-Arab (mlt. hab pr aut add.)

25:17 τριακοντα] *viginti* Boh-Arab

27:3 φαρετραν] + *tuam* Boh-Arab

27:15 om παρ αυτη Boh-Arab

27:15 οικω] + *eius* Boh-Arab

27:16 περιεθηκεν] *ligavit* Boh-Arab

27:17 tr τα δεσματα ... /τους αρτους Boh^W-Arab

29:22 om παντας Boh-Arab

29:23 om λαβων Boh-Arab

29:25 παρελογισω με] *mutavisti verbum tuum* Boh-Arab

29:34 om νυν Boh^W-Arab

29:34 καιρω] + *hoc* Boh-Arab

29:35 ετεκεν] pr *lia* Boh-Arab

29:35 ετι τουτο] *in hoc* Boh-Arab

30:1 τετοκεν] + *ea* Boh-Arab

30:26 fin] + *et*(om Arab) *quanta erant pecora tua qua erant* (*ibi* pro *q.e.*Arab) *mecum* Boh-Arab

30:27 αν] *enim* Boh-Arab

30:29 σου] + *omnia* Boh-Arab

30:32 σου] + *coram te* Boh-Arab

30:38 υδατος] + *ovium* Boh-Arab

30:40 om καθ εαυτον Boh-Arab

30:41 αυτα] *oves* Boh-Arab

31:13 om μοι 1° Boh^L-Arab

31:32 ημων] *eius* Boh-Arab

31:41 εν 1° − σου 1°] *tecum* Boh-Arab

31:43 ταυταις] *filiis meis* Boh-Arab

32:28 om δε 1° Boh^L-Arab

32:29 om δε Boh-Arab

33:4 om περιλαβων Boh-Arab

33:11 μου] *has* Boh-Arab

33:13 om αυτω Boh^W-Arab

34:8 εμμωρ] + *pater sichem* Boh-Arab

34:28 πολει] + *et quae erant in domibus eorum* Boh-Arab

34:30 γην] + *hanc* Boh-Arab

37:7 ωμην ημας] *ecce eramus* Boh-Arab

37:9 om και 3° Boh^L-Arab

37:17 om δε Boh-Arab

37:20 εσται] *facient* Boh-Arab

38:5 υιον] + *alium* Boh-Arab

38:18 ραβδον] + *tuum* Boh-Arab

38:23 om δε Boh-Arab

38:30 ην] *ligatum est* Boh-Arab

39:12 ιματιων] + *eius nudavit eum iis* Boh-Arab

39:20 κατεχοντι] *erant* Boh-Arab

40:2 om επι 2° Boh^V-Arab

40:19 την κεφαλην] *collum* Boh^VW-Arab

41:12 διηγησαμεθα] + *visiones nostras* Boh-Arab

41:24 ειπα] + *visionem meam* Boh-Arab

41:34 om της γης αιγυπτου Boh^W-Arab

41:43 om των αυτου Boh-Arab

41:46 fin] + *et venerunt septem anni abundantiae in omni terra aegypti* Boh-Arab

41:50 om πολεως Boh^VW-Arab

41:54 om ερχεσθαι Boh-Arab

42:3 δεκα] + *fratres eius* Boh-Arab

42:5 εν] + *omni* Boh^VW-Arab

42:6 fin] + *adoraverunt eum* Boh-Arab

42:7 αγορασαι] + *nobis* Boh-Arab

42:27 fin] + *sui* Boh[VW]-Arab

42:38 καταλελειπται] + *mihi ex uxore mea* Boh-Arab

42:38 και 2°] *ne* Boh-Arab

43:2 fin] + *ne moriamur* Boh-Arab

43:7 fin] + *ad me* Boh-Arab

43:9 σε 2°] *patrem meum* Boh[VW]-Arab

44:17 δε] + *eis* Boh-Arab

44:20 γηρως–αυτω] *quem genuit in senectute sua* Boh-Arab

44:20 αυτου 1°] + *non est* Boh-Arab

44:26 ειπαμεν] + *patri nostro* Boh-Arab

44:27 γυνη] + *haec* Boh-Arab

44:30 om τουτου Boh-Arab

44:34 μεθ ημων] *mecum* Boh-Arab

45:5 ζωην] + *vobis* Boh-Arab

46:5 αυτων] + *et*(om Boh) *imposuerunt ea* Boh-Arab

46:6 πασαν–ην] *omnia quae* Boh-Arab

46:32 βοας] + *eorum* Boh-Arab

46:34 om και 1° Boh-Arab

47:5 σου 2°] + *et pecora eorum* Boh-Arab

47:24 om και 1°–αυτης Boh-Arab

49:3 σκληρος 1°] pr *et* Boh-Arab

f   Other affinities with Boh

1:18 om ανα μεσον 2° Boh[W] La Arab

4:7 om ουκ Boh Achm Tht Ambr Aug PaulNola Max Arab

9:15 εις κατακλυσμον] *diluvii* Boh Pal Arab

10:30 μασση] μανασση Boh 55[c] 509 Eus Arab

12:5 εκτησαντο 1° ⌢ 2° Boh Eth Chr Arab

14:2 om μετα 2° Boh Sa[20] Arab

15:2 λεγει] ειπε Boh 106 Chr Sa Arab

15:12 om αδου Boh Arm[codd] Arab

16:3 om αυτω Boh 246* 370 Chr Sa Arab

16:16 ετεκεν] + αυτω Boh 343 54 Arm Arab

16:16 om τω αβραμ Boh 343 54 Arm Arab

17:12 αρσενικον] + *vestrum* Boh Eth Arab

18:29 om ετι Boh 911 Arab

19:2 om ιδου Boh DialTA Eth Arab

19:7 αδελφοι] + μου Boh 59 Eth Arab

19:8 των δοκων] *domus* Boh Eth Arab

19:12 πολει] + *hac* Boh Sa Arab

19:15 πολεως] + *huius* Boh Eth Arab

19:17 περιχωρω] + *sed* Boh La[s] Arab

19:21 πολιν] + ταυτην Boh 376 Pal Arab

19:25 om ταυτας Boh Sa Arab

19:34 ημων] *mei* Boh Arm Arab

21:2 γηρας] + αυτου Boh 17' Sa Arab

21:3 om αυτου Boh 59 Eth Arab

21:5 εγενετο] εγεννηθη Boh 72' Eth La[I] Arab

21:6 κς] ο θς Boh 527 Chr Arm Arab

21:11 περι] + ισμαηλ Boh 129-246 Arab

22:6 χειρα] + *eius* Boh Pal Arab

22:9 ξυλα] + *super eam* Boh Sa Arab

22:10 σφαξαι] + *isaac* Boh Sa
La^{iii} Arab

24:8 τουτου] μου Boh 413 Arab

24:14 παυσωνται] + πασαι Boh
Chr Arab

24:35 παιδισκας] + και Boh 31
Eth Arab

24:42 om συ Boh 392′ Arm
Arab

24:46 om κ. επιον–fin Boh Eth^{-c}
Arab

24:55 om ωσει Boh Eth Arab

24:65 k̅s̅ μου] + *isaac* Boh Sa Arab

25:28 βρωσις] + ην Boh Chr
Arm^{txt} Arab

25:28 αυτω] αυτου Boh 135 108*
318 Arab

26:2 ειπεν] + *ei* Boh Eth Arab

26:3 om γαρ Boh 125 54 Phil Arab

26:10 ημας] *me* Boh^W Eth Arab

27:1 om δε Boh 108 Arab

27:3 τοξον] + σου Boh 319 509
Arab

27:8 om εγω Boh 618 Eth Arab

27:10 om ο πατηρ σου Boh^W 125
458 Eth Ps-Phil Vulg Arab

27:21 om δε Boh^W 458 Arab

27:23 tr ως–αυτου/δασειαι Boh
73 Eth Arab

27:24 fin] + ειμι Boh 30 Arm
Arab

27:27 οσμη 1°] + των ιματιων
Boh DialTA Arab

27:27 om δε Boh^W 135 31 Arab

27:39 om ο πατηρ αυτου Boh 44
La^I Arab

27:41 του πενθους] *mortis* Boh
Fayy Arab

28:4 om σοι 2° Boh La^E Arab

28:11 τοπου] + *illius* Boh Sa La^s
Arab

28:12 κεφαλη] + *eius* Boh Syh
Arm^{txt} Sa Arab

28:13 fin] + μετα σου Boh 56* 75
Quodv Jub Arab

28:15 διαφυλασσων] *et custodiam*
Boh Eth Arab

28:15 οτι] και Boh^W 527 Chr Eth
Arab

29:13 διηγησατο] + ιακωβ Boh
344′ 527 Arab

30:7 om ετι Boh^W Jub Arab

30:10 tr τω ιακωβ/υιον Boh La^s
Arm Arab

30:20 αιρετιει] *diliget* Boh Arm
Arab

30:25 om εις 2° Boh 911 Arab

30:30 επι τω ποδι μου] *in in-
gressu meo ad te* Boh Sa Arab

30:38 πιειν 1° ⌐ 2° Boh 376
Arab

31:2 και ιδου] οτι Boh 509 Eth
Arab

31:13 om και 2° Boh Arm^{txt} Arab

31:31 om γαρ Boh Arm Arab

31:43 om συ Boh La^s Arab

32:17 om δια χειρος Boh^L 376
Eth Arab

32:27 ειπεν 2°] + *ei* Boh^L Eth
Arab

33:5 παιδια 2°] + *mei sunt* Boh
Eth Arm Arab

33:10 ενεκεν] + γαρ Boh Chr
Arab

34:3 ψυχη] + αυτου Boh 15-376
Arab

34:12 om μοι Boh 319 509 Arm
Arab

34:13 om δε Boh^W 509^{txt} Sa Arm
Arab

34:21 tr μεθ ημων/οικειτωσαν
Boh 72 Sa Arab

35:1 om τον τοπον Boh G Eth
VigThap Vulg Arab

35:3 θλιψεως] + *meae* Boh Eth
Arab

35:8 το ονομα αυτης] *eam* Boh
Eth^CRa Arab

35:9 ετι] οντι Boh 53-56^mg 74
Arab

35:11 om εθνη Boh^W 458 Arab

36:43 κατωκοδομημεναις] + αυτων Boh 58 Syh Arab

37:11 fin] + τουτο Boh 458 Arab

37:22 αυτω] + ειπε δε (om Arab)
ουτως Boh Cyr Arab

37:27 on τουτοις Boh La^I Arm
Arab

37:30 om ετι Boh 246 Arm La^S
Vulg Arab

37:36 tr φαραω/αρχιμαγειρω
Boh Syh Arm Arab

38:16 ειπεν 2°] + *ei* Boh Eth Arab

38:17 ειπεν 1°] + *ei* Boh Eth Arab

38:18 ορμισκον] + σου Boh 319
Syh Arab

38:21 εν] + *via* Boh Sa Arab

38:22 ευρον] + *eam* Boh Eth Arab

38:22 om οι εκ Boh Eth Arm La^X
Vulg Arab

38:23 ευρηκας] + αυτην Boh 31
Arab

38:29 χειρα] + αυτου Boh 72
Syh Arab

39:5 om επι 2° Boh 72 Arab

39:5 οικω] + αυτου Boh 72 Eth^-P
Arab

39:13 om και 3° Boh^LM Syh
Arm^txt Arab

40:14 φαραω] pr ενωπιον Boh 76
Arm Syh Arab

40:15 ουδεν] + κακον Boh Tht
Arab

41:8 om αυτης Boh 125 La^X Arab

41:42 δακτυλιον] + αυτου Boh 77
Eth^-P Arm Arab

41:51 om παντων 2° Boh 125
Chr Sa^14 Arab

41:57 εν παση τη γη] επι πασαν
την γην Boh 72 Arab

42:6 om αυτω Boh 130 Arm Arab

42:8 om δε Boh^-V 72 Arm Arab

42:13 ειπαν] + *ei* Boh Eth Arab

42:14 om δε Boh^-W Arm Arab

42:19 αυτοι] υμεις Boh 15 Eth
Arm Arab

42:27 εις] + εξ αυτων Boh Chr
Arab

43:4 σοι] ημιν Boh 72 Arab

44:28 om και 1° Boh^LM Arm Arab

44:34 πατερα] + *meum* Boh Syh
Arm^txt Arab

46:2 om δε Boh^W Arm Arab

46:32 κτηνη] + αυτων Boh 246
Arab

46:34 ερειτε] + *ei* Boh^W Eth Arab

47:19 om ουκ Boh 707 A* B Arab

48:2 tr ο υιος σου/ιωσηφ Boh^W
707 Sa^20 ed. Arab

48:14 χειρα] + *eius* Boh Sa^4 Arm
Arab

48:17 εφραιμ 2°] + (+*et* Arab)
posuit eam Boh Sa^20 ed. Arab

49:17 γενηθητω] εσται Boh
DialTA Arab

50:18 ειπαν] + *ei* Boh Eth Arab

g Affinities with Co-Eth

1:26 ομοιωσιν] + *nostram* Sa^1-
Boh-Eth Achm Pal Arab

7:8 om παντων Co-Eth^R 15-64^txt
392 59 Arab

8:9 om παντι Sa^19-Boh-Eth^P 56*
Arab

8:12 om ετι 2° Co' Pal Aug Arab

9:5 om υμετερον Co' 125 Hi
Iren^var Vulg Arab

18:25 κρισιν] pr *hoc* Co′ Arm
Arab

19:14 ειπεν] + αυτοις Co′ 527
La$^{\text{100var}}$ Arab

20:3 om εμε 3° Co′ 246 458 630
Chr Arab

24:39 πορευσεται η γυνη] βου-
ληται η γυνη πορευθηναι Co′
121-619 961(vid) Arab

30:2 κοιλιας] + *tui* Co′ Arm La^{E}
Arab

32:19 μου] *suo* Co′ Arm^{txt} Arab

34:26 διναν] + *sororem suam* Co′
La^{X} Arab

37:20 λακκων] + τουτων Boh-
Sa$^{3(\text{vid})}$-Eth 527 59′ Arab

39:17 παις] + σου Co′ 59′ Arab

39:23 om αυτος Co′ 44 La^{I} Arab

47:1 κτηνη] + αυτων Co′ 344^{mg}
Arab

48:2 fin] + *meo* Co′ Arab

11   Agreements with Chr and Tht

The large number of these is most surprising.

a   Unique readings with Chr and Tht

2:18 tr ειναι/τον ανθρωπον Chr
Arab

5:29 tr εργων ... /λυπων Arab;
cf. Chr πονων ... λυπων] + και
τ. εργων

5:29 om κυριος Chr Arab

6:6 om και διενοηθη (sub ast Syh)
Chr Arab

6:14 ποιησον ουν] συ (δε) ποιησον
Chr Arab

8:2 om απο Chr Arab

18:29 om προς αυτον Chr Arab

21:4 αυτω ο θεος] κυριος Chr Arab

22:2 om εις ολοκαρπωσιν Chr
Arab

24:45 om και κατεβη–υδρευσατο
Chr Arab

25:26 om αυτους Chr Arab

30:4 om ιακωβ Chr Arab

32:6 om ησαυ Chr Arab

33:18 om σαλημ Chr Arab

38:2 om εκει Chr Arab

43:18 παιδας] + ημας τε Chr
Arab

47:23 om ιωσηφ Chr Arab

49:3 om μου συ Chr Arab

b   Agreements with Chr Tht and scant further support

2:17 φαγητε]–ης Chr Eth^{C} Arab

2:17 αποθανεισθε]–νη Chr Eth^{C}
Hi Aug Vulg Arab

3:1 om των επι Chr 56-664*
JohCass Or-lat Arab

3:10 tr της φωνης σου/ηκουσα
Chr Arm Arab

4:13 αιτια] αμαρτια Chr Tht 72
120′ Or Boh Ruf Arab

9:11 om υδατος 2° Chr 120 La^{M}
Arab

12:5 εκτησαντο 1° ⌒ 2° Chr Eth
Boh Arab

12:11 om αβραμ 2° Chr 14 75
Arm Arab

12:13 om δια σε Chr 318 La^{X}
Arab

13:7 om κτηνων 2° 458 Arab

13:8 om ανθρωποι Chr Eth
Ambr[var] Arab
13:9 tr αριστερα 1° ... /δεξια 1°
Chr Eth-C Ambr[var] Ruf Arab
13:9 tr αριστερα 2° ... /δεξια 2°
Chr Eth-CP Ambr[var] Ruf Arab
15:2 λεγει] ειπε Chr 106 Co Arab
16:3 om αυτω Chr 246*(c.pr.m.)
370 Co Arab
18:1 αυτω ο θ̄ς̄] ο θ̄ς̄ τω αβρααμ
Tht Chr Eth-G Pal Arab
18:10 εξει–σου] εσται τη σαρρα
υιος Tht Chr 121 Sa[20]
LibGeneal Arab
19:29 om πασας Chr Eth[PR] La[I]
Arab[txt]
21:4 om αβρααμ Chr 44 Arab
21:6 κ̄ς̄] ο θ̄ς̄ Chr 527 Arm Boh
Arab
24:27 om κ̄ς̄ 2° Tht Eth Arab
24:32 om ταις καμηλοις Chr 107-
125-610 Arab
24:40 tr γυναικα/τω υιω μου Chr
79 Arab
24:49 om υμεις Chr 630 Eth La[A]
Arab
25:28 βρωσις] + ην Chr Arm[txt]
Boh Arab
27:14 om η μητηρ αυτου Chr
Arm Eth-PR* Arab
27:19 φαγε] + de Boh Arab;
+ εκ Chr; + απο n DialTA
28:15 οτι] και Chr 527 Eth Boh[W]
Arab

30:31 om και 1° Chr Boh Arab
31:42 μοι] μετ εμου Chr 500 53′
Arm Arab
33:10 δια] εκ Chr La[I] Arab
33:10 ενεκεν] + γαρ Chr Boh
Arab
39:6 om αυτος Chr 75 D Arm
Eth Boh Arab
39:20 εις τον τοπον] οπου Chr
Eth Arab
40:15 ουδεν] + κακον Tht Boh
Arab
41:51 om παντων 2° Chr 125
Sa[14] Boh Arab
42:21 om γαρ Chr Eth La[I]
Boh[VW] Arab
42:27 εἱς] + εξ αυτων Chr Boh
Arab
42:38 om η αν πορευησθε Chr 53′
Jub Arab
43:15 om ταυτα Chr 458 962
Arm Sa[21] Arab
44:1 επι 2°–fin] εις τον μαρσιπ-
πον αυτου Chr Eth(sed plur)
Arab
44:31 om δε Chr Arm Eth Arab
45:15 αυτου 1°] + και Chr Arm
La[E] Arab
45:18 υμων 1° ⌒ 2° Chr cII 30
Arab
46:4 om και 1° Chr n Arm La[S]
Arab

12 Instances where Arab is part of a tradition more widespread than a single text group

In these no positive statement on the textual affinities of Arab can
be made.

1:24 γης] + και τα κτηνη και
παντα τα ερπετα της γης

(c var) O[-72] C′[-16-569] b d 56′-664
75 t 424′ 31 55 Chr La[M] Arab

1:25 om καὶ τα κτηνη κατα γενος
72-82 73 *d* 53-56 75 527 54 55
509 Ruf Arab

2:5 την γην 2°] αυτην 82 18 *b d*
53'-56 75 121-392' 122 54 La
Arab

2:8 om κ̅ς̅ 17'-82-135-426 18-79¹-
550-551-569¹ *d* 53'-129 75 *t*
121-424' 31' 319 539 Phil Chr
Hipp Or Procop Sev Tht Arm
La Arab

2:15 fin] + αυτον 135 343-344^mg *t*
319 M Bo^L Eth La Arab

2:19 αυτο] αυτα 15' 18-131** *d* 53
75 74 392**-527 54 59 Chr Sev
Eth La^c Arab

3:6 λαβουσα] + η γυνη 15' C^ꞓ-128**
b d 53'-56 *s* 392' L Arab

3:10 om αυτω 18-414'-500-551 *d*
527 Am Eth^P Bo^K Luc Vulg
Arab

3:13 om κ̅ς̅ 15'-426 14-18 *b d*
56'-129-664** 121-424' 31' 54
L Phil Chr Bo La Pal Arab

3:22 χειρα] + αυτου C^ꞓ-18 *d f*-56**
121-346'-424 31 Chr Genn Tht
Co Eth La^s Arab

5:25 εξηκοντα] ογδοηκοντα 15-
17'-64-707 16-25-77-313^c-422
y-346' *z* 55 A M Eth Arab

5:26 οκτακοσια] επτακοσια κ.
ογδοηκοντα (aut ογδ. και επ-
τακ.) 64-707 C^ꞓ-18-408c 246 *n s*
y-346' *z* 59 509 A M Arm Eth-^P
Syh Arab

6:1 om νωε 2° 18 458 392 *z*-31 Or
Hipp-lat Ps-Phil Vulg Arab

6:9 om νωε 3° 58-72' 107-125 *n*
t-134** 392 59 Chr Eth La^E Arab

6:14 τετραγωνων] + ασηπτων 58
129-246 343 *t* Chr Co Arab:
(+ ασιπτων 53'-56^c)

6:14 την κιβωτον] επ αυτης (aut
−τη aut −την) 72'-82 18 *b d* 127
392 Arab

6:19 και 2° ⌢ 3° 15'-64**-426 18
b d 120' 55 730 Chr Cyr Arm
Bo Syh Arab

6:22 om κ̅ς̅ O'-17'-82-135' 16-57-73'-
408-413^txt *b d f*-129 *n s*-30(mg)-
344(mg) 71-318'-392' Arab

7:4 fin] + απο ανο̅υ̅ εως κτηνους
O-17'-135' *b*(314 ανο̅υ̅ς!) *d* 53'
t 392 54 55 59 730 Chr Arab

7:8 επι 17'-135' C^-16-128-408 56-129^c
121-318-424' *z* 730 A M] pr
ερποντων rell

7:9 δυο 2°] + απο παντων 64 C^ꞓ
b d s 346 54 55^c 730 Chr Arab

7:9 αυτω ο θεος] ο θεος τω νωε
15-64**(vid)-72'-426 73 *b d*-125
54 55 Chr Eth^CFH Arab

7:14 θηρια 17'-58-82-135 *f n y*-346
z 509 730 A D M] + της γης
rell

7:16 εισηλθεν] + προς νωε O-58-376
16 *b d* 53'-246 *s* 54 55 59 Arab

7:16 ο θ̅ς̅] pr κ̅ς̅ 58-64-72'-426
16-761 *b* 246 *s* 346 54 59 319
Eth-^GP Arab

7:17 απο] επι 72'-376 *d* 53'-56^mg
346^txt-392-527^c 54** 319 Sa^19
Arab

7:20 om τα υψηλα 15-58-64**-426
16 *b d* 53' *n s* 392' 55 59 509 L
Arm Bo Pal Sa^19 Syh Arab

7:23 om πασης 58 *b* 129 *t* 54 Bo
Eth Pal Arab

8:3 om ενεδιδου 2° O-64(mg)-82-376-707
b d n 71-392 730 Chr Eth Arab

8:9 πασης 17'-64^c-82 16 56** *s*
71-121^mg-346'-424 *z*-31 55 509
A D M Bo Syh] om rell

8:10 om ετερας 15-64^mg-72'-82^c-

426 Cʼᵔ⁻¹⁶⁻³¹³ *b d* 56* *n t* 392 55
59 730 Cyr Arm Eth Pal
Arab

8:10 om παλιν 15-426 *b d*⁻⁴⁴ *t* 392
Arab

8:11 απο 58-82-376 *f*⁻⁵³ 71-121-424
z 55 319 509 A M Arm Co Eth
La^M] + προσωπου rell

8:12 om παλιν 15-58-64^txt-426
108-314 *d* 392 539 Chr Pal Sa¹⁹
Arab

8:13 απο 82* Cʼᵔ⁻¹²⁸ 56-129-664
n 71-121-424' *z* 509 730^txt A
Co Eth] + προσωπου rell

8:19 om κατα γενος αυτων *b d*⁻¹²⁵
458 392 Arab

8:20 θεω] κ̅ς̅ 15'-64-72'-426 500-
761 *b d* 56' *s t* 346-392 54 L Chr
La^X Arab

8:21 om επιμελως 458 424-619 *z*
Co Eth Syh Aug Hi Arab

8:21 om ετι 64* 25* *b d* 54 911
Chr Bo Ambr Aug Arab

9:2 φοβος 129 458 424' 31' 59
A M Chr Eth La^M Sa Syh]
+ υμων rell

9:5 om εκζητησω αυτο 64 53' *n*
Chr La^E Sa Arab

9:7 πληθυνεσθε 2° 17'-72'-82'-135
57^mg 130^mg-344'^mg 71-121-424
31' 509 A M] κατακυριευσατε
rell

9:8 ειπεν] + κ̅ς̅ 77-79-500-*c*II
f⁻⁵⁶* 71-527 509 730 Arm Sa
Arab

9:9 ιδου/εγω 15-58-64-426 56'
130-344' *t*⁻⁴⁶ 71-121 55 A M
911 Pal] tr rell

9:27 αυτων] αυτου O⁻⁵⁸⁻⁸²⁻¹³⁵ 500 *d*
56'-664* 343 121 122 54 55^c 59
509 L 911 Chr Cyr Genn Eth
La^M Arab

10:1 εγενηθησαν 64-376 78-569
19* 121-346* 319 A M La^I Bo]
εγεννηθησαν rell

10:15 πρωτοτοκον] + αυτου 17'-
72'-82-135' 57^mg-550 108 130^mg
120 319 Bo Eth La^I Arab

10:21 εγενηθη 58^c-135-426 121-
346 319 A] εγεννηθη rell

10:22 om και καιναν 82-376 53'-
56* 318 319 A^c 961 Arm Eth
La^I Arab

11:3 πλησιον] + αυτου O⁻⁴²⁶ 19'
53' *y*⁻⁵²⁷ 31' 319 628 Chr Arm
Bo Aug Hi Hipp-lat Ps-Phil
Vulg Arab

11:4 διασπαρηναι] + ημας 72'
Cʼᵔ *b d* 392 Chr Bo Arab

11:7 fin] + αυτου O⁻¹⁵⁻³⁷⁶' 53' *n* 343
318'-392' 319 509 Or Arm Bo
La^E Arab

11:8 κ̅ς̅] + ο θ̅ς̅ 15-72'-376' 19' *d*
458 *s t* 318'-619 54 319 509 628
730 Chr Arm Hipp-lat Arab

11:9 κ̅ς̅ Cʼᵔ 125 53'-129 *n y*⁻³¹⁸'⁻
⁵²⁷⁻⁶¹⁹ 122 59 M 911 Bo] + ο θ̅ς̅
rell

11:13 τετρακοσια 72' 52-77-128-
422-551 *b* 106 246 121*-318 A
Eth La^A Sa Aug Arab^mg]
τριακοσια Arab^txt rell

11:28 εγενηθη 343 319 A 911]
εγεννηθη rell

12:1 κ̅ς̅] + ο θ̅ς̅ 15 79-569 *d* 129-
246 527 La Arab

12:1 εις 15^txt 129 *t*⁻⁴⁶⁻³⁷⁰ 55 A
911^vid Chr Or Tht Bo Eth⁻^CR
Sa^vid] pr και δευρο rell

12:5 χανααν 1° ⌒ 2° 17'-72'-82*-
135 500-761 *b d*⁻¹⁰⁶ 53 458 343
74 59 509 911 Sa Arab

12:7 om αβραμ 2° O *d* 120' 319
911^vid Arab

12:8 om εκει 1° 15'-376-707 *b* 346
319 911 Arab

12:18 ειπεν] + αυτω 17'-135-426
C'^ *d*⁻¹⁰⁶ 53-129-246 75 *s t* 318-
527 54 55 59 509 730 M 961
Chr Arm La^S Eth Co Arab

13:8 om ανα μεσον 3° 426 *d*⁻¹²⁵
129-246 *n* 343 619 54 959 Chr
Eth^R Ambr Aug^{var} Arab

14:16 αδελφον] –φιδουν 426 B^S *d*
53-664^c 127*-344^c 71-346 Chr
Cyr Eth^C Arab

14:16 και 3° 15'-17'-72' *b* 129 344
319 911 Eth] + παντα rell

14:25 fin] + αυτων O C'^⁻⁷⁷ 53-
664^c 343 370 318' 319 Arm Eth
Sa Arab

15:1 οραματι] + της νυκτος C'^⁻⁷⁷
d 53'-246 75 343 *t* 424'-619 31
54 55 59 M Chr Cyr Arab

15:5 δη C'^⁻⁴⁰⁸* 75 *s*⁻³⁴³ *t y*⁻¹²¹ *z* 55
59 M] om rell

15:5 ειπεν 2°] + αυτο O *f* 343
392^{mg}-527 59 L Or Arm Co Eth
Syh Hi Ruf Arab

15:7 fin] + αυτην O *d f s* 346' 31
Cyr Arm^{codd} Co Eth La^I Arab

15:8 γνωσομαι] + τουτο 422* *d*
664* *n t* 346' 54 M Chr Tht
Arab

16:7 om επι τ. πηγης 2° 135 646
106 *n* 527 120' Chr Cyr Eth
Arab

17:4 om και εγω 72' *d* 130 346 59
730 Eth Hi Arab

17:16 εσονται 15'-72'-426-708 129
n y⁻¹²¹⁻³⁴⁶ *z* 55 59 M 911 961
La^E] εξελευσονται rell

17:17 προσωπον 17'-72-135
*c*I⁻⁴¹³(mg) *d*⁻¹²⁵ *f*⁻⁵³⁻⁶⁶⁴ᶜ *s*⁻¹³⁰(mg)
t⁻³⁷⁰ 121-318' 59 A M 911 961
La^E Bo] + αυτου rell

17:17 om ει 2° 135 C'^ 19 44-125
664 370 346 31 319 Phil Arm
Bo Arab

17:19 αιωνιον] + ειναι αυτω θεος
(c var) 708 C'^ 106-125 *f*⁻⁵³'
130^{mg} *t y*⁻¹²¹(txt)⁻³⁴⁶(txt) *z* 54 55
M^{mg} Bo La^A Arab

18:5 om εις την οδον υμων 15'-
72-708 392 55 319 D 911^{vid} Chr
La^E Bo Arab

18:5 ειπαν] ειπεν C'^ *b* 246 *n s*
t⁻¹³⁴⁻³⁷⁰ 318 54 59 A Arm^{txt} Bo
Arab

18:7 παιδι] + αυτου *d f*⁻⁵⁶*⁻¹²⁹ *s t*
54 55 730 Bo Sa²⁰(cod) Arab

18:9 ειπον] ειπε(ν) *b d*⁻⁴⁴ *f*⁻⁵³ᶜ *n t*
71-121-346-392 120' 54 55 59
319 730 M Arm^{txt} Bo Eth^C
Arab

18:20 πεπληθυνται 15'-72'-376-
708 314 458 *s* 121-318'-392 *z*⁻³¹
59 319 730 M] + προς με rell

18:27 κ̄ν̄] + μου 72'-426 77^c *d* 246
458 130 *t* 346-619 31 54 730 Chr
DialTA Co Arab

19:2 υμων 3°] + ου εινεκεν εξεκλι-
νατε προς τον παιδα υμων
(c var) 413^{mg} 19' *f n* 130^{mg}-343-
344^{mg} 346'-392 319 509 Co Arab

19:12 εξαγαγε] + αυτους C'^ *d*
53-664^c 130^{mg} 54 509 730 Arm
Bo Eth⁻^{P} La^S Arab

19:15 μη C'^⁻⁵⁷'⁻⁷⁸⁻⁷⁹⁻⁵⁵¹'⁻⁶⁴⁶ *b d* 121-
318 A Eth⁻^{PR}] + και rell

19:17 αυτους] αυτον 17'-82-376-*o*I
314* *s* 46 71-346-392 120' 55 509
730 M 961 Bo Eth La^S Arab

19:22 om εκεινης 72'-82-376'-*o*I
14 246 *t* 71-392 120' 55 59 D
961 Just Bo La¹⁰⁰ Arab

19:26 αυτου] (του) λωτ 381 500
d 53' *t* Arm Bo Eth Pal Arab

19:30 ορει *O'*⁻¹⁷'¹³⁵ *n* 121-318-619
  31' 319 A L Eth^P La^I] + αυτος
  961 rell
19:34 την νυκτα ταυτην] τη νυκτι
  ταυτη 25^txt *b* 107' 458 Bo Arab
19:35 om και 1° 376 500* *b* 56'-
  664* Arab
19:38 αμμαν] + λεγουσα *o*I *C'*⁾
  d f 370 121^mg 54 M Chr Arm
  Eth Arab
20:14 διδραχμα] + και *b d*⁻¹²⁵ *n*
  527 59 Chr Arm Eth Arab
20:17 αυτου 2°] + κ. ολον τον
  οικον αυτου *d t* 527 54 55 Bo
  Arab
20:18 κ̅ς̅] ο θ̅ς̅ *C'*⁾⁻¹²⁸ *b* 630^txt
  Procop Bo La^E Arab
21:10 και 1° 15-376-708 129-246
  s⁻¹³⁰ *y*⁻⁷¹⁻⁴²⁴' 122 55 A D 961
  Arm Eth^PR] om rell
21:14 ωμον 129-664* *n* 71'-121-
  318-392 *z* 55* 59 A 961] + αυτης
  rell
22:6 και 2° *C'*⁻⁷⁹ *b d*⁻¹⁰⁶ 53-56^mg-
  129-664^c 130 370 121-318' A
  961 La^I] om rell
22:7 ειπας 128 19' 127^c.pr.m-344
  318 A M La^I Ambr^var Ruf
  Vulg] om Chr rell
22:11 om αυτω 72' *s* 71'-346-392
  z 59 319 730 Chr Phil Arm Co
  La^E Arab
22:19 ορκου 1° ⌢ 2° *C'*⁾ 314 125-
  610 664^txt 370 71 120' Bo Eth
  Arab
23:15 ακηκοα 53-664^c Arm Eth]
  + γαρ rell
23:15 και] + ανα μεσον *O' d f*⁻¹²⁹ *t*
  527 319 D 961 Arm Eth Arab
24:2 υπο] επι 16-78-408 108 44 *f*
  127^sup.lin-130 319 Tht Eth Arab
24:7 εγενηθην 381 16 129* 619 55
  319 S] εγεννηθην Chr rell

24:9 υπο] επι 15-376-*o*I 500 108^I
  44 *n* 71 Eth Arab
24:14 om μοι 2° *O' C'*⁾ *s* 71-346
  630 55 59 319 730 Cyr Arab
24:14 πιε] + συ 25-*c*I *d f n s*
  y⁻⁷¹⁻³⁹² *z*⁻⁶³⁰ 730 Arab
24:15 om δε *O'*⁻⁴²⁶ 14'-77'-500' *b*
  527 59 Arab
24:20 om ετι 17'-72 73 *f* 75 319 A
  Phil Chr Eth Arab
24:27 αληθειαν] + αυτου *O'* 125
  53-664^c 30 59 Bo Eth Arab
24:27 μου 2°] + και 15-426-*o*I
  t⁻³⁷⁰ 527 Arm Eth Syh Arab
24:35 χρυσιαν και αργυριαν] pr
  και 708 53' 121-619 31' A 961
  962 Chr Eth Arm Arab: + και
  72' *b* D 962 Chr Eth^c Arab
24:38 tr γυναικα/τω υιω μου 381'
  t 120' Arm Arab
24:43 εξελευσονται] εκπορευονται
  O⁻⁷²' *b* S 911^vid Arm Bo Arab
24:45 διανοια] + μου 551' 74 121-
  527-619 *z* A Arm Bo Eth Arab
24:45 ωμων] + αυτης *O'* 551 53-
  664^c S Chr Arm Bo Arab
25:3 και 1° ⌢ 2° 72'-82 19' Hi
  Vulg Arab
25:12 αγαρ] + η αιγυπτια *O' C'*⁾
  53' 424' Arm Arab
25:33 πρωτοτοκια] + αυτου 15-
  376-*o*I 551' *b d t* 59 Arm Bo^W
  La^K Aug Arab
26:3 om πασαν 82-135'-708 *C'*⁾⁻¹⁸⁻
  ²⁵⁻⁵⁴⁻¹²⁸⁻³¹³ *b* 53' 75 *s* 346'-424 31
  319 509 730 911 Chr Eth Tyc
  Arab
26:15 αυτου 1° ⌢ 2° 72 *C'*⁻²⁵⁻⁵⁴⁻⁴¹³⁻
  761 19' 107'-125 53 911 Ps-Phil
  Arab
26:18 om αβρααμ 3° *b n* 130^txt
  318'-619 122 55 319 370 509 961
  Bo La^I Arab

26:24 ηυλογηκα] ευλογησω 72′
  b f n 318 59 A Chr Arm Co La^E
  Arab
26:28 ειπαν] + αυτω b^{-118*} f 59
  911 Eth Arab
27:7 και 2° O′^{-17} b d s^{-130(mg)} 346
  911 La^E Syh] ινα rell
27:13 μητηρ] + αυτου O′^{-72} 106
  f^{-56*} 71′-527 31 961 Arm Bo La^I
  Arab
27:14 μητρι 16 b 129 s 71′-318′
  z 55 509 A 911] + αυτου rell
27:28 ο θ͞ς] pr κ͞ς cII^{-18-313} n Arab
27:31 πατρι 2°] + αυτου 15′-135′-
  426-708 A 911 Arm Bo Syh Arab
27:33 εστω] εσται 72′-426 16-79-
  550^c b 125* 53′ n 76 527* 59
  Phil^codd Bo Aug Ps-Phil Vulg
  Arab
27:36 ειπεν 1°] + ησαυ 72′ 500-
  761 d 53-664^c t 527 55 Chr Bo
  Eth La^E Arab
28:1 χανααν] των χαναναιων 376
  b^{-314} 46′ 911 (om των) Chr Bo
  La^E Eth Arab
28:7 πατρος] + αυτου 72′ 56′ 509
  911 Co La^E Arab
28:7 om συριας b 75 318 A 911
  Co Eth La^E Arab
28:9 αυτου] + αυτω O′^{-135} f 46 55
  Arm Co Eth La^E Arab
28:13 κ͞ς 2° O′ b^{-108-B^S} 129-246 30
  911 961 Arm Eth^{-R} La^E Sa Syh]
  om Chr rell
28:18 om εκει f^{-56*-246} n 509 Eus
  Eth Aug^var Arab
29:6 fin] + του πατρος αυτης
  (c var) 17′-135-426-oI b^{-118-537}
  d f t 619 59′ 509 A Co Eth La^S
  Arab
29:9 και 1°] + ιδου 58 b 56^c-129-
  246 t 527 509 961 Arab
29:9 αυτης 1° ⌒ 2° 400^txt 107′-

125 129^txt 30′-343 71 509 Bo^W
  Eth Arab
29:10 και τα προβατα λαβαν του
  αδελφου της μητρος αυτου
  (c var) O′^{-15-17-135} 57-413^{mg} d^{-106}
  53-246 130^{mg}-343-344′ 392 z M
  911 Or Arm La^E Co] om 961 rell
29:17 fin O^{-58} 129^I n 30-130^txt-
  343^{II}-730 71-318-527 319 961
  977 Arm Eth La^E] + σφοδρα
  rell
29:21 αποδος] + μοι 72 d f^{-129}
  s^{-344′} t 318′-392′ 319 A Chr Cyr
  Arm Co Eth La^S Arab
29:21 om μου 2° b d 458 527 319
  509 911^vid Chr Arm La^S Arab
29:27 om ετι 72-135 25 b d 53 59′
  509 Cyr Co Eth Arab
29:28 om αυτω C′^{⌐-128′} f^{-56*} 59 509
  A Co Arab
29:32 tr μου 1° post ταπεινωσιν
  b d Arm Eth Arab
29:32 ταπεινωσιν] + και εδω-
  κε(ν) μοι υιον (c var) 58-381′
  C′^⌐ d f t 71′-392′ z 55 59′ 509
  M Co Arab
29:35 om ετι 1° 15-72-376-oI C′^⌐
  108 44 s^{-344′} 84 318 509 Hi Arab
30:1 τεκνα] τεκνον b t 59′ 509
  Eth^P La^{100} Ps-Eus-lat Arab
30:5 tr τω ιακωβ/υιον 16 d s^{-344′}
  346 Arm Bo Eth La^S Arab
30:12 ετι 58-426-708 C′^{⌐-14′} 129
  130-343-730 74-76-84 71′-346-
  392 630 55 Arm^codd La^S] om rell
30:13 fin] + (ο εστι) πλουτος 58-
  135^{mg}-426 57^{mg} d f 318 509 911
  Arm La^S Sa Arab
30:18 εδωκεν] + μοι 58 C′^{-25} b f^{-129}
  130^{mg} 74-84 71′-346 59′ A 961
  Chr Arm La^E Arab
30:22 om ο θ͞ς 2° cII 125 n Chr
  Arab

30:23 tr τω ιακωβ/υιον 15-376-oI
b d 527 Arm Bo Eth Arab

30:26 παιδια] + μου 58 79 b-B^S
f^-129 30' 71'-392' 31 59' M
Arm^codd Bo Eth La^E Arab

30:27 om γαρ C'' b Bo Eth Arab

30:28 fin] + σοι 17'-82 53' n t 59'
A Co Eth La^E Arab

30:43 om σφοδρα 17'-72-135 761
53' n 619 31 55 Cyr Sa Ambr
Arab

31:10 προβατα] + εν γαστρι
λαμβανοντα 57^mg b f 130^mg-343
t 71'-318-392' 55 509 M Chr
Just Bo Arab

31:10 οφθαλμοις 14 d^-370c 56-129
71' 31' 509 911] + μου Chr rell

31:10 om αυτα 17' d f^-56-129 n
s^-130(mg)-344' t y^-424 55 319 707^II
Chr Arm Eth La^100 Aug Arab

31:11 ιακωβ] bis scr 17'-58-381'
C'' b f 730 46 392' 509 A M
Just Bo^W Eth^-P La^E Sa Arab

31:12 ειπεν] + μοι b 71' 59'
Phil^codd Sa^20 Eth Arab

31:14 tr ραχηλ et λεια 58 b d f
75 30-344' 630 509 961 Sa Arab

31:23 om μεθ εαυτου 17'-72-135
73 d 30 71 Eth Arab

31:28 init] pr και 15'-58-72-376-oI
344' 318 z 961 Arm Bo Eth Arab

31:32 αυτω 2° A 911 Co La^X] om
rell

31:46 om και επιον 72-82 128
56^txt 75 s^-130-730 71'-346-392 z 55
319 707^II Cyr Eth^C La^E Arab

31:46 om εκει 54 d s^-130-730 59' 509
Bo Eth La^O Arab

31:54 αυτου 2°] + (του) φαγειν
αρτον O' f^-129 130 46 71'-318-
527 319 M^mg Arm Syh Arab

32:7 tr τον αδελφον σου/ησαυ d

343-344' 346' 707^II Arm Bo Eth
La^S Arab

32:11 μου] + ταυτη 58-135 57-
73-128-422 b^-19-314 d 53'-56 75
130 t 71'-318 630 55 59' Chr
Cyr Tht La^A Arab

32:19 init] pr και b-B^S 44 130 t 71'-
392 630 55 59' A Bo La^A Arab

32:20 om τουτων d n Arm Co Eth
Arab

32:22 παρεπορευοντο G-15'-
426 b^-19' d 911] προεπορ. (c var)
rell

32:29 om αυτω 25-128-408 t z^-630
911 Sa^20(ed) Arab

33:1 και 4° O^-82-708 125-610
f^-56-129 75 630 911 961 962 La^S
Sa] + επι rell

33:1 και 5°] + επι 376 25-128 246
s^-730 t 346'-392 630 55 59' M
Arm Bo Eth La^O Arab

33:10 δωρα] + ταυτα C'^-128' 53'
458 730 707^II Co La^I Arab

33:14 παιδος] + αυτου O'^-G-72 b d
53' n s^-130-730 t 71-318'-424' 31
55^c 59 Arm Bo^L La^S Sa Arab

34:5 εμιανεν] + συχεμ b 246
s^-127-130-344(txt) t 71'-392 630 55
59' Co La^S Arab

34:9 fin] + εις γυναικας 54^mg d
53-664^c 75 343-344'^mg t 71'-318-
392' 630 55 59 Bo Arab

34:10 tr η γη/ιδου 376-381'
C'^-128-569 d n 730 74 71' A Chr
Co La^S Arab

34:10 επ αυτης] εν αυτη 14'-77-
500'-761* b d 56-129-664* t 318
Arm La^S Arab

34:11 ευροιμι] ευρον d^-370* 53' n
Bo Arab

34:22 ανθρωποι] + ουτοι b f 130
318-392 961 962 Bo Arab

34:23 τετραποδα] + αυτων 15'-
17-376 b⁻¹⁰⁸ d n 30-343 t 346'
59' A 962 Arm Bo Eth Arab
35:2 om τους μεθ ημων O⁻¹⁵ b s⁻³⁰'
71'-346 z 59 509 A Arab
35:5 ιηλ] ιακωβ 413'ᵐᵍ d n 619
630 962 Co Ethᴿ Arab
35:7 τοπου] + εκεινου 376 C'ᴐ⁻⁷⁹*
d⁻¹⁰⁷*⁻¹²⁵ n 730 t y⁻³¹⁸' 630 55
59' 319 509 911 Just Arm Co
Laˢ Arab
35:12 om σοι εσται C'ᴐ 118'-537
107'-125 30' y⁻³¹⁸⁻⁴²⁴ 120'-122
509 962 Chr Bo Eth Laᴵ Arab
35:27 αυτου O⁻⁷² 128 b 129 121
120' 509 A Arm Boᴸ Eth Laᴼ
Sa] + ετι ζωντος αυτου rell
36:6 υιους] + αυτου 72-135-381'
25 b d⁻¹²⁵ f n t 318'-392' 31 55 59'
Co Eth Arab
36:6 θυγατερας] + αυτου 618 53'
n 346'-392* 31 Arm Co Laᴵ
Arab
36:31 εδωμ] pr γη O 128 d n 30'
t 318'-527 31' 55 319ᶜ 961 Arm
Sa Syh Arab
36:39 αραδ] αδαδ O 551 56' s⁻¹³⁰
318 Arm Syh Arab
36:40 αυτων 2°(om in Arab)]
+ εν τοις ονομασιν αυτων
(c var) 17'-72-135 128 346 z
Syh Arab
37:2 προβατα] + του πατρος
αυτου (c var) 58-oI C'ᴐ⁻¹²⁸⁻⁴¹⁴ b f
130-730 46 y⁻¹²¹⁻³⁹² 31 55 319 961
Bo Eth Arab
37:2 αυτων] αυτου 58-72-82-618*-
708 79 19'-108 d f⁻⁵⁶* 458 71'-
121-527* L Bo Eth⁻ᶜ Arab
37:8 αδελφοι 82-135-426 cI d 56*
75 s⁻¹³⁰⁻⁷³⁰ t 392 59 A L] + αυτου
rell

37:13 ιδου] pr ιωσηφ 82 d 53' n
Arab
37:24 ερριψαν] + αυτον 79-313-
615' t⁻⁴⁶ 346-392 z⁻⁶³⁰ 59' Bo Eth
Syh Arab
38:14 σηλωμ] + ο υιος αυτου oI
C'ᴐ⁻¹²⁸ f⁻⁵⁶* s⁻¹³⁰ t 71'- 121-318-392
630 55 59' Cyr Arab
38:17 προβατων] + μου b f⁻⁵⁶*
130-343 t 71'-346' 31 55 319 509
Arm Arab
38:19 θεριστρον] + αυτης O b 130
527 319 Arm Bo Syh Arab
38:21 om τους εκ O 458 Arm Bo
Eth Syh Jub Vulg Arab
38:28 χειρα O f⁻⁵³' s 121-346' z
319ᴵ 707ᴵᴵᴵ A 961 Laᴵ] + αυτου
rell
39:7 ειπεν] + αυτω 72 125 f⁻⁵⁶*⁻¹²⁹*
346' 31 59 962 Arm Co Eth Laᴵ
Arab
39:11 om των 376 18-25 53' n 121
31 319 A Bo Eth Arab
39:19 om και 58-72 107' n 509
Bo⁻ᵂ Eth Arab
40:3 om παρα τω αρχιδεσμο-
φυλακι 120 b 56ᵗˣᵗ 30' 71'-346
z Eth Arab
40:17 επανω 2°] επι 58 d 56* n
509 961 Bo Arab
41:4 εκλεκτας] + ταις σαρξι
(+suis Verss) 17-135 129 t Bo
Eth⁻ᴿ Arab
41:8 ενυπνιον] + αυτου O' C'ᴐ⁻¹²⁸
f⁻⁵⁶* 130-343 71'-392' Or Arm
Boᴸᴹ Eth Laˣ Sa Arab
41:16 tr τω φαραω/ειπεν 128
b d⁻¹²⁵ f n s⁻¹³⁰⁻³⁴³ 962 Arm Co
Laˢ Arab
41:21 αυτων 1° ⌒ 2° 17'-72 77-
422-cII⁻⁵⁶⁹ 19'-108 610 53'-56ᵗˣᵗ
74 318 59' Phil Boᴸᴹ Arabᵗˣᵗ

41:22 om μου O'⁻⁵⁸⁻⁷²⁻⁸² C'ᴐ⁻⁴¹⁴' ⁻⁵⁵¹
458 s⁻¹³⁰⁻³⁴³ 120'-122 Arm Eth⁻ᶜᴾ
Laᴱ Sa Arab

41:30 πλησμονης] + της εσομενης
C'ᴐ f 30'-344ᵐᵍ t 71'-346' z 59'
509 L Bo Laᴬ Arab

41:32 om το 3° O⁻⁷²⁻⁴²⁶ 500 129 n
59' 319 Bo Eth Arab

41:33 επι] + ολης (c var) 82-426
d f⁻¹²⁹ n t 962 Eth Arab

41:51 μανασση] + λεγων 58-426
53'-56ᶜ n t 121-346' 31 55
Aᶜ(vid) Arm Eth Arab

41:52 εφραιμ] + λεγων 17'-58-
135-426 d f⁻⁵⁶*⁻¹²⁹* 75-458ᶜ·ᵖʳ·ᵐ
t 346' 31 Eth Laᴵ Arab

41:54 ησαν] pr ουκ 17'-58-707ᶜ-oI
C'ᴐ⁻¹²⁸ 314 f⁻⁵⁶* s y⁻³¹⁸ 31-630 55
59 319 509 M 962* Arm Bo Eth
Arab

42:1 πρασις] + σιτου 58-72 d n t
Chr Bo Ruf Arab

42:1 ειπεν] + ιακωβ 15-135'-426-
707 C'ᴐ⁻²⁵⁻¹²⁸ 56' 130 t 71-392-
424 962 Arm Bo Arab

42:9 ενυπνιον] + αυτου oI C'ᴐ⁻¹⁶⁻
¹²⁸⁻⁵⁵¹ 106-370 246 n 30'-344ᵐᵍ
t y⁻¹²¹⁻³¹⁸⁻⁴²⁴ 31 55 59 319 509
M Arm Boⱽ Eth La Arab

42:28 αργυριον] + μου 15-72-376
19' Bo Laˢ Arab

42:35 αυτων 2°] αυτου 15-72 500
d 53' 75 t 71 Bo Arab

43:2 αυτοις] + ιακωβ d f⁻¹²⁹ n
30'-344ᵐᵍ t 392' 630 55 59 319
D Fᵇ Arab

43:17 ειπεν] + αυτω d 53' n t Fᵇ
Bo Eth Laˢ Sa³ Arab

43:30 om εκει b f Bo Eth Laˢ Arab

44:7 om αυτω 707 52'-77-128-615'
b⁻¹⁹' 125 Arab

44:16 κυριω] + ημων 72 551' 344'
Fᵇ Bo Laˢ Syh Arab

44:22 πατερα 1°] + αυτου 72'
b d t Arm Bo Syh Arab

44:23 om οτι 58-426 14 b 509 Chr
Arm Bo Laˢ Syhᵗˣᵗ Arab

44:25 om ημιν 376' 16-646 b 44
56* n Arm Bo Laˢ Syh Arab

44:29 οδω] + η αν πορευησθε
57ᵐᵍ-550 d n 344ᵐᵍ t 71'-392 55
59 509 F Bo Arab

45:4 ηγγισαν] + προς αυτον d n
s⁻¹³⁰⁻³⁴³ t 71'-392 630 55 59 509
F Bo Eth Ambr Arab

45:10 τα] pr και O⁻ᶠᵇ 79 53'-56*
n 30' 59 509 962 Arm Bo Syh
Arab

45:17 υμων] + σιτου 82 b d f n
(-ον 458) 127 t 121 55 76 Fᵐᵍ*
Chr Boᵂ Laᴱ Arab

45:21 βασιλεως] + αιγυπτου 58-
82-oI C'ᴐ⁻¹²⁸' d f⁻¹²⁹ 75 s y⁻¹²¹⁻⁵²⁷
120'-122 55 59 F Bo Eth Arab

46:3 λεγων] και (om Boh Arab)
ειπεν 426-Fᵇ 128 d n t 71'-121
Bo Eth Laᴱ Arab

46:5 ισραηλ] + ιακωβ O⁻⁸²⁻⁴²⁶
d⁻¹⁰⁶⁻¹²⁵ t Or Arm Boᴸ Syhᵗˣᵗ
Arab

46:7 om μετ αυτου 17'-72-oI b 44
n s⁻¹³⁰ 134 M Boᵂ Eth Laᴬ
Arabᵐᵍ

46:7 υιων 2° 17'-135-707 A Syhᵗˣᵗ]
θυγατερων rell

46:8 αιγυπτον] + αμα ιακωβ τω
πατρι αυτων (c var) 17'-58-
64ᵐᵍ-82-135 128' b d⁻¹²⁵ f⁻¹²⁹ n
s⁻¹³⁰ 346'-392-619 31-630 55 76
Mᵐᵍ Bo Laᴬ Arab

47:3 fin] + εκ παιδος εως του νυν
(c var) 29-82 d f⁻⁵⁶(ᵗˣᵗ) 75 30'-

343-344^{mg} y$^{-318-424'}$ z 55 59 A
M^{mg} Or Bo Arab
47:12 πατρι] + αυτου 72 128 f^{-129}
346' 31 76 B Co La^{SA} Syh Arab
47:15 om ημων O^{-72} d t 71'-392
120'-122 55 59 76 M Arm Bo
Syh Arab
47:17 κτηνη] + αυτων F^b f^{-56*} 346'
31 Or Bo Eth Arab
47:18 και 4°] + παντα F^b d^{-125}
53'-246 n t Arab
47:18 κυριον] + ημων 58-376
C$^{'ɔ-128-739}$ 19-108 30' 71' M^{mg}
La^8 Arab
47:19 δος] + ημιν C$^{'ɔ-128}$ b 30'
71'-527 630 Bo Eth Arab
47:28 om γη 15'-17'-29-135 422*
246 509 Bo Arab
47:29 tr τον υιον αυτου/ιωσηφ
29 n 30' 527 55 76 319 509 Bo
Arab
47:29 υπο] επι 72-376 16-18-78-
408 107'-125 71'-346 z Arab
48:5 γενομενοι] γεγεννημενοι
d$^{-107-125}$ 46-134 392 59 Arab
48:5 εν] + γη 58-oI C$^{'ɔ}$ d 129-246
n s$^{-127-130}$ t 71'-392 z 55 59 A M
Cyr Sa$^{20(ed)}$ Arab
48:5 αιγυπτω] -πτου
C$^{'ɔ-25-73-79-128-422'-550}$ 458 z^{-630}
Sa$^{20(ed)}$ Aug Hi Vulg Arab
48:8 om σοι 135 57-500 b 44 30'-
127-343 84 71'-318 Arab
48:11 om και 3° 135-618 25*-
414*-551-cI 19-108 Bo La^8 Sa^{20}
Arab
48:13 δεξια] + αυτου f^{-56*} 458 30
La^{MS} Sa$^{20(ed)}$ Arab
48:14 fin] + οτι μανασση ο πρω-
τοτοκος (c var) O$^{-400-707^c}$ d^{-106}
Arm Sa$^{20(ed)}$ Arab

48:15 νεοτητος 17-29-64'-82-707
C$^{'ɔ-128-551}$ 56* n s^{-130} 121 319 A
B] + μου rell
48:17 πατηρ 707-oI C$^{'ɔ-25-128}$ b f^{-129}
s^{-130} 71 B M Arm] + αυτου rell
48:18 επιθες] + την χειρα d f^{-129}
n s^{-130} t 392 630 55 59 L Co Eth
EpBarn-lat Arab
48:18 tr την δεξιαν/σου 53'-246 n
Bo Eth EpBarn-lat Arab
49:31 εκει 2° O^{-82} n 121 B L Arm
Bo] pr και Tht rell
50:4 περι εμου 29-707 56* 121 A
B Bo Eth Sa$^{19(vid)}$] om rell
50:11 εκαλεσεν] -σαν 72-135-
426-oI C$^{'ɔ-414-551*}$ b$^{-19-108}$ d f$^{-56-129}$
127 t 71-392^c-424' 31-630 Eth^{-P}
La^E Arab
50:11 αυτου 15-17-135-426-707
B^8 Arm Eth] του τοπου εκεινου
29-72 b f 84 121-346' 31 59 F Co
La^E Arab: om 414-551*; του
τοπου rell
50:12 αυτου] ισραηλ 376 73-646
d f^{-129} n s$^{-85(mg)-130-344'(mg)}$ t A
Arm Arab
50:12 αυτου B Eth] + καθως
ενετειλατο αυτοις (c var) (tr
ad fin 129 Bo Sa^{19} Arab) rell
50:13 om το σπηλαιον 2° 72-135
25-52'-128 b$^{-19-108}$ 44 53' n 46
71'-392 630 Arm Eth La^{102} Arab
50:16 λεγοντες O b$^{-19-108}$ B^8] ειπαν
Chr rell
50:18 οιδε] ιδε 58-72-135'-426
14'-52'-77'-422'-615^c-739-761
18 71'-392-527^c 55 59 76 Chr
Arm Eth La^{102} Spec Arab
50:24 om ο θεος 2° 15-58-72-381'
73 71'-346' 76 319 Arab

III CONCLUSIONS

As might have been expected Arab betrays strong Egyptian influence, particularly on the part of Boh. In large part this was undoubtedly due to the wide use of the Arabic version translated from Co, i.e. the one used by the Jacobites. It might even seem reasonable to suggest that Arab is actually based on Boh, but this is not the case. Arab was directly rendered from the Greek as two examples will demonstrate. In 24:8 τον οικον is rendered by *populum domi*. This is best explained as based on a *Vorlage* with την οικειαν, not attested in any extant text. Since Boh here translates rather than transliterates, Arab could not be based on it. Even more convincing is 13:2, where Arab has *tabernaculi* for the Greek κτηνεσιν which was probably misread as σκηναις. The error can only have been based on the Greek since Boh has NTEBNH (MT has *miqne[h]*). In contrast, some influence of the popular Saadia version has resulted in a number of unique readings in which Arab is closer to MT than is LXX.

The textual affinities to the Greek families are largely mixed, but some tentative conclusions can be stated. Arab is certainly not part of the old *d* and *t* traditions. The two major affinities are with the *O* and the *b* traditions. The former would seem to be clear from the inclusion at the end of 31:50 of a long plus, as well as from a number of passages sub ast. as at 7:14, 9:24, 20:10, 24:67, 31:53, 35:20, 42:4, 43:24, and 44:22. Of particular interest in this connection are 35:20 and 43:24, both of which contain fairly lengthy plusses neither of which is supported by any of Co/Eth.

The clear affinities with *b* do not constitute a large group, but they do include some of significance. The variants cited for 22:2, 27:4, 32:16, 44:2, and 46:26 demonstrate more than a casual relation to the group.

Most striking of all are the large number of affinities which Arab shows with Chr and Tht. Most of the variants unique to Tht/Chr-Arab are omissions. In one case Tht-Arab provides the only witnesses to the omission of an asterisked passage, 6:6.[10]

Arab's relations to the A groups and to *n* and *s* are not particularly significant. Somewhat more important is the influence of the old *f* group (with which Cod. B stands in closest alignment), as in 11:25, 18:11, and 37:10, but the influence is clearly minimal.

---

10 It will now be necessary to restudy the Chr and Tht citations in view of the new collations. In the meantime I have avoided any reference to Lucian, since that would be begging the question.

Energic Verbal Forms
in Hebrew

RONALD J. WILLIAMS

This study is offered as a small tribute to the esteemed scholar who, more than thirty years ago, helped to guide the writer's earliest attempts to master the intricacies of Hebrew and Arabic. It is a product of the lively interest in grammatical matters which he firmly instilled in his pupil.

The presence of an energic form of the verb in biblical Hebrew has long been recognized by scholars.[1] The extent to which this form is employed as well as its syntactic function, however, requires some clarification. To accomplish this, we would do well to begin by reviewing the evidence for energic forms in the other Semitic languages.

That classical Arabic possessed two energic forms of the imperfect (/yaqtulan/ and /yaqtulanna/), and of the imperative (/uqtulan/ and /uqtulanna/), is well known to Semitists. The energic imperfect occurs most frequently in oaths and with the emphatic particle /la/, where it always has a future meaning, as well as in questions and prohibitions with the negative particle /lā/.[2] It is likely that a certain emphasis is imparted to the meaning by the use of the forms, although the contrast between /lā taqul/ and /lā taqulanna/, 'do not say,' is admittedly slight.

When we turn to the comparatively small body of texts which

---

1 H. Zimmern, *Vergleichende Grammatik der semitischen Sprachen* (Berlin, 1898), § 43a; C. Brockelmann, *Grundriss der vergleichenden Grammatik der semitischen Sprachen* (Berlin, 1908–13), vol. I, pp. 557, 641; E. Kautzsch, *Gesenius' Hebrew Grammar*, rev. by A. E. Cowley (Oxford, 1898), § 58i; H. Bauer and P. Leander, *Historische Grammatik der hebräischen Sprache des Alten Testaments* (Halle, 1918–22), § 48q–s, c'.

2 W. Wright, *A Grammar of the Arabic Language*, 3rd ed. rev. by W. R. Smith and M. J. de Goeje (Cambridge, 1896–8), vol. II, pp. 24, 41–4; C. Brockelmann, *Grundriss*, vol. II, p. 159 (§ 80).

have survived in the inscriptions recorded in the Old South Arabian dialects, we encounter a similar situation. Two of the dialects, Sabaean and Minaean, exhibit energic forms side by side with those which do not have a final /n/,[3] though such energic forms are less frequent in Minaean than in Sabaean.

For the third person masculine singular we may cite in Sabaean *yšᵓmn*, 'he buys' (R 3910/3), *ymwtn*, 'he shall die' (C 126/12), *ᵓl yᶜṭnn*, 'he should not neglect' (R 4176/1), and the Minaean *yqnyn*, 'he will acquire' (R 3350/6). The precative in Sabaean appears as *lyzᵓn*, 'may he continue' (C 3/9f.), to be contrasted with *lyzᵓ* (R 850/6) with no difference in meaning. The energic may even have a final sense, as in *ydᵓn*, 'that it may go forth' (C 570/6). Forms with pronominal suffixes are rare, but we may mention the Sabaean examples *yšᵓmnhw*, 'he buys it' (R 3910/5), and *tsqynhw*, 'it irrigates it' (C 657/3).

The plural of the third person displays two nuns at the end, e.g. Sabaean *ytᵓwlnn*, 'they returned' (Ry 535/7), with which may be contrasted *ytᵓwlw* in the following line with identical meaning, and *yšᵓmnn*, 'they buy' (R 3910/2f.), as well as Minaean *trdnn*, 'they descend,' and *tᵓnṭnn*, 'they shall marry' (R 3306/5f.).

Assyriologists have followed Landsberger in regarding the Akkadian termination /am/ (/nim/ after long vowels in the plural) appended to the present, preterite, imperative, and third person of the stative forms as producing a ventive force.[4] Thus *il-li-kam*, 'he came' (LIH 88:9), in contrast to *il-lik*, 'he went' (Gilg. I iii 46). The ventive may follow the jussive particle /lu/, e.g. *li-ib-lam*, 'let him bring' (TCL 18 102:39), and *li-il-lik ... lu-bil-u-ni*, 'he should come ... they should bring' (ABL 474 r 3f.). These forms were described by earlier scholars as energic.[5] More recently Castellino has argued that, since the ventive is employed with verbs other than those of motion, a designation such as 'emphatic' would be more appropriate.[6] It is significant that von Soden, after commenting on the use of pronominal suffixes after the ventive, remarks: 'ein Bedeutungsunterschied zwi-

---

3 M. Höfner, *Altsüdarabische Grammatik* (Leipzig, 1943), §§ 59–64; A. F. L. Beeston, *A Descriptive Grammar of Epigraphic South Arabian* (London, 1962), §§ 21:6–11. The texts are cited in accordance with Beeston's system of abbreviations.

4 W. von Soden, *Grundriss der akkadischen Grammatik* (Rome, 1952), § 82. The text citations follow the abbreviations of the Chicago Assyrian Dictionary.

5 B. Meissner, *Kurzgefasste assyrische Grammatik* (Leipzig, 1907), § 52c; G. Ryckmans, *Grammaire accadienne* (Louvain, 1938), §§ 239–42.

6 G. R. Castellino, *The Akkadian Personal Pronouns and Verbal System in the Light of Semitic and Hamitic* (Leyden, 1962), pp. 79f.

schen Ventiv und Ind. ist zumal vor den Dat.-Suff. sehr oft nicht feststellbar (z.B. scheinen *iddiššum* und *iddinaššum* "er gab ihm" ganz gleichbedeutend).'[7] He also observes that the ventive is more common in poetry on rhythmic grounds.[8]

The addition of a final /n/ to imperfect forms is a notable feature of most Western Aramaic dialects. It is maintained by many scholars that these forms are always indicative, and contrast with those lacking the /n/ termination which are precative in their meaning.[9] It will soon be apparent that this rule is not always observed. We may add that the longer forms do not confer any special emphasis, as Bauer and Leander assert when speaking of the suffixed forms: 'Die dem Energie-Aor. charakteristische Nebenbedeutung von Nachdruck ist dabei verloren gegangen.'[10] Because in the course of time all final /n/ terminations after short vowels were elided, to be followed by the short vowels themselves, only those forms ending in long vowels retain the /n/ (except before pronominal suffixes), e.g. in later Aramaic, third masc. pl. /yiḵtᵊḇūn/ and second fem. sing. /tiḵtᵊḇīn/.

In Old Aramaic[11] a good illustration of the normal contrast between indicative and precative can be seen in the forms *yṣrn*, 'they will keep' (KAI 222 B, 8), and *yṣrw*, 'may they keep' (KAI 222 C, 15). Examples with pronominal suffixes are *yqtlnh*, 'he will kill him' (KAI 222 B, 27) and *ykṭlwk*, 'may they kill you' (KAI 225/11). Exceptions to the rule are *ʾḥṣlk*, 'I shall rescue you' (KAI 202 A, 14), and *ʾl yhrgn*, 'they will not kill' (KAI 222 A, 24). In the second case the modal negative particle /ʾal/ should be followed by the precative, as in *ʾl tḥzw*, 'do not look' (KAI 233/17).

In the Yaudic dialect similar anomalies are to be found. The shorter form is employed for an indicative, e.g. *ytnw*, 'they will give' (KAI 214/4), and *thrgh*, 'you shall kill him' (KAI 214/33), whereas the longer form accompanies the precative particle *l* in *lktšnh*, 'let one batter him' (KAI 214/31), contrasting with the normal form *lktšh* earlier in the same line.

---

7 *Grundriss der akkadischen Grammatik*, p. 109, § 84c, Anm.

8 *Ibid.*, § 82b.

9 P. Leander, *Laut- und Formenlehre des Ägyptisch-Aramäischen* (Göteborg, 1928), pp. 40f.; S. Moscati, *An Introduction to the Comparative Grammar of the Semitic Languages* (Wiesbaden, 1964), § 16.34; G. Garbini, *Il semitico di nordovest* (Naples, 1960), pp. 146f.

10 H. Bauer and P. Leander, *Grammatik des Biblisch-Aramäischen* (Halle/Saale, 1927), § 26b.

11 G. Garbini, 'L'aramaico antico,' in *Atti della Accademia Nazionale dei Lincei, Memorie*, ser. VIII, vol. VII, fasc. 5 (Rome, 1956), pp. 239–83; R. Degen, *Altaramäische Grammatik* (Wiesbaden, 1969).

Imperial Aramaic presents us with a very much larger body of material.[12] As evidence for the indicative/energic forms we quote *yqblwn*, 'they will bring' (c 6/16), *tntnn*, 'you (fem. sing.) shall give' (k 9/21, c 8/10), *tṣbyn*, 'you (fem. sing.) shall wish' (c 13/16), and *ʾ ykhlwn*, 'they shall be unable' (c 20/11). The precative is found in a wish, *yšʾlw*, 'may they seek' (c 37/2); as a vetitive, *ʾl tntnw*, 'do not give' (d 6/6); or expressing purpose, *yntnw*, 'that they may give' (d 8/3), the latter contrasting with *yntnwn*, 'they shall give' (k 3/18). Nevertheless, exceptions to this rule are not lacking, as we see from *yʾklw* (kai 270 b, 3) which, though precative in form, means 'they will eat,' and *tntnw*, 'you will give' (c 25/14), which should be indicative like *tzbnwn*, 'you will sell,' in the same line.

We also encounter unexpected instances of the energic in singular forms where the termination would normally be lost. These are *yʾhdn*, 'he will take' (c Aḥ 171), *ʾšbqn*, 'I shall leave' (c Aḥ 82), *ʾšlmn*, 'I shall reimburse' (c 35/5), and *ʾl tlqḥn*, 'do not take' (c Aḥ 119). In the last example the vetitive particle should be accompanied by the precative form. It is perhaps significant that three of these unusual vestiges occur in the Aḥiqar text.

Energic forms with pronominal suffixes preponderate, e.g. *ygrnk*, 'he will sue you' (c 6/14), *ʾšlmnhy*, 'I shall repay it' (c 11/3), *yršwnkm*, 'they will bring an action against you' (c 20/13). Again we must note that the normal rule is not rigidly observed. The indicative is used where a precative would be proper in the greeting formula *yšymnk*, 'may he set you (for favour),' i.e. 'accord you favour' (c 30/2), and also after the modal negative particle *ʾal*/ in *ʾl nqṭlnhy*, 'let us not kill him' (c Aḥ 61). Conversely, the precative is employed where an indicative is required in two passages: *yrškm*, 'he shall bring an action against you' (c 25/15), and *ʾ nkl ngrky*, 'we shall be unable to sue you' (c 1/4). The latter may be contrasted with the similar statement *ʾ ykhl ... ygrnk*, 'he will be unable to sue you' (k 3/16f.).

The Aramaic of the Old Testament is in all essentials identical with Imperial Aramaic. Examples of indicative/energic forms without pronominal suffixes are /yištaḵlǝlūn/, 'they will be completed' (Ezek. 4:13), /yiškǝnɔ̄n/, 'they (fem.) dwell' (Dan. 4:18), and /tǝqabbǝlūn/, 'you shall receive' (Dan. 2:6). For the precative we may cite /yēḇaḏū/, 'may they perish' (Jer. 10:11), and /ʾal-yištannɔ̄/,

12 Texts are quoted with the following abbreviations: c – A. Cowley, *Aramaic Papyri of the Fifth Century B.C.* (Oxford, 1923); k – E. G. Kraeling, *The Brooklyn Museum Aramaic Papyri* (New Haven, 1953); d – G. R. Driver, *Aramaic Documents of the Fifth Century B.C.* (Oxford, 1954), abridged and rev. ed. 1957.

'let them not change' (Dan. 5:10). The indicative form of the latter is /yištannōn/ (Dan. 7:28). An unusual feature of this dialect is the preformative /l/ instead of /y/ for the third person of the verb /hᵃwʒ/, 'to be.' One instance of this verb in the third fem. pl. has the indicative/energic form in a context where a precative is required, viz. /lɛhɛwyʒn/, 'let them be' (Dan. 5:17). The parallel clause has an imperative.

When pronominal suffixes are added to the indicative, the resulting forms are /yᵊšēzᵊbinkōn/, 'he will rescue you' (Dan. 3:15), /yᵊbahᵃlunnanī/, 'they were alarming me' (Dan. 4:2), /ᵖᵃhōdᵊʕinneh/, 'I shall inform him' (Dan. 5:17). Precative examples are /ᵖal-yᵊbahᵃlōk/, 'let it not alarm you' (Dan. 4:16) and /ᵖal-yᵊbahᵃlūk/, 'let them not alarm you' (Dan. 5:10).

The earliest of the northwest Semitic languages to have an extensive literature is Ugaritic. Gordon has distinguished three moods in the verb (like classical Arabic) on the basis of the final vowel or lack of it as revealed by roots, the final consonant of which is aleph. These appear to be /yaqtulu/, an indicative; /yaqtula/, morphologically identical with the Arabic subjunctive, but in meaning indicative or cohortative; and /yaqtul/, which is both precative and preterite.[13] To these forms may be added an energic ending /n/, yielding a form which may be vocalized either as /yaqtulan/ or /yaqtulanna/.[14]

We are fortunate, as a result of the repetitive nature of Ugaritic epic poetry, to have a number of identical passages. These reveal the fact that there is no discernible difference in meaning between the energic and the forms lacking final /n/. We are forced to conclude with Gordon that the former was merely a variant for the sake of style.[15] The following examples are conclusive:

yphn, 'he perceived' (1 Aq 135): *yph* (1 Aq 120)
t[t]bn, 'you will return' (51.vii.24): *ttb* (51.vi.2, 15)
iqrdn, 'I shall proclaim' (52/23): *iqrd* (52/1)
aštn, 'I shall put' (1 Aq 140): *ašt* (1 Aq 112, 126)
tlhmn,[16] 'they eat' (124/23): *tlhm* (124/21)
tkbdnh, 'she honoured him' (49.i.10): *tkbdh* (51.iv.26)
tšan, 'they both lifted up' (Krt 303): *tša* (67.ii.16)
tshn, 'they both cried out' (Krt 304): *tsh* (67.ii.17)

13 C. H. Gordon, *Ugaritic Textbook* (Rome, 1965), § 9.10.
14 *Ibid.*, § 9.11. The text references which follow use Gordon's system of designation.
15 *Ibid.*, p. 73, fn. 1.
16 In the third person masc. pl., the preformative /t/ often occurs in place of the expected /y/; cf. Gordon, *Ugaritic Textbook*, § 9.14.

The regular assimilation of /n/ to a following consonant (except
when /n/ is the third radical of a verb) makes it impossible to distinguish energic forms when first or second personal suffixes are added,
e.g. *yblk* (51.v.79) and *tblk* (51.v.77), both meaning 'they will bring
you.' In the case of the third person, the consonant /h/ frequently
disappears in the written form because of the phenomenon of regressive assimilation. We might compare, in identical passages, *áqbrnh*
(1 Aq 140) and *áqbrn* (1 Aq 126), meaning 'I shall bury him.' Sometimes a second /n/ may appear, eliminating the ambiguity, e.g.
tbqᶜnn, 'she split him' (49.ii.32).

Examples of the precative after the modal particle /ʾal/ are *ál tqrb*,
'do not both approach' (51.viii.15f.), and *ál yᶜdbkm*, 'let him not
make you' (51.viii.17). It would appear that the energic ending may
occur on precative forms also, for we find *ál tbkn*, 'do not weep'
(125/25). Affirmative uses of the precative are *tispk*, 'may it gather
you' (1 Aq 66, 73), and *tšlmk*, 'may they preserve you' (117/8).

In common with classical Arabic, Ugaritic has an energic form of
the imperative, e.g. *qḥn*, 'take' (1 Aq 215). More surprising is the use
of this termination on the perfect, perhaps better termed the suffix conjugation. Here may be recorded *šlbšn*, 'he clothed (him)'
(67.v.23),[17] and probably *ṯtᶜ.nn*, 'he dreads him' (67.ii.7), which is
paralleled in the preceding line by *yráun*, 'he fears him.' It is less
certain whether we should so interpret the strange form *ldn*, 'she was
victorious' (127/14), from the root *ʾy*.

The earliest form of what may confidently be described as Canaanite is preserved in the fourteenth century B.C. archive of cuneiform
tablets which was discovered at Tell el-Amarna.[18] The distinctively
Canaanite material is contained in those letters emanating from the
Phoenician cities of Byblus and Beirut. Moran postulates three
moods in Amarna Canaanite, corresponding to those in Ugaritic: an
indicative /yaqtulu/, a 'volitive' /yaqtula/, and a precative /yaqtul/.[19]

The evidence for an energic form is overwhelming.[20] For instance,
yú-wa-ši-ru-na, 'he will send' (EA 112/19), contrasts in the same letter

17 Although Gordon shows a break immediately before this form in his transliterated text, the cuneiform text shows that it was preceded by *l*, and hence we
may not restore this verb as a preformative conjugation.
18 F. M. T. Böhl, 'Die Sprache der Amarnabriefe mit besonderer Berücksichtigung
der Kanaanismen,' LSS, V, 2 (1909); E. Ebeling, 'Das Verbum der El-Amarna-
Briefe,' BAS, 8/2 (1910); E. Dhorme, 'La langue de Canaan,' in *Receuil Edouard
Dhorme* (Paris, 1951), pp. 405–87, earlier published in RB, 22 (1913), 369–93;
23 (1914), 37–59, 344–72.
19 W. L. Moran, 'Early Canaanite *yaqtula*,' *Orientalia*, N.S. 29 (1960), 1–19.
20 E. Ebeling, 'Das Verbum,' § 21.

with the simple form *yú-wa-ši-ru* (EA 112/37); *la-a yi-eš-mu-na*, 'he does not listen' (EA 85/7), with *la-a yi-eš-mu* (EA 118/54); *ti-eš-tap-ru-na*, 'you have written' (EA 117/8), with *ti-eš-tap-ru* (EA 124/36); *ti-il-qú-na*, 'they will seize'[21] (EA 104/32), with *ti-il-qú* (EA 84/32); *la-a ti-li-ú-na*, 'they are unable' (EA 108/45), with *la-a ti-li-ú* (EA 83/20); and finally *yú-ú-ul-qú-na*, 'it/he will be taken' (EA 117/68), with *yú-ú-ul-qú* (EA 117/33), also in the same letter.

When pronominal suffixes are attached we have forms such as *yú-te-ru-na-ni*, 'he shall send back to me' (EA 251/11f.), which contrasts with the equivalent *yú-te-ru-ni* (EA 137/82). Other instances are: *uš-ši-ru-na-ši*, 'I shall send it' (EA 143/16), and *tu-ša-ab-li-ṭú-na-nu*, 'you give us life' (EA 238/31).

The 'volitive' is normally without the energic ending, as we see from the following examples: *ia-di-na*, 'let him give' (EA 85/19), *ti-na-ṣa-ru*, 'let them protect' (EA 112/35), *ú-ul yi-eš-ma*, 'let him not hear' (EA 82/23), and *ú-ul yú-uq-ba*, 'let it not be said' (EA 83/16). One exception, however, is *ul ti-ma-ḫa-ṣa-na-ni*, 'lest they slay me' (EA 77/37). The rare precative does not appear to receive the energic termination, e.g. *ta-ap-šu-uḫ*, 'let it be calm' (EA 107/31), *ia-az-ku-ur*, 'let him remember' (EA 228/19, a marked Canaanite gloss). In contrast, as in Ugaritic and Arabic, the imperative may have the energic ending as is evident from a comparison of *uš-ši-ru-na-ni*, 'send to me' (EA 71/23), with *uš-ši-ra-ni* (EA 108/66).

The Phoenician inscriptions themselves attest to the fact that the energic was a feature of the language, as we have already inferred from the Amarna letters. The claim by scholars that the energic with final /n/ is indicative, and thus to be distinguished from the precative, as in the case of Aramaic, seems to be substantiated from the small amount of textual material available.[22]

In the matter of the precative, the orthographic conventions preclude any distinction between singular and plural, since final /ū/-vowels are not indicated by means of waw. The following are recognized as plural only from their contexts: *ycbd*, 'may they serve' (KAI 26 C, 10), *ydc*, 'that they may know' (KAI 60/7), and *ʾl ykbd*, 'let them not honour' (KAI 24/14f.). Examples of indicative/energic forms are: *yšʾn*, 'they shall pay' (KAI 60/6), *yqṣn*, 'that they cut off' (KAI 14/22), expressing purpose, and with the negative particle, *bl tdrkn*, 'you must not tread' (KAI 27/8). It is quite startling to discover that Phoe-

---

21 As in Ugaritic (cf. fn. 16), the third masc. pl. commonly has the preformative /t/ in place of /y/.

22 Z. S. Harris, *A Grammar of the Phoenician Language* (New Haven, 1936), pp. 40f.; J. Friedrich, *Phönizisch-punische Grammatik* (Rome, 1951), § 135.

nician, like Imperial Aramaic, has preserved an example of an energic in a singular form which should have lost the termination, viz.
ʾpqn, 'that I may find' (KAI 50/3).[23]

The same modal distinction is apparent with pronominal suffixes,
e.g. ydbrnk, 'they talk to you' (KAI 14/6), compared with ypᶜlk, 'may
they make you' (KAI 50/3), and ybrkm, 'may he bless them' (KAI 40/5,
47/4), to be contrasted with ysgrnm, 'they shall deliver them up' (KAI
14/9, 21). The latter form, probably to be vocalized /yasgīrūnēm/,
originated from an energic form with the addition of the suffix /hēm/.
The /h/ then disappeared, perhaps by regressive assimilation. The
significant fact is that in the course of time the ending /nēm/ was
understood to be the pronominal suffix, and could even be added to
substantives![24]

In the light of this wealth of material from other Semitic languages, we are in a more favourable position to understand the situation as it confronts us in biblical Hebrew. The evidence for a termination in /n/ is not inconsiderable: including forms with attached
pronominal suffixes, some 775 examples are preserved, of which over
300 are forms without suffixes.[25] Since Hebrew, in common with Aramaic and, at a much later period, Arabic, lost all /n/ terminations
after short vowels (at the same time as mimation was dropped) and
eventually also suffered the elision of all short final vowels,[26] the
energic forms are only identifiable when terminating in a long vowel
or followed by pronominal suffixes.

Examples of the first type are the second fem. sing. form /tištak-
kɔrīn/, 'will you play the drunkard?' (1 Sam. 1:14), the second masc.
pl. /təḏabbərūn/, 'you shall say' (Gen. 32:20), and the third masc. pl.
/yaḥsərūn/, 'they will be lacking' (Gen. 18:28). When pronouns are
affixed, sometimes the usual assimilation of final /n/ to the following
suffix does not take place. For instance, contrast /yəsōḇəḇennū/, 'it
surrounds him' (Ps. 32:10), with /yəsōḇəḇenhū/ (Deut. 32:10);
/yōᶜīḏɛnnī/, 'he will summon me' (Jer. 49:19), with /yəḵabbəḏɔ̄nənī/,
'he honours me' (Ps. 50:23), or /ʾɛttəqɛnkɔ̄/, 'I would pluck you off'
(Jer. 22:24). This lack of assimilation is regular with the third masc.
pl., for instance /yiqrɔ̄ʾūnənī/, 'they will call on me' (Prov. 1:28),
/yiśśɔ̄ʾūnəḵɔ̄/, 'they will lift you up' (Ps. 91:12), /yəśɔ̄rətūnɛk/, 'they

23 Friedrich, *Phönizisch-punische Grammatik*, p. 72, interprets the final nun as the
    particle which appears in Hebrew as *n*', vocalized /nɔ̄/!

24 Cf. Z. S. Harris, *Development of the Canaanite Dialects* (New Haven, 1939),
    pp. 77f.

25 These approximate statistics are the result of a hasty count of forms in
    Mandelkern's Concordance.

26 Cf. Harris, *Development*, pp. 32f., 59f.

shall serve you' (Isa. 60:7, 10), /yaᶜabᵊrūnhū/, 'they will pass over it' (Jer. 5:22), /yimṣᵊ²ūnhɔ̄/, 'they will find her' (Jer. 2:24), and once with an original connecting vowel, /yilkᵊdūnɔ̄/, 'they capture him' (Prov. 5:22), derived from */yilkᵊdūnahū/.

The general rule that verbal forms terminating in /ūn/ or /īn/ were indicative in contradistinction to precative forms in /ū/ and /ī/ has been claimed for biblical Hebrew as well.²⁷ If this be so, then it must be confessed that by the biblical period Hebrew no longer observed the distinction with any regularity, since the great majority of indicative forms have no /n/ termination, although this consonant would not have been lost after long vowels, and it should have been retained before pronominal suffixes.

The converse is also true, for there are nearly fifty examples of precative forms with the energic ending. These are found: (1) with the modal negative /ᵊal/, e.g. /ᵊal-yaṭṭɛkkɔ̄/, 'let it not deflect you' (Job 36:18; cf. 9:34, 13:21); (2) with 'simple' waw to express purpose,²⁸ e.g. /wᵊyɛˀᵉhɔ̄bɛkkɔ̄/, 'that he may love you' (Prov. 9:8), /wᵊnaᶜaśɛnnɔ̄/, 'that we may do it' (Deut. 30:12f.; cf. 1 Sam. 11:1, Judg. 19:22, 2 Kings 6:28f.), /waᵊᵃṣawwɛnnū/, 'that I may commission him' (Deut. 31:14; cf. Judg. 7:4, Ps. 119:33f.); or (3) in a jussive sense, e.g. /yisᶜɔdɛkkɔ̄/, 'may he support you' (Ps. 20:3; cf. 72:15, 140:12), /tᵊsɔ̄bᵊbɛkkɔ̄/, 'let it surround you' (Ps. 7:8), /našqɛnnū/, 'let us make him drink' (Gen. 19:34; cf. Num. 6:25).

Moreover, some thirty instances reveal that the energic ending is also appended to the preterite, with or without 'consecutive' waw.²⁹ Without the conjunction we note /yᵊnūsūn/, 'they fled' (Ps. 104:7; cf. 74:6, Job 4:4), /yimṣɔ̄²ɛnnū/, 'he came upon him' (Hos. 12:5, cf. Isa. 26:5, Deut. 32:10), /ᵊanḥɛnnɔ̄/, 'I guided her' (Job 31:18). With the conjunction may be cited /wattaggīšūn/, 'you brought near' (Amos 6:3), /wayyɛˀᵉtɔ̄yūn/, 'they came' (Isa. 41:5; cf. Judg. 11:18, Deut. 1:22), /wɔ̄²ᵃhallᵊṣɛkkɔ̄/, 'I rescued you' (Ps. 81:8; cf. Isa. 49:7).

There are eight cases of the imperative with the energic ending: /qɔ̄ḥɛnnū/, 'take him' (Jer. 39:12; cf. 1 Sam. 16:11, 20:21, Num. 23:13), /qᵊrɔ̄²ɛnnɔ̄/, 'read it' (Jer. 36:15; cf. Job 5:27, Jer. 36:14, 1 Sam. 21:10). Less expected are four instances of the construct infinitive with the energic termination.³⁰ These are /lᵊyaḥmɛnnɔ̄/, 'to

---

27 Kautzsch, *Grammar*, § 48g; G. Beer and R. Meyer, *Hebräische Grammatik* (Berlin, 1952–5), vol. II, p. 11.

28 Cf. R. J. Williams, *Hebrew Syntax: An Outline* (Toronto, 1967), §§ 187, 517.

29 Cf. *ibid.*, § 177.

30 Probably the Ugaritic locution ᶜ*dbnn dnk*, 'I made him' (49.ii.22), is an example of the absolute infinitive with energic nun followed by the independent personal pronoun.

mate them' (Gen. 30:41), /ləyassərɛkkɔ̄/, 'to discipline you' (Deut.
4:36), /ləqaləlɛkkɔ̄/, 'to curse you' (Deut. 23:5), and /ṣaddəqɛkkɔ̄/,
'to justify you' (Job 33:32).

Unique to Hebrew are four examples of participles with the energic
ending: /məyassərɛkkɔ̄/, 'disciplining you' (Deut. 8:5), /ʕōnɛkkɔ̄/,
'answering you' (Job 5:1), and /məṣawwɛkkɔ̄/, 'about to command
you' (Deut. 12:14, 28). Equally surprising is the fact that Hebrew,
like Ugaritic, preserves six cases of energic endings on the perfect
aspect, two without pronominal suffixes. These are /yɔ̄dəʕūn/, 'they
knew' (Deut. 8:3, 16), /ṣɔ̄qūn/, 'they poured out' (Isa. 26:16; this
may be a corrupted text), /yissərannī/, 'he has disciplined me' (Ps.
118:18), /dɔ̄nannī/, 'he has judged me' (Gen. 30:6), and /ūḇērᵃkɛkkɔ̄/,
'he will bless you' (Deut. 24:13).

Having surveyed the evidence for biblical Hebrew, we may state
several conclusions. It is misleading to describe the energic /n/ before
pronominal suffixes as 'epenthetic,' because it is not inserted and
does not serve to facilitate pronunciation. Nor is it correct to speak
of the Hebrew forms ending in /ūn/ and /īn/ as 'archaic' or 'archaiz-
ing,' as has frequently been done, since these are not older forms but
existed concurrently with those in /ū/ and /ī/, and the /n/ would not
have been elided after long vowels.

Perhaps we have been guilty of depending too heavily on classical
Arabic for our reconstruction of Protosemitic forms. We have
assumed that because Arabic has the imperfect indicative forms
/yaqtulūna/ and /taqtulīna/, these were the only original forms. We
have seen that the Sabaean and Minaean dialects of Old South
Arabian, Amarna Canaanite and Ugaritic alike, employed forms in-
discriminately with the /n/ ending or without it. There are also clear
instances of the indicative without /n/ in Imperial Aramaic. Instead
of a reconstructed Protosemitic conjugation in which forms identical
with the much later Arabic energic /yaqtulunna/ and /taqtulinna/
contrast with the indicative /yaqtulūna/ and /taqtulīna/, it would be
at least as likely to assume that in Protosemitic the sing. /yaqtulu/,
/taqtulī/ and pl. /yaqtulū/ contrasted as indicative forms with the
energic /yaqtulan/, /taqtulīn(a)/, and /yaqtulūn(a)/ respectively.

It is an accepted linguistic fact that a morpheme may lack any
semantic significance, and later be specialized for a particular purpose. For instance, mimation or nunation in nouns has no semantic
function except in the case of classical Arabic, which alone uses nunation to indicate indefiniteness. In like fashion the energic, in the same
language, imparts a degree of emphasis. In the other languages that
we have examined, it is clear that the energic is merely a stylistic

variant which is employed when required for the natural rhythm of the sentence. It serves, in other words, to provide a longer and heavier form comparable to the English expressions 'to' and 'unto,' or 'I have' and 'I have got.'

The Hebrew /ɔ̄/ ending frequently added to the imperfect and imperative forms, and occasionally even on the preterite with 'consecutive' waw (cf. Gen. 32:6, Judg. 6:9f., etc.), is often regarded as a vestige of the energic ending.[31] The lengthening of a final short vowel in Hebrew is totally at variance with the phonological history of the language, and a different explanation must be sought.

We must also make mention of the puzzling third fem. sing. forms /tišlaḥnɔ̄/, a preterite meaning 'she stretched' (Judg. 5:26), /tēraḏnɔ̄/, 'it will go down' (Job 17:16), and the second masc. sing. precative /ʾal-tišlaḥnɔ̄/, 'do not send' (Obad. 13). These have been interpreted as energic forms derived, for instance, from an original **/tišlaḥanna/.[32] The same problem confronts us with respect to the final vowel. In this connection, the Hebrew particle *nʾ*, vocalized /nɔ̄/, has been explained likewise as a vestige of the energic in /anna/ by various scholars.[33] In view of the same phonetic situation, caution is also advisable here.

---

31 E.g., B. Kienast, 'Das Punktualthema **japrus* und seine Modi,' *Orientalia*, N.S. 29 (1960), 151–67.

32 Cf. W. F. Albright, JPOS, 2 (1922), 78ff.; C. F. Burney, *The Book of Judges* (London, 1930), pp. 152f.; D. N. Freedman, ZAW, 31 (1960), 102.

33 Cf. Zimmern, *Vergleichende Grammatik*, § 43a; S. T. Byington, JBL, 64 (1945), 340; Gordon, *Ugaritic Textbook*, p. 72, fn. 2; Garbini, *Il semitico*, p. 146.

Israel's Eschatology
from
Amos to Daniel

W. S. M C C U L L O U G H

In his book *He That Cometh*, S. Mowinckel surveys the discussion of the term 'eschatology' in Israel's literature,[1] and argues that this term is properly applicable only to the ideas found in Daniel and other apocalyptic works, though the beginnings of it can be traced back to Isaiah 40–66. For the pre-Daniel period Mowinckel prefers the phrase 'the Future Hope.' To the present writer this seems a doubtful distinction, and he is therefore taking the position, as others have, that there is a kind of incipient eschatology in the eighth-century prophets. In any case we must remember that eschatology is always a relative term, and is conditioned by the scope of the experience and imagination of the age in which it appears.

I THE PRE-EXILIC PERIOD

Any hope for the future which pre-exilic Israel had was based on two main premises: first, that Yahweh was not only the supreme God but also the controller of history, and second, that there was a covenant between Yahweh and Israel. If Amos shared in these convictions, it is understandable why, although he considered it his main business to condemn Israel's sins, he could not disengage himself from the hope of something beyond the impending punishment (Amos 5:14–15). This point was appreciated by most of the prophets who followed Amos, and its force was enhanced by the temple cultus. For part of the purpose of the temple rituals, especially at Sukkoth (which may

1   Translated by G. W. Anderson (Oxford, 1956), pp. 125–8.

have been the occasion for covenant renewal), was to confirm the expectation that Yahweh's good purpose for Israel would some day be realized.

The eschatological passages in the prophets have long been identified,[2] though there is considerable difference of opinion among scholars as to their genuineness. In one sense this is an immaterial point, for whoever the authors, their ideas became part of Israel's eschatology and their authorship does not really matter. If, however, we are concerned with the historical development of this type of religious thought, then the authenticity of a given passage is of considerable importance.

If we consider the prophets down to and including Ezekiel, it is not difficult to isolate their chief eschatological themes.

1 / *Judgment.* The coming judgment was a basic element in the words of the prophets (Amos 2:6–8; Isa. 5:1–7; etc.), and, projected into the distant future, it remained a constant feature of all later eschatology.

2 / *The national revival of Israel.* Wherever it originated, Isaiah's idea of a remnant which will weather the coming catastrophe (Isa. 7:3, etc.; cf. Amos 5:15), proved to be fundamental for all later pictures of Israel's future felicity. Connected with this is the hope that exiled Hebrews will return home, and that the two former kingdoms will become the one people of God. This expectation is generally earth-centred, as Jer. 32:6–15 illustrates.

3 / *A Davidic king will rule.* The restored community will require leadership, and Israel's political experience pointed to some form of monarchy. Since the house of David had served for over four hundred years and had exploited religious traditions to gain both priestly and popular support (e.g., Ps. 132:11–18), it was almost mandatory that the future king should be thought of as of Davidic lineage (e.g., Jer. 23:5–6).

4 / *Death.* Pre-exilic Israel seems to have shared with other peoples in western Asia, notably the Babylonians, the view that at death everyone entered a very restricted existence in the underworld (*Sheol* in Hebrew). The appropriation of the Ugaritic myth involving Mot (Ps. 49:15[EV 14]; Isa. 25:8) does not seem to have affected the view that Sheol was man's destination. Unlike the contemporary Egyptians whose records reflect a considerable interest in death and the hereafter, Israel was prepared to take death as the inevitable end of life.

2 *Ibid.,* pp. 146–7, footnotes 1–20.

II ISAIAH 24–27, 34–35, 40–66

It is here assumed that these chapters, along with the writings of the eighth-century Isaiah, were brought together by an editor, probably around 520 B.C. The chapters in question illustrate rather well the difficulty of weaving Israel's variegated eschatological ideas into a rational and coherent pattern.

1 / *Judgment* continues to be important, and in Isa. 26:21, 34:1–4, 66:15–16 it is extended to all the inhabitants of the earth. In 66:24 the bodies of apostates are to be burned in an unquenchable fire. In 24:17–23 there is to be, apparently in conjunction with this judgment, a cataclysm of nature, and in v. 21 a punishment of 'the host of heaven' is referred to. The latter phrase may be a reference to rebellious members of Yahweh's entourage, and if so it is one of the earliest elaborations of Gen. 6:1–4 (cf. 1 En. 6–11). In Isa. 27:1 there is a curious reference to the punishment of Leviathan. Although the crushing of Leviathan in Ps. 74:14 points to a primaeval conflict with Yahweh (cf. the Ugaritic myth), in Isa. 27:1 the Leviathan idea has been projected into the future, and it designates a powerful being opposed to Yahweh who will be punished 'in that day.' This is a novel conception in Israel's thought.

It is of interest that the theme of judgment can be associated with fire, as in Isa. 66:15–16. This is consonant with Yahweh's connection with fire in various theophanies (Exod. 3:2 and 19:18; Ps. 50:3–4 and 97:3–4; etc.); this fire could, when the occasion demanded, be destructive (Num. 11:1–3; 2 Kings 1:10–14).

2 / *The national revival* remains of primary importance, although the various ideas advanced are somewhat of a medley. Apart from the assurance that the exiles will return (Isa. 43:5–6, etc.), Yahweh's salvation is said to involve dramatic cosmological changes (51:6 and 60:19–20), and in 65:17 and 66:22 there is mention of a new heaven and a new earth. Since there are numerous references to the revived Israel living in its old homeland (44:3, 49:8–13, 51:3, etc.), it seems best to take these cosmological passages as poetical, designed to emphasize the drastic difference between the present age and the new one to be instituted by Yahweh.

3 / *Universalism.* Although the subservience of the nations to Israel is referred to in the material under review (Isa. 60:10–12; cf. 45:14, 48:23, etc.), universalism is a more distinctive feature. Israel's religion in the future is to be shared (the details are not spelled out) with the Gentile world (42:1–9, 45:22, 49:6, etc.). Whatever the spe-

cific antecedents of this ideal, it is obviously a deduction from the character of Yahweh, and this clearly explains why we find this ideal in Second Isaiah.

4 / *No Davidic king appears.* It is notable that there is no reference to a kingly figure who will give guidance to the restored community: attention is focused on the actions of Yahweh himself (24:1, 21; 34:2, 6; 40:10; 43:14; etc.). Indeed in 24:23 we are told that 'the Lord of hosts will reign on Mount Zion and in Jerusalem.' The two references to Cyrus, 44:28 and 45:1, indicate that Cyrus had an ad hoc mission to perform, but this must not be confused with the role of the Davidic king. This indifference to the tradition about a future Davidic ruler suggests that some Jewish circles set little store by this tradition (as in Daniel, the Assumption of Moses, 3 Baruch). Even in 2 Esdras 7 where 'my son the Messiah' appears and lives for four hundred years before he dies, he has no vital function to perform, and in the subsequent resurrection and judgment he plays no role at all.

5 / *Death.* Second Isaiah has only the traditional Hebrew view of death (51:14, 53:12). Although some assume that 53:10–12 imply a resurrection of the Servant if he is to experience what is described in vss. 10–11,[3] it can be argued that what is meant is the restoration of the nation (as in Ezek. 37), not the revival of an individual. However, when we turn to 25–26 we find some new material. The date of these chapters, and particularly 26:7–9, can only be surmised. The present writer finds R. B. Y. Scott's second century B.C. date for the latter poem impossible,[4] and he has no difficulty in putting this material in the late sixth century. If this date can be accepted, it means that two important eschatological views emerged early in the Persian period. First, in 25:8 there is a reference to Yahweh's swallowing up death for ever. While this phraseology must owe something to the well-known Ugaritic myth, in its Hebrew context it presumably means exactly what it says: in the future, death will be no more. Second, in 26:19 the dwellers in the dust are to awake and sing for joy, for they shall live. This is probably the earliest reference in Israel's literature to a resurrection of the dead, but it is characteristic of similar statements in later sources that it appears without elaboration (Dan. 12:2; 1 En. 51:1; 2 Esd. 7:32; 2 Bar. 21:22–23). The *idea* of rising from the dead, found in Isa. 26:14, 19, may be older than this chapter. The best example is Ezek. 37 where Yahweh, in v. 12,

---

3 C. R. North, *The Second Isaiah* (Oxford, 1964), pp. 242–6.
4 *The Interpreter's Bible* (New York and Nashville, 1956), vol. 5, p. 307.

is to raise Israel from its grave and bring it into its own land. While this is presumably a metaphor, the use of the metaphor suggests that the *idea* of being raised from the grave was not unfamiliar in Ezekiel's time.

III   520–300 B.C.

A   *The History of Judah*

From 539 B.C. down to Alexander the Great's time Judah was a part of Achaemenid Persia. Politically the situation was not greatly changed from what it had been under the Assyrians and Babylonians, except that the Davidic monarchy was not revived. We know very little about the secular life of the Jews in these two centuries, even with the augmentation of the meagre biblical sources by the Elephantine papyri. We know that they paid tribute to Persia (Ezra 4:13, 6:8, etc.), and we suspect on the basis of a reference in Josephus (*Against Apion* I, 194) that they may have been involved in a Phoenician rebellion against the Persians in 351 B.C. There is some evidence to support the view that in this fourth century the high priest emerged as the titular head of the Jewish community.

B   *Eschatological Views in the Jewish Sources*

I
Jews living in the years following 516 B.C. must have been sadly aware that the return of some of the Babylonian exiles after 538 B.C., the rebuilding of the temple in 520–516 B.C., and the renewal of Judah's corporate life did not inaugurate the great national revival of which earlier prophets had spoken. Whatever expectations might have been centred on Zerubbabel in 520 B.C. (cf. Hag. 2:20–23; Zech. 3:8, 6:12–13), the fact remained that Judah was a small tax-paying state in a large empire. The conclusion was therefore inevitable that the fulfilment of earlier promises for Israel still lay in the future. The prophet Zechariah (Chs. 1–8) may have been one of the first to make this adjustment: his words of hope in ch. 8 are but a reiteration of some of the basic ideas of Second Isaiah.

Although Zechariah's eschatological views are mediated to him in the usual way ('Thus says Yahweh of hosts,' 8:2), it is a curious fact that the visions which he experienced in 1:7 to 6:8 are interpreted for him in each case by an angel, and that in one of these visions (3:1–10) Satan appears in much the same role as in Job 1–2. As these angelic figures are mentioned casually, it would seem that their existence was a matter of common belief.

2

The contribution of the book of Malachi (ca. 450 B.C.) to eschatological thought is twofold. In 3:1 reference is made to a messenger
who will prepare the way for Yahweh's appearance in judgment; in
3:23-24 (EV 4:5-6) this messenger is identified, possibly by a later
editor, as Elijah. In this connection R. C. Dentan is wrong in asserting that 'the figure of Elijah came to have a considerable role to play
in later apocalyptic thought.'[5] Apart from the Gospels and about a
half dozen references in the Mishnah (*Shekalim* 2:5; *Sotah* 9:15; etc.),
Elijah has no part at all in most Jewish apocalyptic writings.

Malachi's other contribution is his reference to Yahweh's 'book of
remembrance' (3:16). Actually this is a much older Near Eastern
idea, and reflects the highly anthropomorphic view of God which
Israel had developed (Exod. 32:32-33; Ps. 69:29 [EV 28], 139:16;
Isa. 65:6). The association of this book in Malachi with 'the day
when I act' (3:17) helped to assure its survival in later literature
(Dan. 7:10; 2 Esd. 6:20; 1 En. 47:3, 90:20; 2 Bar. 24:1).

3

It is here assumed that Ezekiel 38-39 are a later addition to the book,
probably made between 516 B.C. and Nehemiah's time. The burden
of these chapters is that Gentile forces from the north will launch an
all-out attack upon Yahweh's people, and that Yahweh himself will
decisively defeat them. Israel does not take any part in this operation, except in a scavenger and burial capacity after the struggle is
over. Then the fortunes of Israel will be restored, though the limits
of the restoration will still be terrestrial. The main point of these
chapters, however, seems to be that all forces opposed to God in this
world ('Behold, I am against you, O Gog,' 38:2) will eventually be
annihilated. The idea of a final struggle between good and evil, accompanied by woes and tribulations, was destined to live on in later
writers (Joel 4:9-11 [EV 3:9-11]; Zech. 14:1-5; Dan. 12:1; 1 En.
56:5-8, 90:13-19; etc.). In the Qumran War Scroll, in contrast to
Ezek. 38-39, Israel takes a very active part in the war against the
Sons of Darkness; in 6:6 of this scroll it is stated that God works
'through the saints of His people' (Yadin).[6]

The Gog material in Ezekiel is but one example of an awareness in
ancient Israel that there were real forces in the world working in opposition to Yahweh and his people. Quite apart from the challenges

5 *The Interpreter's Bible* (New York and Nashville, 1956), vol. 6, p. 1144.
6 Y. Yadin, *The Scroll of the War of the Sons of Light against the Sons of Darkness*,
   translated by B. and C. Rabin (Oxford, 1962), p. 286.

presented by the Canaanite Baal and the Tammuz-Ishtar cult, we
may here note: (1) Azazel: although the Day of Atonement material
in Lev. 16 is post-exilic in its present form, there is no doubt that it
represents an old tradition. The precise origin of Azazel is uncertain,
but the fact that he was an alternative to Yahweh in the lot-casting
in Lev. 16:8 suggests that he was a demonic power of some stature,
as is borne out by his later importance in 1 Enoch. (2) Satyrs (Lev.
17:7), demons (Deut. 32:17), and liliths (Isa. 34:14) are other illustrations of the recognition by Israel (as by all the cultures of the
ancient Near East) of the existence of various demonic agents in
this world.

4

The book of Joel probably belongs around 400 B.C. As noted previously, in 4:9–11 (EV 3:9–11) it appears to be echoing Ezek. 38:39
in the account of a final battle between the nations and Yahweh, the
latter to be aided by his heavenly hosts. This Day of Yahweh is to be
preceded by various cosmic portents (3:3–4 [EV 2:30–31]), and is apparently to be followed by a universal judgment in the valley of
Jehoshaphat (4:2 [EV 3:2], 4:12 [EV 3:12]).

5

Zechariah 9–14 contain such a hodgepodge of prophetic utterances
that it is difficult to see how they could have come from one writer.
We here assume that they were brought together in the last third of
the fourth century B.C.

Although in Zech. 9:9–10 there is a lyrical description of the coming of Zion's king and of his establishment of universal peace, in the
later chapters this ruler is either referred to obliquely (12:8), or he
does not appear at all. In 12:1–9 it is Yahweh who gives the primary
lead in opposing the attack of the nations upon Judah, and the clans
of Judah then follow suit. In 14:1–21, which is another account of this
eschatological war, it is Yahweh who fights against the nations in
v. 3; in v. 5 he is accompanied by 'all the holy ones.' Yahweh's victory is followed by changes in the natural world (14:6–8), which are
reminiscent of Ezek. 47:1–12 and Isa. 51:6 and 60:19–20. It helps to
redeem this somewhat nationalistic material to find in 14:9, 16
references to Yahweh's receiving from the remnant of the peoples
recognition as king over all the earth.

6

If we can date Chronicles to 350–300 B.C., one reference in it is pertinent to our present inquiry. In 2 Sam. 24:1 it is said that Yahweh
incited David to undertake a census of Israel and Judah, but in
1 Chron. 21:1 Satan is said to have done this. As Satan in the latter
passage appears without the article (cf. the article in Job 1–2 and

Zech. 3:1–2), it can be argued that Chronicles represents a step towards making Satan the proper name of an important member of the heavenly establishment. Further, since Yahweh was displeased with David's action (1 Chron. 21:7), it is evident that Satan's standing among the angels might easily deteriorate.

c *Persian Religion in the Achaemenid Period*

I

Zoroaster, the founder of the religion which bears his name, is thought to have flourished around 600 B.C.[7] One view supported by Frye[8] and others is that he lived and taught in eastern Iran. It was a polytheistic society, but Zoroaster came to believe himself to be a prophet of the god Ahura Mazdah. His subsequent career is best explained as an effort to reform religion and to bring it into line with the demands of Ahura Mazdah. Such a program inevitably evoked opposition from vested interests, and Zoroaster's progress was slow until the conversion of a political figure, Vishtaspa, and thereafter his message was more favourably received. For any acceptable reconstruction of his teaching we have to depend basically upon the Gathas, poems or songs said to go back to Zoroaster himself (Yasna 28–34, 43–51, 53).[9]

Zoroaster's message was, for various reasons, modified by later generations. An important factor here was the influence of the Magi, a fraternity thought to have been of Median origin who exercised sacerdotal functions in Iran. It is theorized that the Magi, in embracing the new teaching, brought back older beliefs and practices. This seems to account for the differences between the Gathas on the one hand and the religious views reflected in the inscriptions of the Achaemenid kings, in the Gatha of the Seven Chapters (Yasna 35–42), in the comments of Herodotus on Persian religion, and in the Avestan Hymn to Mithra (450–400 B.C.) on the other.

2

The only parts of Zoroaster's teaching that concern us here relate to (a) Ahura Mazdah and the Amesha Spentas, (b) dualism, and (c) eschatology. All references are to chapters and verses in the Yasna.

7 The dates 628–551 B.C. are supported by R. C. Zaehner, *The Dawn and Twilight of Zoroastrianism* (London, 1961), p. 33, and by R. N. Frye, *The Heritage of Persia* (London, 1962), p. 29.
8 *Heritage*, p. 30.
9 The present writer, who is not an Iranian scholar, has used J. H. Moulton's translation in his *Early Zoroastrianism* (London, 1913), pp. 343–90, and has supplemented this occasionally with *Songs of Zarathushtra*, by D. Framroze, A. Bode, and P. Nanavutty (London, 1952).

(a) *Ahura Mazdah and the Amesha Spentas.* In an Iranian world which believed in a number of gods (*ahuras*), Zoroaster took over one deity who may have simply had the name Ahura, and expanded his significance by adding the epithet *mazdah*, 'wise.' The prophet then ignored other gods and treated Ahura Mazdah as the only god that really mattered.

Light and fire are basic elements in many cosmogonies, and we should not be surprised that they appear in Zoroastrianism in close association with Ahura Mazdah, the creator god (31:7, 44:5). In the Avestan Hymn to Mithra, fire is the son of Ahura Mazdah;[10] in Yasna 36:3 fire is identified with the Holy Spirit; and in 37:4 Asha is associated with fire (cf. 34:4 and 43:4, 9). Fire thus became an accepted symbol of Ahura Mazdah, and the fire altar served as the physical centre of Zoroastrian worship. The close association of fire, light, and sun doubtless explains why in the inscription of Darius I at Besitun Ahura Mazdah is represented by a conventional sun symbol.

An obvious feature of the Gathas is the appearance in them of a number of beings (or 'entities,' as some prefer) closely associated with Ahura Mazdah. Six of these are mentioned together with Ahura Mazdah in 45:10 (cf. 34:11 and 47:1): Armaiti ('Devotion' or 'Right-mindedness'), Asha ('Truth' or 'Law'), Vohu Manah ('Good Mind'), Khshathra Vairya ('Power' or 'Kingdom'), Haurvatat ('Perfection' or 'Wholeness'), and Ameretat ('Immortality'). Another prominent being is Spenta Mainya ('Holy Spirit'), who is important enough to have a whole Gatha (47) largely devoted to him. In 47:1 another one appears, Vahishta Mana ('Sovereign Mind' or 'Best Thought'). Of these beings, two, Wholeness and Immortality, would appear to be Ahura Mazdah's gifts to mankind; the others are modes or instruments through which Ahura Mazdah operates in the world. It is only in the post-Gathic period, notably in the Gatha of the Seven Chapters, that the phrase Amesha Spentas (possibly 'Bounteous Immortals') appears, and is generally applied to these beings, but even here its meaning is not precisely defined. In 39:3 the Bounteous Immortals seem to be differentiated from the Good Mind, which suggests that the phrase was a loose one at that time.

There are parallels to the Amesha Spentas in Israel's religious thought. Yahweh often operates through his Spirit (Judg. 6:34; Mic. 3:8; etc.); in Prov. 8:22–31 Wisdom appears as Yahweh's first creation; in Pss. 57:3 and 85:9–10, steadfast love, faithfulness, righteousness, and peace are almost personified. Such language must not be

10 I. Gershevitch, *The Avestan Hymn to Mithra* (Cambridge, 1959), 1:3, p. 75.

pressed for hidden metaphysical meanings. Rather, it serves a peda-
gogic purpose, in that it is an attempt to present Yahweh and his
demands in an effective way to Israel. It is not unreasonable to sup-
pose that the beings or 'entities' which appear in the Gathas had a
similar role with respect to Ahura Mazdah and Iran.

(b) *Dualism.* Zoroaster lived in a world in which there was much
opposition to Truth as he understood it, and at some point in his life
he adopted or created the idea that all the evils he was fighting were
due to the activities of the Lie (*Druj*, a word that occurs about
twenty times in the Gathas). The Spirit of the Lie is Aka Mainyu,
and in Yasna 32:3 the daevas (demons and false gods) are said to be
the offspring of this Spirit. Once in the Gathas (45:2) the Lie is referred to as the 'hostile one' (*angra*), and in the post-Gathic period
mainyu ('spirit') was added to this, to get the phrase Angra Mainyu,
the antecedent of the name Ahriman. In 30:8 it is stated that at the
'Consummation' the Lie will be delivered into the hands of Right (or
Truth), and it would therefore appear that the malevolent actions of
Druj will ultimately be brought to an end.

(c) *Eschatology.* Zoroaster's interests embraced, among other things,
the consummation of human life and of history. To what extent there
were current traditions about such matters we can only surmise, but
if there were, probably Zoroaster contributed to them his own views.

(i) Regarding the end of the individual life. Here Zoroaster uses the
idea that death brings one to the Bridge of the Separator (*Chinvat*),
46:10–11, 51:13; possibly this was an element in the religious folklore
of the age. Seemingly Zoroaster's novelty was that he made the cross-
ing of the Bridge an occasion for moral judgment. Those condemned
will proceed at once to the House of the Lie, a place of darkness,
misery, ill food, and woeful cries (31:20, 53:6; cf. 45:3). In 45:7 and
46:11 it seems that they will remain there for all time. Those who have
been wise (46:17) and who have lived in accordance with the Truth
(31:2) will go permanently to the House of Song (45:7–8); in 30:11
it is called the abode of Good Thought, of Mazdah, and of Truth
(cf. 33:3, 5 and 53:4), and in 46:19, the reward of the Other Life.

Some of the details connected with the Bridge are curious. In 46:17
Ahura Mazdah is the judge, though Zoroaster himself appears to be
present. In 46:10 Zoroaster speaks of accompanying believers across
the Bridge. Moulton's interpretation of 31:2, 33:1, and 34:1, whereby
Zoroaster is thought to act as a judge (*ratu*) at the Bridge, seems to
the present writer to be debatable.[11] In 43:12 there is a reference to

11 *Early Zoroastrianism*, pp. 118, 166.

certain heavenly beings, Sraosha and Ashi, having a role in the judgment.

(ii) The consummation of the present age appears in the Gathas, but the references are not always free from ambiguity, for it is sometimes uncertain whether the allusion is to death or to the end of history. In 43:5 and 51:6 the goal of creation is referred to. In 30:11 we read: 'the long punishment for the liars, and blessings for the righteous – then hereafter shall ye have bliss.'[12] This appears to refer to an era *after* the one inaugurated at the Bridge of Judgment. In 48:2 there is an expression of faith in the ultimate victory of Asha. The very fact that one of the Amesha Spentas is Immortality suggests that eternal life (at least for those worthy of it) is part of Ahura Mazdah's grand design. One obscure reference in 30:7 has been thought to point to some form of bodily resurrection, but this is not elaborated anywhere else in the Gathas. A complicating factor in all this is the reference to a flood of molten metal or fire (30:7, 31:19, 32:7, 34:4, 51:9). This appears to be some current eschatological notion that Zoroaster utilized, but precisely how it fitted into his other views is not clear. We can only theorize that it is a colourful way of affirming that at the end of history the evil in the world will be eliminated. Incidentally, the term *Saoshyant*, 'deliverer' (pl. *Saoshyants*), found in 45:11 and 48:9, 12, refers to Zoroaster or his disciples, and in 34:13 to future leaders.

D   *Early Judaism and Early Zoroastrianism*

In the period under review, the religion of Israel was developing into Early Judaism. Whatever initial impulses in this direction came from the Jewish settlements in Babylonia, it is clear that it was largely Palestinian Jews who guarded and expanded the religious traditions. As we learn from Malachi, Ezra, and Nehemiah a more rigid orthodoxy was slowly emerging, and we can suspect that ideas and values associated with any form of non-Yahistic religion would be coolly received.

When we ask 'Did the Zoroastrianism of the Achaemenid age influence the Jews?' the honest answer is simply that we do not know. We do not know whether in the days of the Medes Iranian religious ideas had filtered into western Asia, or whether any of Zoroaster's teachings had drifted westwards. When we come to the Achaemenid period, we do not know to what extent Zoroaster's views, or modified versions of them, were known either in Mesopotamia or on the Medi-

12 *Ibid.*, p. 351.

terranean seaboard. We are equally ignorant about the zeal of the Magi in Zoroastrian propaganda. Such evidence as there is in the Achaemenid inscriptions and in the Old Testament suggests that the Persian authorities followed a policy of laissez-faire in religious matters. In view of these considerations, we must be cautious about the influence of Zoroastrianism (in any form) on the Judaism of this period. To the present writer it is clear that the Jewish literary sources of this age, which we have examined in section B above, can be fully understood without reference to any known Zoroastrian material.

IV 300–165 B.C.

A *Judaea's History*

Alexander the Great's initial conquest of western Asia led, after his death, to wars among his successors, and Palestine, with its Jews and Samaritans, suffered from this situation. When Ptolemy I gained control of Phoenicia and Palestine in 301 B.C., inaugurating a century of Ptolemaic rule, he in fact began the exposure of the Jews to Hellenism, and from this time on Hellenistic culture was one of the realities of the world in which Israel had to live. The replacement of the Ptolemies by the Seleucids in 199 B.C. did not materially alter the political and cultural picture for the Jews. It was the accession of Antiochus IV in 175 B.C. that really disturbed the life of Judaea, and eventuated in 167 B.C. in the Maccabaean Revolt.

B *Jewish Literature*

Five writings, pertinent to our present inquiry, belong in this period, viz., Ecclesiastes, Tobit, the Book of Noah (fragments in 1 En. 6–11, 54:7–55:2, 60; 65–69:25, 106–107), Ben Sira, and Daniel. What they have to contribute will be dealt with under four headings.

1 / *Judgment.* The Book of Noah is principally concerned with the fallen angels getting their deserts, and it does not expand the reference in Enoch 10:6 to the day of the great judgment which follows Azazel's long detention in a dark abode. Ben Sira alludes to Isaiah's references to 'last things' and 'the end of time' (48:24–25), but such matters were of limited concern to the Jerusalem scholar. It is in Daniel that God's coming judgment receives fuller treatment: in ch. 2, as the crushing power of the supernatural stone; in ch. 7, in the vividly portrayed meeting of the heavenly council; in ch. 8, as the breaking of a notorious Greek king; in ch. 9, as 'the decreed

end ... on the desolator'; in ch. 12, as the opening of the heavenly book (cf. 7:10).

2 / *Angels good and bad, and demons.* As angels came to have various roles in Israel's eschatology, it may be useful here to sum up the basic data about them.

Ben Sira seems to have been indifferent to angels. In 16:7 he betrays some acquaintance with the tradition that the errant angels and the giants of Gen. 6:1–4 were punished, but he does not embroider this, and in 42:17 he indicates the limitations of the angels in Yahweh's economy.

Other Jews, endowed with more imagination, did not have to search far in the growing corpus of Israel's scriptures to find material illustrative of the complexity of the angelic world. That Yahweh was surrounded by a heavenly retinue numbering tens of thousands was an old Hebrew idea (Deut. 33:2; 1 Kings 22:19; Isa. 6:1–7; Job 1:6 and 2:1). It was a natural supposition, possibly on the analogy of a human court, that there would be differences, presumably of function, among these angels, and support for this was found in the scriptural references to the commander of Yahweh's host (Josh. 5:14; cf. Dan. 10:21), cherubim (Gen. 3:24), seraphim (Isa. 6:2), 'angel of his presence' (Isa. 63:9); even the eyed, spirit-filled wheels of Ezek. 1:15–21 were later to become the Ophannim (1 En. 61:10).

The earlier reference in this essay to Satan as an angel of doubtful repute (1 Chron. 21:1) should remind us that there were others of the same ilk in the heavenly assembly. 'Destroying angels' appear in Ps. 78:49 (cf. 2 Sam. 24:16–17 and 2 Kings 19:35), and in Judg. 9:23 an evil spirit was on hand who could be sent by God on a mission (cf. 1 Sam. 18:10 and 1 Kings 22:21–22). The abstract noun 'worthlessness' could be used as 'worthless one' or 'destroyer' (Nah. 2:1 [EV 1:15]; 2 Sam. 23:6; Job 34:18), but its application to one of the wicked angels, giving us Belial or Beliar, is not found until later (Jub. 1:20).

It is Tobit that supplies two references of considerable interest. The first is to a named angel, Raphael (5:4 and 12:11–21). The fact that Raphael's status and role are described to Tobit and his son in 12:14 may mean that this angel was a relative stranger in the pious circles of Judaism. The other reference in Tobit is to the demon Asmodeus (3:8; 6:6–7, 15–17; 8:1–3); this simply illustrates the demonology of the world in which the Jews lived.

It is in the Book of Noah that there is a striking proliferation of named angels. This must be one result of the Jewish penchant for meditating imaginatively on scriptural materials, a characteristic which, at a later date, produced the Midrashim. The pericope in Gen. 6:1–4 was couched in such vague language that it invited elaboration, and this is what we have in the Book of Noah. We may suspect that names were first given to the fallen angels, and here, for a start, Azazel and Satan were at hand. Indeed in 1 En. 9:6 and 10:8 Azazel was made responsible for all sin, although elsewhere in the Book of Noah Semjaza (Semiazaz) is the leader of the sinful angels (1 En. 6:3, 10:11, 69:2); lists of his associates are given in 6:7–8 and 69:2–3. To form some sort of a balance it was evidently felt necessary to attach names to some of the good angels. In 9:1 Michael, Uriel, Raphael, and Gabriel are mentioned: their role is to bring men's prayers to God (9:3). Michael and Uriel are Hebrew personal names (1 Chron. 6:9 [EV 6:24], Num. 13:13); the other two may also have been human names, or they may have been formed, on an established pattern, for the author's purpose. In Tobit Raphael declares that he is one of the seven who transmit prayers (12:14; cf. 1 En. 20:1–8). Clearly the precise number of these leading angels was uncertain.

Angels appear in Daniel 7–12, where their function is essentially the same as in Zech. 1–8: they interpret the visions. Gabriel (8:16) and Michael (10:13, 21) are mentioned in such a way as to suggest that the naming of angels was now well established.

3 / *Death.* Ben Sira accepts the usual view of Sheol (10:11, 14:16–19, 41:1–4). It is in Ecclesiastes and Tobit that we have a modification of this older idea. In Eccles. 12:7 we learn that the body at death returns to the dust, whereas the spirit returns to God (cf. Ps. 104:29 and Job 34:14). This may imply that such judging as is necessary is done in life, in experiences of prosperity and adversity. Tob 3:6 appears to reflect the same thought. The Book of Noah, being largely concerned with the recalcitrant angels, has little to say about the death of human beings. In 1 En. 60:8 (Book of Noah) there is a reference to a garden where the elect and righteous dwell, and this notion appears also in 32:3 and 77:3, but no details are given.

Daniel 12:1–2, which comes, as does the rest of the book, from a period of religious crisis in Judaea, is unique in that it speaks of a resurrection from the dead, but a resurrection of a limited kind. Those resurrected (and these are not identified) are to experience either everlasting life or shame and everlasting contempt. Such statements raise a number of questions, and we can only conclude that resurrection was a relatively novel idea, at least in the circles which produced the book of Daniel, and that its full meaning and implications had not yet been worked out.

4 / *Hope for the future.* The book of Tobit has a simple outlook for

the future. There will be a return of the diaspora (13:5), the future glory of Jerusalem is portrayed with pardonable exaggeration (13:16–18), and even the Gentiles will worship the King of Heaven (13:11 and 14:6–7). The Book of Noah gives essentially the same picture. The future age of prosperity, peace, and righteousness is earth-centred, and will be shared by all the children of men, for all the nations will worship God (1 En. 10:16 to 11:2; 107:1).

In Daniel the main concern is what God is about to do in history, and in chs. 2, 7, 8, 9, 11 the secular events in western Asia, as affecting the Jews, are surveyed as a prelude to the expected action of God. There is no struggle here between Yahweh of Israel and a cosmic antagonist. It is human kings who are the trouble-makers. After the judgment (see 1 above), the Kingdom is to be established (2:44–45; 7:13–14, 27; 12:1–3), but the data regarding it are very meagre: in ch. 7 it seems to be an earthly realm. It is noteworthy that God is the actor in bringing in the new age, and that he delegates none of this work to any human leader.

c   *Foreign Influences on Jewish Eschatology*

Since the period beginning with Alexander was the age when Hellenism made its first serious impact on the life of the Near East, it is apparent that Hellenism has to be considered in any effort to identify the non-Jewish factors in Israel's eschatology down to the time of Daniel.[13] Another factor that we might suspect is Persian religion, but, unhappily, any examination of this is handicapped by the fact that our knowledge of Zoroastrianism in the later Achaemenid Empire, as in Seleucid and Parthian times, is very sketchy. It is usually assumed that some of the Magi perceived the real nature of Zoroaster's mission and kept the faith more or less intact, and because of them Zoroastrianism experienced a revival in the third century A.D. But the Magi were a mixed bag, and some could be described by Herodotus as magicians and interpreters of dreams (I, 107, 120, 140; VII, 19, 113, etc.), while others, appropriating some of the prophet's teaching, compounded it with Babylonian magic and other accretions.

The one form of post-Achaemenid Persian religion that we know about is Mithraism. Mithra was an old Iranian god whom Zoroaster completely ignores in the Gathas. But Mithra could not be so cavalierly disposed of, and as we know from the Achaemenid inscriptions and the Avestan 'Hymn to Mithra' he was soon rehabilitated, in

13 See T. F. Glasson, *Greek Influence in Jewish Eschatology* (London, 1961).

which revival some of the Magi were active. The worship of Mithra in Asia Minor is attested to by Ctesias as early as the fourth century B.C.[14] It would seem to be Mithraism that Strabo (*Geog.* XV, 3.13f.) and Plutarch (*Isis and Osiris*, 46–47) both describe.

Although western Asia, in the period under discussion, harboured Hellenism and Mithraism, it was also familiar with an assortment of Asiatic and Egyptian cults which had gained prominence since Alexander's conquests. Among the deities involved were Serapis, Isis, Osiris, Atargatis, and Cybele. In short, the religious world during these centuries was an immensely complicated one, and the action of one cult upon another and a strong tendency towards syncretism make the tracing of ideas and even practices almost impossible.

This was the religious environment of the Palestinian Jews, and with minor modifications it was also the environment of Babylonian Jewry and of the Egyptian Jews. Although the Jews, wherever they lived, had developed very effective measures against the adoption of pagan practices (as *Abodah Zara* in the Mishnah testifies), they could not isolate themselves completely from Gentile society. One example of what happened is the enrichment of the vocabulary of Jewish Aramaic by numerous Greek and Latin words. Furthermore, although this exposure to paganism may have galvanized Israel into a fresh awareness of its own resources and values, there was a danger in this confrontation, and the wonder is that the Jews survived as a distinctive religious community. One of the reasons they survived was that their whole style of living rested in a considerable measure upon the hope and faith which found expression in their eschatology. That there are pagan elements and myths from far-off days in these eschatological writings cannot be denied. But it is the burden of this paper that all the really important features in this eschatology, at least down to Daniel, can be most satisfactorily accounted for by carefully scrutinizing Israel's own traditions.

14 M. J. Vermaseren, *Mithras the Secret God* (London, 1963), p. 21.

Oral Tradition and
Historicity

ROBERT C. CULLEY

The debate over the historical value of the biblical accounts of the Patriarchs, the Exodus, and the Conquest which has continued during the past few decades is well known.[1] It is generally assumed that the biblical narratives which refer to these early periods have passed through a period of oral tradition. This prompts the question of the reliability of oral tradition. What happens to stories transmitted orally and in what sense or to what degree can such stories be considered historical sources? It is generally conceded that these early prose narratives are legends, at least in the sense that they contain both historical and non-historical elements. But there is disagreement about the nature of the historical and non-historical material, the relative amount of each, and the way in which they are mixed. This present study seeks to contribute to the discussion in a very limited way by asking the question: what do we know about the historicity of oral tradition? But this first question leads to another question which will be dealt with briefly towards the end: in what context has the question of the historicity of oral tradition been raised in biblical studies?

It is perhaps not necessary to emphasize the fact that oral tradition is a very complex process which has not yet been thoroughly in-

It affords great pleasure to be able to pay tribute to Professor Winnett who was head of the Department of Near Eastern Studies during my many years there as a student. This paper is a revised version of one read before the Canadian Society of Biblical Studies in May 1968. Mr Murray Henderson, B.A., a student in the Faculty of Divinity, McGill University, was a very helpful as a research assistant in tracing and checking bibliographical material.

1 For a useful summary see R. de Vaux, 'Method in the Study of Early Hebrew History,' in J. Philip Hyatt (ed.), *The Bible in Modern Scholarship* (Nashville, 1966), pp. 15–36.

vestigated as a whole.² For example, it is known that there are different ways of composing and transmitting oral works of poetry and prose. Some traditions are transmitted in a fixed form and others are transmitted in an unfixed form. These facts, as well as several other aspects of the complex process of oral tradition, should certainly be kept in mind when asking about the ability of orally transmitted material to preserve historical information.

But how do we proceed? When we consider the traditions about the earliest stages of Israelite history such as the Patriarchal legends, the most obvious means of testing their historicity is to assemble whatever relevant external evidence is available and compare it with the texts in question. Thus it is that comparisons of the results of archaeological investigation, including here all pertinent written material, with the Patriarchal stories have loomed so large in recent discussion. There can, of course, be no objection to the validity of this approach as such or to the continued pursuit of this line of inquiry. Yet, although the theory is sound, the results are disputed. This difference of opinion is apparent not only in the familiar division between some American scholars and some German scholars reviewed in the article by de Vaux noted earlier but also in a recent article, 'The Problem of Childlessness in Near Eastern Law and the Patriarchs of Israel,'³ by J. Van Seters challenging the use hitherto made of some comparative evidence and calling for a 'radical re-examination' of this approach to the problem.

However, the scope of the question might be broadened. Instead of inquiring after the historicity of a particular group of narratives from the past in so far as it may be ascertained from external evidence, we might well ask what we know about the historicity of oral tradition in general, both past and present. We would then be able to turn to oral traditions in periods which supply a great deal more of the information needed to check the reliability of oral tradition. This approach has been advocated and followed in a limited way by John Bright, although the comparative material was limited to a few examples from his own experience and American history.⁴

2 For a discussion of this problem, see my article 'An Approach to the Problem of Oral Tradition,' VT, 13 (1963), 113–25; and a more detailed study by me of one method of composition and transmission, *Oral Formulaic Language in the Biblical Psalms* (Near and Middle East Series, no. 4; Toronto, 1967).

3 JBL, 87 (1968), 401–8.

4 *Early Israel in Recent Historical Writing* (Studies in Biblical Theology, no. 19; London, 1956, pp. 93ff.; also W. F. Albright's very brief references to local traditions he collected from Arabs in southern Palestine, 'The Israelite Conquest of Canaan in the Light of Archaeology,' BASOR, 74 (1939), 13.

There are possible objections to such an approach. Some may question the value of comparing traditions from widely separated times and places, or at least insist that the greatest caution should be exercised in order that significant differences may not be overlooked.[5] It might also be argued that some advantage would be gained by restricting analogies to the ancient Near East or periods and peoples closely related to it, the theory here being that the further we get from the ancient Near East in time and space the less convincing the analogies become since oral tradition may have operated differently under different conditions and in different environments. In support of the comparison of biblical and ancient Arabic material, J. R. Porter points to the fact that the ancient Hebrews and pre-Islamic Arabs were both 'Semites.'[6] It is clear that caution is well advised in all comparisons, but the use of ancient materials is usually burdened with the limitation of an absence of information about how traditions grew and were transmitted. The same problem faces us in dealing with biblical traditions.

In what follows a small number of studies of historicity and oral tradition will be reviewed. These will include oral traditions from both the past and the present and will represent widely separated geographical areas. The best descriptions will come from contemporary investigations of living traditions, field studies based on careful observation of oral tradition in action. Not only is the impulse to investigate and describe scientifically a process such as oral tradition a phenomenon of relatively recent times but in addition the recording equipment necessary for thorough analysis has only become available in the electronic age. The broadening of the scope of the study of oral tradition to include reports of modern traditions is aimed primarily at attempting to map out and define all known ways in which historical information has been preserved and transmitted. Surely there must be some advantage in being able to define this process in terms of what we are fairly certain does happen on the basis of careful observation rather than in terms of what we guess might have happened. Any application to biblical material of what we learn will, of course, have to be carried out carefully and cautiously. The hope is that if biblical texts are studied in the light of what we know are the likely possibilities we may be able to comment more intelligently

---

5 See, for example, the remarks of G. W. Ahlström, 'Oral and Written Transmission: Some Considerations,' *Harvard Theological Review*, 59 (1966), 70, n. 7.

6 'Pre-Islamic Arabic Historical Traditions and the Early Historical Narratives of the Old Testament,' JBL, 87 (1968), 18.

about the nature of these texts and how they may have been influenced and shaped by oral composition and transmission.

The studies to be discussed are not as numerous or as detailed as might be desired. Nor are any claims made for completeness, since articles and books on the subject of the historicity of oral tradition or which refer to this subject are widely scattered over various disciplines and areas of study. I have simply included a selection of the best of those which came to my attention. In the main, studies of oral prose transmission were sought, but some discussion of poetic transmission has been included. The discussions have been grouped roughly in the following way: a well-known study of Scandinavian tradition, an important study of African traditions, a survey of the significance of American traditions, three studies of particular literary categories, and finally a grouping of examples of historical memories which have survived for long periods.

It is appropriate to begin by referring to the views of Knut Liestøl as presented in his book *The Origin of the Icelandic Family Sagas*.[7] His study is hardly a report on field-work since the sagas he has investigated come from the thirteenth century. Nevertheless, his book is known to biblical scholars and his views have been referred to in discussions of oral tradition and the Bible. With regard to historicity, Liestøl takes care to point out that the family sagas present their historical material in a form which has been shaped by the creative artist. He concludes: 'obviously, then, we can neither say of oral tradition that it is essentially reliable or unreliable, nor that it is essentially short-lived or long-lived. *Everything depends on the conditions in which it lives.*'[8] However, having made this general statement, he is inclined for various reasons to argue that historical facts have been much better preserved in Iceland than most other places and that the sagas are particularly reliable in this respect, although there is much that is unhistorical in them.[9]

Liestøl's study appears to be careful and well balanced. Yet he worked with texts from the past and in this respect is in the same position as the biblical scholar in that he lacks full and precise information about how the texts were composed and transmitted. What is more, his discussion should be seen in its proper context, as a rather long debate on the nature of the saga. It is not easy for an outsider to judge, but a glance at a book such as *The Problem of Icelandic*

7 Trans. A. G. Jayne (Oslo, 1930).
8 *Ibid.*, p. 234.
9 *Ibid.*, p. 235.

Saga Origins by T. M. Andersson gives some indication of the divergence of opinion regarding the historicity of the sagas.[10] Andersson comments that 'the belief in historicity has always been a matter of persuasion rather than demonstration and therefore cyclical. In 1800 it was anathema, only to become gospel again in 1900.'[11] Incidentally, another issue in this debate is the extent to which the sagas are oral or written, an issue which has played a part in the debate about biblical traditions.

The best general study at present is certainly Jan Vansina's book, *Oral Tradition: A Study in Historical Methodology.*[12] Although the author of this book hopes that it will be a contribution to the general problem of historicity in oral tradition, his discussion is based largely on field-work in a small number of African territories. He states his aim in the following way: 'I hope to show that oral tradition is not necessarily untrustworthy as a historical source, but, on the contrary merits a certain amount of credence within certain limits.'[13] This statement reflects the balanced judgment and cautious approach which marks the book. Vansina is writing as a historian and it would seem that his study was prompted, at least in part, by the particular situation facing the historian of African peoples for which oral tradition is a major source.

The importance of Vansina's investigation for the present discussion is the view already indicated that oral tradition cannot be ruled out a priori as useless for the historian, even though the valid historical use to be made of oral traditions can only be established after rigorous investigation. Vansina puts it this way:

> I have attempted to show that oral traditions are historical sources
> which can provide reliable information about the past if they are
> used with all the circumspection demanded by the application
> of historical methodology to any kind of source whatsoever. This
> means that study of the oral traditions of a culture cannot be
> carried out unless a thorough knowledge of the culture and of the
> language has been previously acquired.[14]

This last point poses a problem for biblical scholars since the text of the Bible is itself a primary source for the reconstruction of the culture.

10 Yale Germanic Studies, no. 1 (New Haven, 1964).
11 *Ibid.*, p. 82.
12 Trans. H. M. Wright (Chicago, 1965).
13 *Oral Tradition*, p. 1.
14 *Ibid.*, p. 183.

Some of Vansina's comments on prose narratives are worth mentioning in order to illustrate his approach. For the purposes of his study, he proposes a division of such narratives into four categories: historical, didactic, artistic, and personal tales. All tales share one thing in common: they 'all record history to some extent, but this aim is subordinate to another, the main aim being either to instruct, edify, give pleasure or vindicate rights.'[15] He believes that the historical tales are on the whole less reliable historical sources than other kinds of sources. Vansina argues that, since these historical tales have as their main object the serving of propaganda, they are 'mainly useful as sources of information about military, political, social, institutional and legal history.'[16] According to Vansina, official traditions are extremely open to distortion because they represent the interests of a group. Nevertheless, he claims that they sketch the outline of past history and thus are useful. Curiously enough, he points out that 'an official tradition is less trustworthy as a historical source than a private one in so far as it is official, but more trustworthy in so far as it is much more carefully transmitted.'[17]

A similar judgment is made by Vansina with regard to another of the categories mentioned above, the artistic tale.[18] Since the aim of such tales is to please the hearer, other elements in the story, including historical information, are subordinated to this primary purpose with the result that historical facts and details are changed and distorted. Details are added. Historical figures are given a personality or made into ideal types. Traditions are often combined or even split up. The transmission of this sort of tale is not subject to strict control and such a tale may change considerably in the course of time. Vansina suggests that stories of this type might be used to establish the psychological attitudes of some period in the past, if there has been careful transmission. Otherwise, and this is usually the case, the stories reflect the views of the period in which they are collected.

In speaking of the limitations of oral tradition, Vansina emphasizes that it is important to be alert to the way in which societies condition the literature found in them. He is thinking especially of literature closely related to structures of the society. He stresses the point that political, and to a lesser extent social, structures produce traditions which function within them and which are shaped and influenced by the bias of these same structures. Here Vansina is speak-

15 *Ibid.*, p. 154.
16 *Ibid.*, p. 154.
17 *Ibid.*, p. 85.
18 *Ibid.*, pp. 159f.

ing of entities which might be called states and which have a definite
political structure. This is not so true of simpler groups such as the
tribe, the town, or the family. Traditions from these smaller groups
are not particularly useful, if they exist at all, in reconstructing the
course of historical events. Thus, in the face of the limitations of oral
tradition, the historian must turn to whatever information can be
provided by auxiliary disciplines, of which archaeology is not the
least. Vansina calls archaeology 'the most necessary and the most
useful of the auxiliary disciplines that the historian of oral traditions
can make use of.'[19] Nevertheless, only a fragmentary knowledge is
apt to be gained even with the use of all the resources at the disposal
of the historian. The historian must, however, work carefully and
intelligently with what he has and not abandon his research because
the results are meagre.

This study by Vansina, then, is cautious all round. He tries to take
oral tradition seriously as a potentially valuable historical source, yet
he is well aware of the many limitations and problems confronting
the historian. It is likely that a great deal more useful information
about oral tradition will come from the general area of African
studies. As an indication of this, some recent discussions of an interesting problem might be mentioned.

These studies refer to a problem encountered in the study of genealogies. G. I. Jones has argued that East Nigerian traditions treat
time structurally rather than historically.[20] He claims that there are
two categories of past time: 'remote past' and 'recent past.' What
belongs in between is either pushed into one of these two divisions or
forgotten.[21] E. J. Alagoa counters Jones's view by suggesting that a
wider sampling of traditional sources would have shown a fuller
knowledge of the past than was evident in the politically conditioned
genealogies.[22] J. S. Boston also speaks of a telescoping or 'structural
amnesia' in the genealogies and draws attention to the Igala convention of reciting only nine names of kings, an early ruler and the eight

19 *Ibid.*, p. 176.
20 'Time and Oral Tradition with Special Reference to E. Nigeria,' *Journal of
    African History*, 6 (1965), 153–60.
21 W. F. Albright has noted that a similar phenomenon has been found in some
    other parts of the world and has suggested that such a phenomenon may ac-
    count for the gap between the early patriarchs and Moses; see *New Horizons in
    Biblical Research* (The Whidden Lectures for 1961; London, 1966) p. 11, n. 1.
22 'Oral Tradition among the Ijo of the Niger Delta,' *Journal of African History*,
    7 (1966), 405–19.

most recent ones, even though a fuller list is known.[23] Boston suggests that this phenomenon likely stems from the fact that oral traditions serve not only a historical function but also a political one.

Turning to another kind of study about a different geographical
area, we find that in his article 'Oral Tradition and Written History:
The Case for the United States,' Richard Dorson lists five ways in
which oral tradition may be helpful to the historian, illustrating these
points with references to American history.[24] The most relevant sections from our point of view are those headed 'Disentangling Fact
from Fancy' and 'Verification of Incidents.' Like Vansina, Dorson
argues that oral tradition is not to be rejected a priori as useless to
the historian. Dorson claims that 'historical facts may lie embedded
in narratives filled with distorted and folkloristic elements.'[25] It is his
claim that a 'knowledge of the folklore properties of oral tradition'
would permit a historian to distinguish between historical fact and
fiction.[26] Great care is necessary because local tradition tends to take
legendary motifs and turn them into real events associated with real
persons and places. Even when a group tells stories which obviously
reflect common folklore themes found all over the world, it selects
the themes which are appropriate to its historical situation so that
such traditions may be, strictly speaking, historically false yet psy-
chologically true.[27] Thus, these stories may still be a very valuable
source to the historian in that they offer insight into the psychology
of the groups in which they are told. Dorson remarks: 'Oral traditions may well exasperate the historian of a literate, or at least print-
glutted society, with their quicksilver quality and chronological slip-
periness. But they can be trapped, and they offer the chief available
records for the beliefs and concerns and memories of large groups of
obscured Americans.'[28]

It is worth noting that Dorson, like Vansina, indicates that oral
tradition may be a useful source to the historian in two ways. It may
reflect original persons and events or reflect the community's reac-
tion to what has happened, or what they think happened, at later
periods. Another folklorist, Américo Paredes, has summed it up this
way: 'For if history is the history of peoples as a whole, then folklore
has something to contribute to it, even when there is enough docu-

23 'Oral Tradition and the History of Igala,' *Journal of African History*, 10
    (1969), 29–43.
24 *Journal of the Folklore Institute*, 1 (1964), 220–34.
25 *Ibid.*, p. 231.   26 *Ibid.*, p. 228.
27 *Ibid.*, pp. 229–30.   28 *Ibid.*, pp. 233–4.

mentary evidence about a period to make the investigator feel he knows it well. There are attitudes and feelings, undercurrents of emotion in the masses of people, which are not recorded in official documents but which may have a profound effect upon events.'[29]

Three further studies of a more limited or specialized nature may be mentioned. The first is an analysis of legends collected from towns along the route of the retreat of the British army from Kabal to Jahalabad in 1842 by Louis Dupree.[30] His statement is tentative but he makes some points of general interest. He refers to the 'accordion effect' observed in the tales with regard to chronology. There is a certain amount of confusion about persons and happenings. However, the investigator claims that the tales compare favourably with the British accounts. There is also the 'educational aspect' in that the tales are used to instil the values and attitudes of the group, but this appeared to be equally noticeable in the written accounts of the British. Then there is the 'evolutionary aspect' illustrated by one story-teller who introduced modern elements such as machine guns and airplanes into his accounts of the retreat. Finally, the 'entertainment aspect' is not to be overlooked since the audiences apparently enjoyed and responded to the telling of these tales.

The second is a study of the family sagas of Greenlanders which tends to emphasize the limitations of oral tradition. Eigil Knuth has compared a collection of family sagas with extant parish records and has come to the conclusion that the change from correct history to fiction was rather rapid, within one hundred and fifty years according to his estimate.[31]

The third study, 'Some Popular Views of Four Mediaeval Battles,' by Douglas J. McMillan, is an examination of five mediaeval Anglo-Scottish ballads comparing them with the earliest historical sources in order to see what happens to history when it is transmitted in ballads.[32] Although it is true that this concerns poetry rather than prose, the main interest of the present study, the article is of sufficient interest to warrant brief mention. McMillan points out that he does not claim to be comparing the ballads with what actually happened but only the historical account with the ballad account so that

---

29 'Folklore and History,' in M. C. Boatwright (ed.), *Singers and Storytellers* (Publications of the Texas Folklore Society, no. 30; Austin, 1961), p. 62.
30 'The Retreat of the British Army from Kabal to Jahalabad in 1842: History and Folklore,' *Journal of the Folklore Institute*, 4 (1967), 50–74.
31 'Singajuk's Family Saga,' *Folk (Dansk Etnografisk Tidsskrift)*, 5 (1963), 209–18.
32 *Southern Folklore Quarterly*, 30 (1966), 179–91.

the differences between the two may be measured.[33] Although he hesitates to draw general conclusions from such a limited study, he suggests tentatively that the ballads 'at core are historically true' but that the details deviate as much as thirty to seventy per cent from historical truth (i.e. the historical sources). Usually only the basic outline remains, and instability and change are seen in the confusion of names, places, and dates, in an apparent weakness with regard to chronology, and in the invention of conversations.

The final group of material to be referred to is a small number of examples of apparently accurate historical information which has been passed on for considerable periods of time. These examples would seem to be informal in the sense that they do not appear to have any particular literary form. Undoubtedly many instances of this kind of transmission of historical memories exist.

A good illustration of this phenomenon, and this was referred to by Dorson, is a report by two archaeologists, David M. Prendergast and Clement W. Meighan.[34] When these archaeologists were working on an American Indian site in Utah, Paiute informants made statements to them about a people who had lived where the excavation was taking place more than eight hundred years before. These statements offered general information about such things as the stature of the people, the kind of homes they lived in, and the way they ground their food, and were substantiated by deductions based on the results of the archaeological excavation. It should be pointed out, however, that the material from the informants seems to have come in the form of short statements rather than stories and no one informant had all the information. In a reply to a criticism by Lord Raglan, Meighan refers to a statement by F. de Laguna concerning reports from certain natives in Alaska telling about times in the past when ice covered part of their territory.[35] The writer estimates through comparison with geological reports that the oral reports must refer to the presence of glaciers in the fifteenth century and later in the eighteenth and nineteenth centuries.

33 Douglas J. McMillan, 'Folk Projection and Historic Truth,' *American Notes and Queries*, 2 (1964), 149–50.

34 'Folk Traditions as Historical Fact: A Paiute Example,' *Journal of American Folklore*, 72 (1959), 128–33. Also Lord Raglan's comments and Meighan's reply in the following year in the same journal.

35 'Geological Confirmation of Native Traditions, Yakutat, Alaska,' *American Antiquity*, 23 (1958), 434. See also Albright's suggestion that the Mesopotamian flood tradition is a memory of the floods in Asia Minor following the Glacial Age, dated around 9000 B.C. in *History, Archaeology, and Christian Humanism* (New York, 1963), p. 95, n. 27.

Two examples of this type are given by Thorleif Boman in his book *Die Jesus-Überlieferung im Lichte der neueren Volkskunde.*[36] Peasants in Norway told an archaeologist in 1876 that a knight with horse and weapons was to be found under a large rock. The archaeologist dug and discovered the remains of a man, horse, and weapons which could be dated one thousand years earlier. Around the same time, peasants in Denmark reported that a wagon filled with gold was buried in a certain place. The archaeologists found no gold but did come across two wagons which they dated to the pre-Roman iron age, about two thousand years earlier.

The last two examples come from Martin P. Nilsson, although the length of time during which the memories were preserved is much shorter than in the previous cases.[37] As a child, Nilsson was told by his mother that the soldiers of a certain general had passed by his home village, had camped in a nearby wood, and had been fed by the people of the village. Later a colleague confirmed that the expedition led by this general probably passed near Nilsson's home village in the year 1709. Thus, the memory of this event had been kept alive in the village for about two hundred years. The other example concerned an old peasant who told of a dispute over some land between the people of his district, where his family had lived since the sixteenth century, and a neighbouring district. A wall had been removed by the people of the neighbouring district but restored again after a court case. Nilsson reports that court records contain such a case from the year 1621. In this instance the memory was passed on for some three hundred years, although some of the details had become confused. The removal and subsequent restoration of the wall was correct, but the land was not the property of the people of the old peasant's district, being rather land held commonly by both parties.[38]

This concludes the brief survey of studies which treat in one way or another the problem of the historicity of oral tradition. The general impression gained is that the problem is extremely complex, comprehending many variable factors. Great caution is to be recommended. Oral tradition can be a reliable source of historical informa-

---

36 Göttingen, 1967, p. 23.
37 'Über die Glaubwürdigkeit der Volksüberlieferung mit Besonderem Bezug auf die Alte Geschichte,' *Scientia*, 40 (1930), 322f.
38 John Bright's account of the 'Battle above the Clouds,' in *Early Israel in Recent History Writing* (London, 1956), pp. 97ff. would appear to be just such an informal oral tradition although of much shorter duration than the examples mentioned above.

tion and therefore cannot be dismissed as useless by the historian. At the same time, however, it can be very unreliable and thus requires very careful scrutiny. It is clearly too early to set up guidelines for the evaluation of the historicity of various kinds of oral tradition. However, the above studies may offer some clues in this direction. The more complex problems seem to arise from texts having a literary or similar formal structure which serves a purpose other than the simple preservation of historical information, be it political, social, religious, educational, or entertainment, or a combination of two or more of these. It seems highly likely that there is a tension between these other purposes and the historical, leading to a distortion of the historical material to a greater or lesser degree. But even if the original persons and events are obscured, the oral tradition is not rendered useless for the historian, since it may be extremely valuable in revealing beliefs, opinions, and attitudes prevailing at various stages of transmission. The simpler problem is presented by what may be called informal traditions which do not appear to have any formal structure, literary or otherwise. These traditions seem to be found in smaller groups such as families, towns, or districts and do not have any obvious purpose which would work against the preservation of historical information. Finally, one weakness which has been mentioned more than once is the frequent confusion of names, dates, and places and an uncertainty with regard to chronology.

Much of the information found in the studies referred to above has been known or surmised by biblical scholars. For example, W. F. Albright has been particularly perceptive in his comments on the nature of oral tradition and the problem of its historicity. He has drawn attention to the mixture of folkloristic elements and history.[39] He has emphasized the fact that oral tradition selects, sifts, and refines the material it passes on.[40] He has noted that historical material is often omitted while literary or religious material is retained.[41] He has also referred to the uncertainty of the chronology.[42] Further, there are the two small points already noted with regard to chronology and historical memories.[43] However, along with these statements, which appear to recognize and concede the great difficulties inherent in evaluating and making use of oral tradition, runs the continual re-

39 *From the Stone Age to Christianity*, 2nd ed. (New York, 1957), pp. 69f.
40 *Ibid.*, p. 268.
41 *New Horizons in Biblical Research*, p. 10.
42 *The Biblical Period from Abraham to Ezra* (New York, 1963), p. 5.
43 See above, notes 21 and 35.

frain affirming Albright's belief in the substantial historicity of the
early traditions of Israel. Clearly this means more than a simple
affirmation of the fact that reliable historical information may be
preserved for long periods of time. A strong claim is made for the
reliability of the oral tradition. To support this claim, Albright accepts the theory that a poetic epic lies behind the prose traditions
and argues that poetry is preserved in oral tradition much better
than prose.[44] Even if the theory of the epic were true, there is little
evidence so far to suggest that poetry has more or less historical reliability than prose. The only point that needs to be made here is
that oral tradition as such cannot be used as an argument for or
against historicity. It is, of course, clear that the alleged reliability
of oral tradition is only one element in Albright's argument for the
substantial historicity of the early traditions of Israel.

This is perhaps as far as the main question to be examined in this
paper can be taken. However, there still remains for brief consideration the second question of how the problem of historicity has been
raised in biblical studies. In what context has it been asked? Turning
again to Albright, we find that he operates as a historian using the
biblical texts as sources for a historical reconstruction. Furthermore,
he focuses his attention rather more on establishing the original persons and events. Since he has considerable confidence in the traditions, he sees no great tension between the tradition outline and his
reconstruction.

The approach of Gerhard von Rad appears at first glance to be
very different. His ultimate aim is to produce a theological treatment of the traditions of early Israel. Nevertheless he seeks to base
his theological approach upon and derive it from a method of an-
alysing texts which has been widely used by a number of scholars.
Since these early traditions are legends, he concedes that they are
likely to contain historical kernels. But, for him, the isolation of these
kernels remains an insurmountable problem, although at one point
he does agree that the Patriarchal legends preserve the atmosphere
of the pre-Mosaic era.[45] Conscious of how legends function within a
community, von Rad argues that they reflect real historical experiences of the community, since the beliefs and attitudes of the com-

---

44 See, for example, *History, Archaeology, and Christian Humanism*, pp. 84f.; and
   the comments made in the introduction to the paperback edition of Hermann
   Gunkel, *The Legends of Genesis*, trans. N. H. Carruth (New York, 1964), p. viii.
45 For this and what follows, see especially *Genesis*, trans. John H. Marks (London, 1961), pp. 32ff.

munity have shaped and influenced its legends from their origins to the time of the narrator. According to von Rad, preserving legends is a way in which a people talks about its own history. It is true that he calls this history an 'inner' history, a history of the people with Yahweh, which is clearly only acceptable as a theological statement, but the basis of this view is the assumption, expressed by several of the folklorists referred to above, that legends can reflect the attitudes, feelings, and reactions of groups or communities at various stages of their history. Thus, at this level, von Rad is operating as a historian, just as Albright is, except that von Rad focuses on a reconstruction of the beliefs of the community or the history of the inner life of the community. Although he sees a wide gap between the historical-critical reconstruction of biblical history and the biblical tradition, he does not see any great tension between his reconstruction of the history of the faith of the community and the biblical traditions. His awareness of the fact that texts continue to live and find response in succeeding ages makes him very much interested in reflecting on the nature of legends and the fact that they are able to do this.

If the preceding analysis of Albright and von Rad is correct, then one would have to say that both are operating as historians using the texts as a source for reconstruction, although they focus on different elements in the texts and aim at different kinds of reconstructions. This is the context in which the question of historicity has been discussed. It would seem to be natural for historians to be interested in historicity in either of the senses mentioned above at least: establishing actual events and persons or establishing beliefs and attitudes. The enterprise is valid. The texts may be and should be approached in this way.

But why the dominance of this historical approach? Is it enough to say that the texts demand it before other kinds of analysis have been fully explored? It has been said at the beginning that legends are a mixture of historical and non-historical material. The non-historical material is the product of the imagination at work in the creation and transmission of the legends. If we have been at pains to examine the elements in the texts which point and refer to an original historical context or to later contexts in which the texts have functioned, should we not be equally interested in exploring those elements in the texts which enable them to be understood and enjoyed in a great many succeeding historical contexts? Such an approach would mean discovering and using analytical methods which seek to reveal the structure of texts. This does not mean supplanting the historical approach by another 'superior' method. But it does mean that the historical approach and its results should be seen and evaluated alongside of other analytical methods aimed at illuminating the structure which the imagination has produced in these texts. Perhaps the problem of historicity and the historical approach might be better evaluated in this broadened context.[46]

46 An important article by Richard M. Dorson, 'The Debate over the Trustworthiness of Oral Traditional History,' in F. Harkort, K. C. Peeters, and R. Wildhaber (eds.), *Volksüberlieferung*, Festschrift für Kurt Ranke (Göttingen, 1968), pp. 19–25, was discovered after the manuscript had been submitted for publication. He aims, as I do, at a survey of the problem.

Abraham and David?

N. E. WAGNER

In a recent stinging indictment of Old Testament scholarship as it exists today, Morton Smith points out the virtual disarray on the scene.[1] Disagreement is now rampant in almost every branch of biblical scholarship. The reasons for such widespread disagreement are not immediately obvious. Smith, however, has hit close to home when he shows how the once generally held theories have been gradually modified by a number of individual scholars whose presuppositions are far from uniform. A strange, almost ambivalent position has emerged. For example, although many scholars have loudly attacked Julius Wellhausen, they have not only failed to replace his position with more acceptable theories, they have rather quietly taken much of it over as their own.[2] Such action is understandable, and in many respects pays tribute to the fact that research is constantly concerned with building on the work of former scholars. What is too often overlooked is the fact that the former system has been modified almost imperceptibly until it has become drastically changed. Such a development is perfectly legitimate provided that new evidence is brought to bear which radically changes the former position.

In our research we are thus forced to return to the basic evidence as well as to a study of the underlying presuppositions used by critics in arriving at their conclusions. As an illustration of what is involved, we propose to examine one aspect of the history of the Patriarchs which has come in for considerable debate during the past several generations. This has to do with seeking a legitimate context for the traditions concerning Abraham in the life of ancient Israel.

It is a well-known fact that Wellhausen and his followers reconstructed the development of Hebrew history and religion by giving

1 'The present State of Old Testament Studies,' JBL, 88 (1969), 19–35.
2 *Ibid.*, p. 25.

great prominence to the classical prophetic movement. The great
Jahwistic epic was seen as a product of the same general era. The
ninth and the eighth centuries B.C. were, therefore, viewed as the
context in which one must seek to understand the J traditions.[3]

Two decisive moves have taken place within the past seventy
years which force us to re-examine this situation. A notable number
of scholars have decreed that the J material is to be dated during or
immediately following the time of David and Solomon, i.e. nearly
two centuries earlier than Wellhausen had suggested. These views
will be discussed in greater detail below. Another group of scholars
has insisted that the stories of the Patriarchs reflect neither the
eighth nor the tenth century B.C., but fit in well with what we know
of the customs and practices in the mid-second millennium B.C. The
words of John Bright might serve as an illustration of this point of
view 'the stories of the Patriarchs fit unquestionably and authentically in the milieu of the second millennium, and not in that of any
later period.'[4] Since adherents to both approaches just noted still
subscribe in broad measure to Wellhausen's *literary* analysis, one is
surely justified in going back to examine the evidence which led to
the original position as well as modifications to it. No attempt will be
made to engage in a debate on how authentically the Patriarchal traditions do in fact fit the second millennium B.C., except to suggest
that R. de Vaux's words of caution are worth bearing in mind.[5] The
fact that much of the reconstruction of the early history of Israel
offered by critics such as Bright stands at variance with the picture
presented by the Old Testament itself is too little appreciated.[6] This
question leads to a full discussion far beyond the scope of the present
study.

Two aspects of the problem will be raised in the present paper.
These are, first, the presuppositions regarding the scope and extent
of the literary source material concerning Abraham, specifically the
so-called J traditions, and second, the attempt to connect the Abrahamic traditions with the court of David and Solomon.

The first of these may require a degree of explanation since literary
criticism is often glossed over today as being irrelevant. It is worth

3 Julius Wellhausen, *Prolegomena to the History of Ancient Israel* (New York,
   1957), pp. 360–2.
4 *The History of Israel* (Philadelphia, 1959), p. 70.
5 'Method in the Study of Early Hebrew History,' *The Bible in Modern Scholarship* (Nashville, 1965), pp. 26–7; also Smith, 'The Present State of Old Testament Studies,' p. 30.
6 De Vaux, 'Method in the Study of Early Hebrew History,' pp. 21–2.

noting that literary criticism can and often still is a basis for proper form-critical and traditio-historical studies. One need only think of Gunkel or von Rad as illustrations from two quite different periods in the present century. Although few scholars would care to defend classical literary criticism in isolation, it is precisely when a scholar seeks to penetrate the historical context in which a particular tradition arose as well as the possible reinterpretations which were attempted at various junctures in history, which may in themselves be radically different from both the historical event which lies behind the story and the initial description of that event, that he must seriously consider the scope of the material with which he is dealing. The task of searching for the different historical contexts of a given tradition is thus primarily still possible by means of literary criticism.

When one seeks the historical context in which the Patriarchal stories in Genesis arose an immediate problem is encountered, namely, the delineation and definition of the literary source material which is accessible. It is in Genesis that the critical literary approach has been endlessly applied for over a century, and whether or not one agrees with the results of literary analysis, it is a truism that different traditional complexes or strata are to be found there. More than one simple picture of the Patriarchs is therefore also to be found. Whether or not the traditionally accepted symbols J, E, P are the most fortunate choice is now beside the point. A span of several centuries is irrefutably represented in the development of the material. In order to study the accurate context of any one picture of the Patriarchs one must carry forward the never-ending task of attempting to unravel the literary development of the sources. Despite some uncertainty regarding the exact dating of the sources, it is now generally accepted that a Yahwistic version, dated by many scholars in the early years of the United Monarchy, stands at one end of the spectrum, and a Priestly account derives from a time at least four or five centuries later. For the present purposes it is not necessary to go into the question of the pre-literary stage of this material. M. Noth,[7] and more recently E. A. Speiser,[8] argued for an underlying *Grund* source which gave rise to both J and E versions, but this too may be ignored at this point. Since this study will deal primarily with the Yahwistic formulation of the tradition, we may also exclude from the discussion the suggestion of G. von Rad that the stories may origi-

---

7 *Überlieferungsgeschichte des Pentateuch* (Stuttgart, 1948), pp. 41–4.
8 *Genesis*, pt. i, vol. i of *Göttinger Handkommentar zum Alten Testament* (Göttingen, 1922) pp. xxxviii–xxxix.

nally have been the expansion of ancient credal themes.[9] We are thus concerned with the history of tradition from the Yahwist onward. The day is past when it could be maintained that 'late' sources included only later material.[10] It is sufficient to be reminded that through the centuries of Hebrew history various radical changes in outlook did take place and that these different contextual situations must be ascertained.

If we turn our attention to the accounts of the Hebrew Patriarchs sufficient questions emerge which beg answer. As we have just noted, the first problem to be met is that of literary extent. Hans Walter Wolff states that in searching for the kerygmatic intention of the Yahwist we must first of all define the literary limits with which we will work.[11] Wolff feels that he can work 'a critically assured minimum,' namely, a Tetrateuch,[12] extending at least as far as Numbers 25:5, with the further possibility that in Numbers 32 an original conclusion to the Yahwist's work is embedded.[13] Such a working hypothesis is of no small account. It is most significant that Wolff has rejected the theory of a Hexateuch in favour of Noth's idea of a Tetrateuch followed by a Deuteronomic History complex.

Much more than merely the length of a source is involved, since what matters greatly here is that Wolff by the definition of his source material has excluded the Joshua conquest stories from his Yahwistic corpus. This view is diametrically opposed to that of von Rad who saw the Conquest narratives as basic to the entire structuring of the work of the Yahwist. This basic theme then was augmented by the addition of other thematic elements to round out the tradition.[14] Once the Conquest stories have been removed a radical adjustment is required concerning the promises to the Patriarchs, since it has been maintained that the Conquest stories in fact fulfil the promises of the land made to the Patriarchs. The matter of whether these stories are indispensable to an understanding of the Yahwist's work

9 *Das formgeschichtliche Problem des Hexateuch*, BWANT, IV (1938), 26.

10 One thinks for example of J. Pedersen's now famous dictum that all the sources contain both pre-exilic and post-exilic material; see 'Die Auffassung vom Alten Testament,' ZAW, 49 (1931), 179.

11 'The Kerygma of the Yahwist,' *Interpretation*, 20 (1966), pp. 131–58. First published as 'Das Kerygma des Jahwisten,' *Evangelische Theologie*, 24 (1964), 73–97. References are to the English version.

12 *Ibid.*, p. 133.

13 *Ibid.*, p. 134.

14 Von Rad, *Das formgeschichtliche Problem*, pp. 36ff.

would seem therefore to be a question far from resolved.[15] Once Wolff has made his decision regarding the extent of J he is free to draw a conclusion as to why and how the Yahwist has relegated the land promise to an inferior position by not including the Conquest stories and by magnifying the promises of numerous descendants.[16]

The methodological implications here are worth special mention. Wolff states that the Yahwist must surely have inherited a tradition concerning the promise of the land. Furthermore, this land promise theme was already linked to the Exodus-Conquest tradition. Then Wolff concludes: 'It is all the more surprising that this theme of the Promised Land, which was known to the Yahwist and which was prominent in the Palestinian patriarchal tradition and decisive for its connection with Israelite conquest tradition, recedes completely in the introductory word in Genesis 12:1–3.'[17] Whether or not the land promise motif is lacking in Gen. 12:1–3 is only of secondary concern to us here. What is important is to note how, having established arbitrary limits, it becomes easier, or perhaps necessary, to explain the absence of certain motifs. Wolff is driven to conclude that since the Yahwist must have inherited a tradition in which the Exodus and Conquest themes were already combined, the Yahwist has intentionally ignored the conquest tradition because 'this does not belong to the realm of his particular interest.'[18] One can only be amazed at such a line of reasoning.

A similar question can be raised, however, at the very beginning of the Patriarchal stories as well. Von Rad[19] and, more recently, James Muilenburg[20] have argued that Gen. 12:1–3 forms a fitting conclusion to the Primaeval History and must be seen as a ray of hope following the dismal Tower of Babel story, not an abrupt beginning to the Abraham account. This view is acceptable only if one has already decided that there is Yahwistic material prior to the Abraham story. One might consider, for example, the view of R. H. Pfeiffer, who suggested that the work of the Yahwist begins only in ch. 12 of Genesis, with much of the so-called Yahwistic material in chs. 1–11

15 One aspect of the discussion may be seen in B. L. Goff, 'The Lost Yahwistic Account of the Conquest of Canaan,' JBL, 53 (1934), 241–9. Cf. also S. Mowinckel, *Tetrateuch-Pentateuch-Hexateuch*, BZAW, 90 (1964).
16 'The Kerygma of the Yahwist,' p. 140.
17 *Ibid.*
18 *Ibid.*, p. 140 n.
19 *Das formgeschichtliche Problem*, p. 61.
20 'Abraham and the Nations,' *Interpretation*, 19 (1965), 389–90.

actually having been added even later than the time of P.[21] Pfeiffer
would thus conclude that although the traditions may have been of
varied origin, some likely non-Israelite, it was not until about 400
B.C. that a solid connection existed between the Patriarchal stories
and chs. 1–11. Even if Pfeiffer's view is not entirely acceptable, it is a
necessary reminder that even within Genesis there is need to define
one's sources.

B. D. Napier once wrote: 'We are struck by an obvious difference
between primeval and patriarchal stories: they differ in quality –
they are not of the same literary stuff.'[22] In their monumental study
of literature H. M. and N. K. Chadwick discuss the differences between the Patriarchal stories and chs. 1–11, and concerning chs. 1–11
conclude that 'these chapters probably have a separate history of
their own.'[23] Unfortunately this idea has not been followed up in detail.[24] It is clear that at some time the Primaeval History was integrated with the Patriarchal stories, but did this take place as early as
the time traditionally assigned to the Yahwist? In a thorough study
of the background of chs. 1–11 C. J. de Catanzaro has demonstrated
that a likely date for the so-called Yahwistic material is no earlier
than the time of Josiah, perhaps shortly after 625 B.C.[25] Some of the
implications of such a view have been worked out by F. V. Winnett.[26] In this connection one might also mention the view of J.
Hempel, who, while still arguing for a basically integrated Yahwistic
product, did see Gen. 1–11 as a later stage (J³) added even after the
Joseph story (J²) had been added to the Patriarchal narratives,
which were the core (J¹).[27]

Although many scholars may argue that matters of literary origin
should give way to newer aspects of research, the present writer
would insist that unless some of these questions are faced anew we
will be compounding errors for some time to come. The whole question of the composite nature of the work of the Yahwist has received
concentrated study from those closely related to the field of Pentateuchal studies, but is glossed over by most other Old Testament

21 ZAW, 48 (1930), 66–73. Also, *Introduction to the Old Testament* (New York,
    1941), p. 141.
22 B. D. Napier, *From Faith to Faith* (New York, 1955), p. 71. Cf. also p. 97.
23 *The Growth of Literature*, vol. 2 (Cambridge, 1936), p. 692.
24 N. E. Wagner, 'Pentateuchal Criticism: No Clear Future,' *Canadian Journal of
    Theology*, 13 (1967), 229–30.
25 *A Literary Analysis of Genesis I–XI* (Toronto, 1957), p. 142.
26 'Re-examining the Foundations,' JBL, 84 (1965), 1–19.
27 *Die althebräische Literatur und ihr hellenistisch-jüdisches Nachleben* (Wildpark-
    Potsdam, 1930), pp. 112ff.

scholars. Even before Gunkel's time scholars were convinced that J was not a unity. Wellhausen himself argued this way,[28] as did the all but forgotten French critic, C. Bruston.[29] When Gunkel introduced the idea of separate centres for the origin of the various parts of J, more emphasis was placed on the pre-literary stage of the tradition.[30] But it will be noted that an impressive list of scholars who were concerned with literary origin and who argued for J being composite can be built up. Gunkel himself was also a thorough-going literary critic.[31]

Although the view that much of composite nature in the material can be explained along the lines suggested by Gunkel has much to commend it, one is left wondering whether or not it is that simple. The fact that Jacob is presented with such frankness while Abraham is glorified as a great man of trust and unswerving faith ought to raise the possibility that these forefathers have been depicted for us by sources which are not identical in origin or development. Napier suggested: 'The cycle of stories which revolves around the character of Jacob differs from that of Abraham. If the idealizing tendency has had only a partial influence on the Abraham material, it is almost absent in the Jacob stories ... Can it be that the two cycles of stories come to their final form with two different historical epochs in mind?'[32] It will be recalled as well that Hempel and others have argued for a separate development of the Joseph traditions.[33]

If some change is made in the assumptions regarding the extent of the literary blocks, other modification may follow. For example, the so-called E material is generally connected with the northern part of Israel, while J is felt to be Judaean in origin. This assumption is due to factors derived from the Joseph story as well as the book of Exodus. But the E material in the Abraham story (chs. 20–21) speaks only of Abraham's activity in the far south of Palestine. It would seem much more reasonable to consider different Elohistic versions with different points of origin. The only obvious conclusion at this time is that the question of literary origin is far from solved.

28 J. Wellhausen, *Die Composition des Hexateuchs und der historischen Bücher des Alten Testaments* (Berlin, 1899), pp. 8, 207–8.
29 C. Bruston, 'Les deux Jéhovistes,' *Revue de Théologie et de Philosophie*, 18 (1885), 5–34, 499–528, 602–37.
30 H. Gunkel, *Genesis*, 5th ed. rev. (Göttingen, 1922).
31 There is no attempt made here to exhaust the list, but the following deserve special attention: Karl Budde, Rudolph Smend, Eduard Meyer, Johannes Meinhold, Otto Eissfeldt, R. H. Pfeiffer, C. A. Simpson.
32 *From Faith to Faith*, pp. 82–3.
33 *Die althebräische Literatur*, pp. 112ff.; also Napier, *From Faith to Faith*, p. 97.

If the internal structure of Genesis is in need of further definition it follows without question that the relationship which the book bears to the remaining parts of the Pentateuch must also be called into question. Aage Bentzen stated: 'Among the narrative material *Genesis* has a position apart, and it is doubtful whether it has anything to do with the other collections.'[34] Y. Kaufmann too argued for a separate history for Genesis, noting even its use of literary forms different from those in the books which follow.[35] The present writer is not able to accept Kaufmann's early dating of this material but it is most interesting to see reference to *literary* differences, not merely vague references to different 'character' without further specification as to exactly what is meant.

It is amazing that for so long scholars have merely assumed that Genesis cannot be separated from what follows. Often the evidence has surely pointed in that direction. For example, Pfeiffer was critical of O. Eissfeldt's theory involving an L source on the grounds that when one carries the analysis beyond the limits of Genesis the source becomes too fragmentary to be very convincing.[36] It would surely have been just as plausible to conclude that Eissfeldt might be on the track of something significant but that the analysis as a whole falls short because it has been applied to other parts of the Pentateuch which have little in common with Genesis.

One also notes studies such as Kurt Galling attempted regarding Israel's election and promise themes, which showed that in Israelite tradition the Exodus-Sinai material played an entirely different role from that of promises to the Patriarchs.[37] One might expect that this would suggest to some critics the possibility that these separate traditions had entirely separate histories, not only at the earliest oral stage. Their roles in much later history surely point in that direction.

Quite clearly, then, one must examine each unit on its own merit. What Gunkel did for the pre-literary stage must be continued to later stages as well. For example, F. V. Winnett, in a book which has received far too little attention, has argued for a separate development for the Mosaic traditions in Exodus-Numbers, holding that these traditions are quite ancient.[38] However, Winnett can also argue that late

34 *Introduction to the Old Testament*, 2nd ed. rev. (Copenhagen, 1952), vol. 2, pp. 20–1.
35 *The Religion of Israel*, trans. Moshe Greenberg (Chicago, 1960), pp. 206–7.
36 *Introduction to the Old Testament*, p. 159.
37 *Die Erwählungstraditionen Israels*, BZAW, 48 (1928).
38 *The Mosaic Tradition* (Toronto, 1949).

Yahwistic revisions have taken place in the book of Genesis.[39] Studies along these lines ought to be followed up.

Such an approach provides a necessary alternative to some of the current views which tend to disregard the problem of literary origin. For example, J. A. McKenzie speaks of J as a massive entity stretching from the creation of man to the accession of David, a literary deposit in which several men shared 'in a common enterprise.'[40] Such a view concedes that the literary origin of the individual sections is either too complicated to be unravelled with any certainty or that its solution is not really that vital to its proper understanding. Quite likely many critics would agree with these sentiments; at least little attention is being given to detailed study in this area. But, as we have shown above, the accurate delineation of one's source material is not an optional exercise.

A number of scholars have argued for a particular date for their source simply because of its particular extent. G. Hölscher, for example, saw the unity of the twelve tribes to be one of J's leading motifs, which would tie in very well with the time of David and Solomon. However, since he thought that J extended as far as 1 Kings 12:19, J must be dated at least as late as the time of which it speaks. Hence one must think of the time of Jereboam.[41] Similarly, D. N. Freedman calls Genesis to 2 Kings 25 'the primary history' and feels that he can date its final compilation by the date of the last event mentioned, i.e. 561 B.C.[42] What validity has such a conclusion and what does it help in coming to understand the material? Surely Freedman would allow for later interpolation, and his stand is well known for the antiquity of much of the traditional material.[43] We have insisted above that the literary extent of one's sources must be given most careful attention, but we must reject the attempts noted immediately above as failing to come to grips with the problem.

It must be admitted, however, that even when one restricts one's evidence to usually accepted parts of the Pentateuch dangers exist when evidence concerning a small part is applied to the whole. For example, Hartmut Schmökel feels that Exodus 14:13ff. likely precedes the events of 1 Kings 14:25, namely, the plundering of the temple by Shishak 1 in 928 B.C. The conclusion he then reaches is that J

39 'Re-examining the Foundations.'
40 'Reflections on Wisdom,' JBL, 86 (1967), 5.
41 *Geschichtsschreibung in Israel* (Lund, 1952) p. 112.
42 'The Law and the Prophets,' VT, Supp. 9 (1963), 250–65.
43 'Pentateuch,' *The Interpreter's Dictionary of the Bible*, (Nashville, 1962), vol. 3, pp. 713ff.

must be dated prior to 928.[44] Similarly, Mowinckel saw J emerging
shortly after the split of the Northern and Southern Kingdoms because the golden calf story is to be taken as a polemic against the
Dan and Bethel sanctuaries of Jereboam I. This leads Mowinckel to
suggest Asa's cultic reformation, circa 800, as a probable time in
which to date J.[45] Even if it could be maintained that these points of
contact are such that they merit serious consideration for purposes of
dating, it does not necessarily follow that all so-called Yahwistic material found elsewhere must be similarly dated.

These illustrations are sufficient to indicate the nature of the current situation. No attempt has been made to offer a solution to the
problem of literary origin but doubts have been raised about the possibility of speaking of J without further discussion concerning the
exact significance of this symbol. In any case, a warning has been
registered against hasty acceptance of a large segment of tradition as
a fixed reservoir of tradition from which one can dip at random until
one's dating scheme is firmly bolstered. One feels constrained to argue that critics must once more tackle the question of literary composition, perhaps with several new options which have been unrecog-
nized as possibilities.[46]

Attention must now be given to the probable context in which at
least some of the traditions to which we have referred may have
arisen. If we restrict our investigation to the Yahwistic traditions in
Genesis we find that there is still ample scope for an illustrative investigation. We can say at the outset that it is almost universally
agreed today that the Genesis Patriarchal accounts, at least those
assigned to J, are to be dated sometime in the early years of the
United Monarchy. This position seems to be taken as being so self-
evident by most scholars that little need is seen to defend it. It is as
if scholars feel this aspect of Old Testament research is settled and
they can busy themselves with other matters. Since the connection
of the Yahwistic material with the time of David and Solomon is
such a pivotal assumption in many discussions of the development of
Israelite religion, it is absolutely essential that the question be raised
in some detail as to whether or not this assumption is valid.

It is of more than passing significance that such a date for J does
not coincide with that propounded by the critics of a few generations

44 ZAW, 62 (1949–50), 319–21.
45 Erwägungen zur Pentateuchquellenfrage,' *Norsk Theologisk Tidsskrift* (1964),
    p. 58.
46 See, in general, N. E. Wagner, 'Pentateuchal Criticism: No Clear Future,'
    pp. 225–32.

ago. It has been noted above that Wellhausen and those associated with the critical school saw connections between J and the early eighth-century prophets, particularly Amos and Hosea. This conclusion was based primarily on affinities in religious and ethical matters.[47] Such is no longer the case. The points of contact sought for today are primarily in the historical field. Such a shift is, therefore, more than merely a change of relative dating. The kind of evidence sought is totally new. This change is no doubt a reflection of our general turning away from 'subjective' ideas of a theological nature in favour of 'objective' historical fact, a topic which could easily occupy us for the remainder of our available space. It must suffice here to have drawn attention to the fact that changes which may appear to have been subtle are in fact of considerable import.

No matter how subtle the shift may have been, today the consensus of opinion is that the Patriarchal stories and the Kingdom of David and Solomon have a great deal in common, and that the latter provides the milieu in which the former gained prominence. The comments of Leonard Rost may be taken as typical: 'So stellte der Jahwist die Ordnung des davidischen Grossreichs dar als ein gottgewolltes, schon in der Urgeschichte und in der Patriarchengeschichte angebahntes System von Beziehungen, das durch Jahwes Führung und Leitung nun im davidischen Grossreich verwirklicht wurde.'[48] If it is of significance for our proper understanding to pin-point the historical context we must investigate this claim more fully. One of the most detailed attempts in recent years to argue for a Davidic date for the Patriarchal material is to be found in an article by H. W. Wolff.[49]

Wolff provides a general outline to justify his assignment of the Yahwist to the time of Solomon.

> The various traditions of the Israelite tribes have long since grown together into a complete unity. The Sinai tradition of the southern tribes is connected with the Exodus tradition of the Joseph tribes; the God of the Fathers is identical with Yahweh, the God of Israel, and is unhesitatingly so named; the originally varied patriarchal traditions, with their various centers of tradition, have become long since the common property of all the tribes. Coalescence of the traditions to such an extent is conceivable, at the earliest, toward the end of the premonarchical

47 See above, note 3.
48 'Zum geschichtlichen Ort der Pentateuchquellen,' ZTK, 53 (1956), 5.
49 'The Kerygma of the Yahwist,' pp. 131–58.

period. On the other hand, there is nowhere any evidence of conflict of two Israelite states such as occurred after solomon's death. Thus the period we have in view is generally that of David's and Solomon's empire.[50]

Such a broad outline seems at first glance to present a reasonable argument. On closer examination, however, one is disappointed. The primary reason for its failure to carry conviction is its extreme vagueness. It must be admitted that Wolff has built his case on a number of suppositions which have to be examined before they can be brushed aside. This we are unable to do in detail at this point. One thinks, for example, of the complex history of the traditions to which he refers. Moreover, it must be shown that the Sinai traditions and those dealing with the Exodus had separate origin.[51] No concrete illustrations are offered to demonstrate the claim that the various traditions have coalesced, if they ever existed separately. How would one find instances of conflict among the tribes in the Abraham story in any case? In a rather unconvincing attempt Nielsen argued that the separation between Abraham and Lot at Bethel (Gen. 13:1ff.) symbolizes the split which occurred between north and south when Jeroboam built his sanctuary at Bethel.[52] This serves to illustrate the lengths to which one must go to find supporting evidence for such a view. All one can say is that the portrait of Abraham and his descendants is one of idealized unity but that it is impossible to date its appearance in this general way.

It is no doubt unfair to attack Wolff at length on such minute evidence. Fortunately he provides other points which are more concrete. He notes that certain peoples are mentioned in Genesis: Philistines, Moabites, Ammonites, Aramaeans, Edomites, Amalekites, and Canaanites, 'the very peoples which, according to 2 Samuel 8, were incorporated into David's empire.'[53] But is the mere fact that these names occur sufficient evidence to draw valid historical parallels? If one reads the story of Lot's daughters in Gen. 19:30–38 it becomes clear that the story merely heaps ridicule on the Moabites and Ammonites by attributing to them an incestuous origin. No contact with Moab is even hinted at. Where does one see a connection with David's amicable working agreement with the Moabites which we hear of in 1 Sam. 22:3ff.? In other words, the mention of Moabites

---

50 *Ibid.*, p. 134.

51 See, in this connection, W. Beyerlin, *Origin and History of the Oldest Sinaitic Traditions* (Oxford, 1965).

52 *Shechem: A Traditio-historical Investigation* (Copenhagen, 1959), p. 214.

53 'The Kerygma of the Yahwist,' pp. 134–5.

in the anecdotal incident in Gen. 19 is simply not the kind of evidence which can be used for dating the time of writing. Similarly, the Aramaeans are introduced on several occasions in the Patriarchal stories. This has little to do with the emergence of the Aramaeans as a potent force in Solomon's time and thereafter. It points rather to the fact that the Israelites looked to western Mesopotamia as their point of origin. So it is with the Philistines. Even from ch. 26 of Genesis, where the Philistines are mentioned more than elsewhere, one does not get the impression that they are or were recent enemies to the extent that one would expect after reading the accounts in Samuel. One must conclude that the writers are telling of peoples from the distant past with only partial concern for accuracy regarding the actual points of origin and their distinctive characteristics, not unlike the treatment of names in the Table of Nations (Gen. 10).

There is one rather unique exception in the matter of names involving a statement concerning Edom. In the *Ersatz* blessing to Esau, Isaac makes the following statement: 'By your sword you shall live, and you shall serve your brother; but when you break loose you shall break his yoke from your neck' (Gen. 27:40). There is no doubt that the writer would have us equate Esau-Edom. This is clear in the name given at birth where attention is drawn to Esau's redness (25:19–26) and also in the incident involving the red soup in the birthright story (25:27–34). The identification is spelled out explicitly in 36:1, 'These are the descendants of Esau, that is, Edom,' and in 36:8, 'So Esau dwelt in the hill country of Seir; Esau is Edom.'[54] No reader or hearer could possibly miss the point. Therefore the specific reference in 27:40 ought not to be overlooked, because it seems to make clear an eventual Edomite rebellion which would free Edom from the control of Israel. Wolff's contention that this is an allusion to Hadad, an Edomite, who annoyed Solomon (1 Kings 11:14ff.) is not convincing.[55] There is no evidence at all for an Edomite rebellion at this time. Nor can one reconcile this reference with David's conquest of Edom (2 Sam. 8). Although our knowledge of Edom's international affairs is sketchy, it does appear as if Edom was able to break Israel's control on several occasions. The first known break in the period of our concern came about 850 B.C. (see 2 Kings 8:20–22). Later, in 735, Edom once more revolted, this time against Ahaz. It

---

54 It is difficult to see how the name Esau is connected with the word for hair, *śʿr*. One possibility is that the name is based on the root ʿatā (hence ʿśw, from which the Arabic aʿtā, 'hairy,' is derived. Since this root is unknown in Hebrew, the writer had to use a Hebrew root with similar meaning, hence *śʿr*.

55 'The Kerygma of the Yahwist,' p. 135.

thus appears as if the one specific reference in the Patriarchal stories which could be used for historical comparison yields nothing at all which would point to the time of David and Solomon. In fact, it is only at a time some years later that one could find the earliest possible date which could warrant serious consideration. It is not surprising that Wolff would take the last part of 27:40 as a later gloss![56] Going on to point to the absence of Egypt or Babylon as major powers, Wolff concludes, 'at no time before David and Solomon or afterwards is this political outlook more intelligible.'[57] One thing is certain. The evidence just examined does not strengthen the case for a Davidic date for the Patriarchal narratives.

Another aspect of the supposed connection with the early years of the Monarchy is the assumed correspondences between the work of the Yahwist and the Court History of David (2 Sam. 7, 9–20; 1 Kings 1–2), perhaps better known as the Succession story. Von Rad drew attention to a connection between the two,[58] and Wolff agrees, speaking of the two sources as having similar 'high literary culture.'[59] The Succession story has received considerable attention since Leonard Rost's well-known study of 1926.[60] Many critics have attempted to isolate the literary techniques used by the writer,[61] and considerable attention has been given to the place which the story plays in the development of history writing among the Hebrews,[62] but it is only very recently that a specific attempt has been made to study the literary relationships between the Succession story and the work of the Yahwist. Such a study was undertaken by J. Blenkinsopp with limited scope.[63] Blenkinsopp applied what he refers to as the 'new stylistics' approach and insisted that this kind of research runs parallel to and not in competition with more traditional literary analysis.[64] He found the basic outline of the Succession story to consist of four variations on a theme of sexual immorality: adultery with Bathsheba, the rape of Tamar, Absolom's occupying of his father's harem,

---

56 *Ibid.*
57 *Ibid.*
58 *Das formgeschichtliche Problem*, p. 66.
59 'The Kerygma of the Yahwist,' p. 135.
60 *Die Überlieferung von der Thronnachfolge Davids*, BWANT, 42 (1926).
61 See recently Jared Jackson, 'David's Throne: Patterns in the Succession Story,' *Canadian Journal of Theology*, 11 (1965), pp. 183–95.
62 An important contribution in this connection has been made by S. Mowinckel, 'Israelite Historiography,' ASTI, 2 (1963), 4–26.
63 'Theme and Motif in the Succession History (2 Sam. xi 2ff) and the Yahwist corpus,' VT, Supp. 15 (1966), 44–57.
64 *Ibid.*, pp. 48–9.

Adonijah's attempt to possess his father's concubine.[65] Once he has laid bare this outline, Blenkinsopp is hard pressed to draw parallels with the Yahwist. By concentrating on the first few chapters of Genesis he is able to relate a few points dealing with sin and death but even here one is not easily convinced that Eve is to be viewed as an undesirable type parallel to the foreign women in David's affairs.[66] What is more far-fetched is to see any real significance in Esau's foreign wives making life miserable for aging Isaac, as if this were a major motif in the Jacob story.[67] More recently this same question has been broached by Walter Brueggemann with much of the same method, i.e. collecting all possible points of contact between David's adventures and the opening chapters of Genesis.[68] It is entirely possible that a minute analysis of expressions and motifs might yield a few minor points of contact between the two narrative sources in question, but hardly anything which could be termed thematically significant. It is clear that the structure of the Patriarchal stories follows a pattern entirely different from that of the Succession story. Whether they both originated in association with the court at similar points in history is a question which cannot be answered by such internal evidence.

Although we have found the evidence drawn from names of peoples mentioned and correspondences with the Succession story to be inconclusive if not negative, it must still be admitted that there is an inviting possibility of seeing a connection between the figures of Abraham and David. Both regard Hebron as home, both entered into covenant relationships with YHWH, and both became gigantic figures in later Israelite tradition. With the tribe of Judah reaching a position of pre-eminence in David's time it would have been advantageous for him to have a figure out of the past to use as a support in his climb to fame. The possible relationship between David and Abraham has been investigated by previous critics, but none speaks so positively as R. C. Clements in a recent book:

> The priority given to Abraham as the great ancestor of all Israel
> reflects the position of pre-eminence which was claimed by Judah
> at this time. It is, therefore, reasonable to look for connections
> between David and the tradition concerning Abraham, and
> to suggest that a number of very important links relate these two

65 *Ibid.*, pp. 47–8.
66 *Ibid.*, p. 52.
67 *Ibid.*, p. 53.
68 'David and his Theologian,' CBQ, 30 (1968), 156–81.

great figures to each other. There are several clues which suggest that the tradition of the Abrahamic covenant contributed to David's own religious and political achievements, and that the importance which has been given by the Old Testament sources to the memory of Abraham has been affected by the part which David played in its preservation.[69]

No one will argue with Clements when he traces the increasingly larger role played by the Judah federation in David's rise to power. Hebron was clearly the chief city in the region and it was from there that David was able to govern even the northern part of the kingdom for some time. If there were ancient traditions known at Hebron which described the great Abraham of old as the founder of the Hebron shrine or at least as having been a local hero, it is likely that David was familiar with them. The question to be answered has to do with how these stories about Abraham could have helped David in his climb to power.

Clements argues that these stories were of tremendous help to David by legitimizing the kind of covenant entered into by David. 'Probably whilst David was still at Hebron members of his entourage associated his greatness with the ancient tradition of Abraham, and linked the two figures together under a scheme of promise and fulfilment. This theme of promise and fulfilment was to provide a basic motif for the great epic history of Israel's origins which was composed by the Yahwist early in Solomon's reign.'[70] It was thus not merely on the level of personal correspondence or merely because both David and Abraham were from Hebron that the two were linked. Clements refers with approval to the statement of G. Mendenhall:

> Therefore, during the Monarchy and according to every indication we have in the time of David, the tradition of the covenant with Abraham became the pattern of a covenant between Yahweh and David, whereby Yahweh promised to maintain the Davidic line on the throne (2 Sam. 23:5). Yahweh bound Himself, exactly as in the Abrahamic and Noachite covenant, and therefore Israel could not escape responsibility to the king. The covenant with Abraham was the 'prophecy' and that with David the 'fulfilment.'[71]

69 *Abraham and David* (London, 1967), p. 47.
70 *Ibid.*, pp. 56–7.
71 'Covenant Forms in Israelite Tradition,' *Biblical Archaeologist*, 17 (1954), 71–2.

We thus have the following picture. The form of the Davidic covenant is similar to that made with Abraham but is different from the Sinai-Horeb law covenant form. By going back to the early form with Abraham David would invoke a form predating other agreements or differences which might be in existence. This would serve to unite all Israel. All David then had to do was to incorporate the concept of a dynastic monarchy and his new kingdom would be established. This latter element may even have come from the Jebusites in Jerusalem.[72]

One would like to believe that it was really this simple. If this is the pattern which was followed is it not strange that there is not even the slightest glimmer of a reference to Abraham in the stories concerning David? No reference at all to the Patriarchs is to be seen in the whole complex which speaks of the growth of the monarchy. What we are given in detail is the account of how by means of the introduction of the Ark of the Covenant David sought to unite the various tribes (2 Sam. 6). This episode is most certainly related to the Sinai-Horeb tradition and has nothing to do with Abraham. When one recalls the birth stories of Jacob's sons in Genesis or the grandiose promises made to Abraham and his descendants it is amazing that these elements are not utilized by David. The picture we have of the tribes in David's time is definitely not the ideally united group of twelve pictured in Genesis. Instead we have the picture of scattered elements held together at least to some extent by common external foes and who can muster no more than a general statement that the Northerners recognized their relationship to David as 'Behold, we are your bone and flesh' (2 Sam. 5:1). Covenantal form has been duly studied by competent scholars in recent years, but when the easy parallels are shown for what they really are, the formal considerations become negligible for dating purposes.

What makes it more difficult to pin-point the development of these traditions is Clements' theory of literary growth. Although David made use of the Abrahamic covenant, the Yahwistic account of that covenant which we now possess is post-Davidic. That is, although the tradition itself may be ancient, J's work is to be seen as having grown up in the generation following David and having been written no doubt in the light of David's achievements. 'It is impossible to avoid the conclusion that the Yahwist himself saw an important connection between Abraham and David.'[73] Although we found no visi-

---

72 Clements, *Abraham and David*, p. 56.
73 *Ibid.*, p. 59.

ble signs of the Abrahamic traditions in the stories concerning David,
if Clements and others who hold this opinion are right it ought to be
possible to find signs of David's activity in the work of the Yahwist.
Clements finds this at the very centre of the Yahwist's work, namely
in the idea that Israel is to be a universal blessing to all mankind.[74]

> The promise of the land was made to point forward to the con-
> quest under Joshua, and beyond this to its effectual conclusion in
> the rise of the Davidic state. Similarly the growth of Abraham's
> descendants into a nation points to a fulfilment in the Davidic
> age when Israel became a territorial state and took its place
> among the nations of the world. Although the Yahwist did not
> continue his story up to David's time it is clear that this was the
> age which formed his own contemporary background, and there is
> no doubt that he was writing with a very positive interest in the
> new political situation which had arisen in his own day. The fulfil-
> ment to which the Yahwist directs the attention of his readers in
> his account of the divine promises reached beyond the events
> of the Exodus and the conquest under Joshua to the founding of
> the Israelite state under David.[75]

Similar conclusions are reached by Wolff in the article discussed
briefly above. Wolff too sees the heart of the Yahwist's work in his
promises to Abraham in Gen. 12:1–3, especially v. 3 which tells of
Israel becoming a universal blessing.[76]

When all is said and done one is still left searching for evidence to
back up this contention. The only concrete evidence Clements can
muster to show that J wrote consciously for the Davidic period is two
references which he feels are 'quite specific predictions of the rise of
the Davidic monarchy from Judah,' namely, Gen. 49:10 and Num.
24:17–19.[77] Unfortunately both are deeply buried in oracles which
are enigmatic to say the least. The sceptre of Judah (Gen. 49:10) and
the star and sceptre from Jacob-Israel (Num. 24:17) may well be
royal symbols, but to assign to them the specific function of predict-
ing the growth of David's monarchy from Judah is a somewhat dubious procedure, especially in view of the fact that no other clear
references point in that direction. Clements continues to argue that
there are 'other indications that the Yahwist was very conscious of

74 *Ibid.*, p. 57.
75 *Ibid.*, pp. 57–8.
76 'The Kerygma of the Yahwist,' pp. 140ff.
77 *Abraham and David*, p. 58.

the existence of Israel as a monarchic state, and was concerned to show the divine providence which had overruled in history to bring this into existence.[78] He gives the following references to support this last point: Gen. 12:1–4a, 13:17, 15:18–21, 22:17, 26:4, 28:14; Exod. 23:31; Num. 24:7f. Yet on closer examination it becomes clear that these references speak only of the promises of land and descendants to the Fathers. There is not the slightest indication that they are related to the time of David's kingdom, or to a kingdom of anyone else.

If one turns to a specific promise it will become clear how shaky the foundations of the line of reasoning outlined above really are. One might ask how the various nations conquered by David are to be the recipients of the promise that 'all the nations of the earth' are to be blessed, or invoke blessing upon themselves, by means of the seed of Abraham? Clements actually argues that this takes place by military conquest and the nations are blessed in the position in which 'under David, Israel exercised hegemony over a number of surrounding vassal states.'[79] Wolff comes up with a conclusion very similar in tone.

> To summarize: the Yahwist expounds his kerygma in the patriarchal narrative. He deals with 'all the families of the earth' through the examples of the Moabites, Ammonites, Philistines, and Arameans. How are they to find blessing *in Israel?* By Israel's intercession with Yahweh on the example of Abraham; by economic aid on the model of Jacob. Yahweh created the prerequisite by fulfilling the promise of increase and expansion. In what way is *blessing* found through all this? By its bringing annulment of guilt and punishment, community life without strife, effective material aid for life.[80]

One can only say that if this is what the Yahwist is really driving at he has been subtle beyond all words. Although James Muilenburg follows a basic line not far different from that of Wolff and Clements it is instructive to note the hesitancy in his comment on this point:

> The nations will bless themselves through Abram and, of course, *mutatis mutandis* through the people of whom Abram is the father and progenitor. The blessing now extends to all humanity ... That such words should be composed in David's time, in a time

---

78 *Ibid.*
79 *Ibid.*, pp. 58–9.
80 'The Kerygma of the Yahwist,' p. 150.

of nationalism and national power and prestige, is indeed surprising. Nowhere do we encounter a single reference to Abram in
all the traditions of the United Monarchy, but the Yahwist
epic, which in all probability was composed at this time, must
reflect the faith of those who were contemporary with David. One
wonders what David would have thought of such programmatic
writing, especially since Genesis 12:1–3 determines the movement of the whole epic from beginning to end.[81]

One wishes that this uncertainty had led Muilenberg to another conclusion, namely, that the supposed connections between David and
the Yahwistic work are decidedly dubious and, in fact, likely non-
existent. All along, not enough attention has been paid to the question of dating the Court History. Carlson, for example, has pointed
to the possibility of a Deuteronomic setting for it. Should this be on
the right track most of the supposed connections discussed above
would cease to be relevant at all.[82]

Whatever one's decision may be regarding the historical allusions
said to be present in the Patriarchal narratives, it must be admitted
that the promises to the Fathers constitute the core of the stories as
we have them today. Wolff has based the centre of his argument,
as noted above, on the Yahwist's having been responsible for Gen.
12:2–3 where above all else his kerygma is to be found.[83] Together
with Gen. 15, we have the distinctive mark of J. It is to be admitted
that the promises provide the thematic bond uniting the present
book of Genesis, even if one confines one's attention to the pre-P tradition. Only by means of the promises once made and subsequently
renewed are the separate episodes tied into a coherent whole leading
to a conclusion, giving us the picture that prior to the Exodus there
existed a traceable blood-bond among the separate tribes. Whether
or not the simple story of Jacob fathering twelve sons reflects historical circumstances is beside the point for our present purposes.
There is no room for doubt left in any reader's mind. The unmistak-
able impression is left that Abraham, Isaac, and Jacob stand in a
direct line of descent illustrating how the Israelites stemmed from
one man. This became a reality only because Abraham heeded the
divine summons to leave his former home to strike out for a new
land. At the very beginning of the Abraham story we are told with
startling simplicity of this divine command and of Abraham's obe-

81 'Abraham and the Nations,' p. 393.
82 R. A. Carlson, *David the Chosen King* (Stockholm, 1964). .
83 'The Kerygma of the Yahwist,' pp. 137ff.

dient acceptance. It is precisely because these opening verses of Gen.
12 are so important that we must examine them carefully. The idea
that Abraham's obedience foreshadowed the destiny of the entire nation is by nature such a fertile concept that it invites constant ampli-
fication as time goes by. In other words, we must once more raise the
question of the historical context in which the present form of the
tradition arose.

One is immediately struck by the fact that it is not until 12:7 that
YHWH promises the land to Abraham. In 12:1 we are told only that
Abraham is to leave his present home in favour of a land which YHWH
would *show* him. If one were to continue the account by reading v. 4
one would learn that Abraham left as directed and then in v. 7, on
his arrival at Shechem, he received the promise from YHWH that this
was in fact the land which he and his descendants would call their
own. If one includes vv. 2–3 in the account, a totally different picture
of Abraham emerges. He is given absolute assurance before leaving
that his mission will be a success. These verses tell him that he per-
sonally will become famous, that he will be the father of a great nation, that the destiny of others will depend on how they respond to
him, and, finally, that all mankind will find a source of blessing in
him. It would take a fool not to respond to this call! But are vv. 2–3
really an integral part of the story? We have been able to sketch a
narrative without including them and found that it is a clear and
coherent whole in itself. C. A. Simpson argued for the secondary nature of vv. 2–3 on the grounds that they anticipate the promise made
to Abraham in v. 7.[84] It might also be noted that R. Kilian has more
recently argued for a source composed of 12:1, 4a, 6a, 7–8, etc. with
vv. 2–3 being an expansion of the basic story.[85] If such key verses can
in fact be taken as secondary it becomes imperative to discover how
and when they may have become part of the tradition, especially if
they provide us with a key to understanding the present purpose of
the narrative. Since these verses contain such diverse ideas it is not
necessary to regard them as a unity unless there is compelling reason
to do so.[86] One can only decide after the separate elements in the tradition have been examined. The problem is further complicated by

---

84 *The Early Traditions of Israel* (Oxford, 1948), p. 69.

85 *Die vorpriesterlichen Abrahamsüberlieferungen* (Bonn, 1966). He does, however,
attribute vv. 2–3 to the Yahwist, with the other verses being more ancient,
pp. 1–15.

86 Simpson called v. 3b 'unnecessary' in the light of v. 2 (*Early Traditions*, p. 69),
whereas O. Eissfeldt assigned v. 2 to his L source and v. 3 to J, *Hexateuch-
Synopse* (Leipzig, 1922), pp. 11, 19*.

the fact that several other key sections of the Patriarchal stories require study at the same time.

It is extremely dangerous to concentrate on 12:2–3 merely because they are encountered first in one's reading and then force subsequent reference into place. The same might be said for taking ch. 15 as the key to the whole puzzle. J. Hoftijzer, for example, did just that by taking chs. 15 and 17 as central cores around which all other promises were later clustered.[87] It is suggested that the investigation must proceed on an even broader base. The reason for saying this is that there are more elements of a promissory nature in the Patriarchal narratives than usually noted. No reader of the Abraham story could really miss the absolutely basic theme of the promise of an heir. In fact, the whole Abraham story hinges on this point, which constantly seems to be in danger of frustration. Beginning with a barren wife (11:30), Abraham saw a gradual improvement in his personal lot, but it appeared as if his heir would be Eliezer, a slave (15:2–3). Abraham is assured that he will have a son of his own (15:4) and it begins to appear as if this will become a reality by means of Hagar the Egyptian slave girl (16:4). The expulsion of Hagar, however, frustrated that hope. Finally, it is stated that Sarah is to become pregnant (18:10–15). After this long-awaited son is born, Abraham is called upon to sacrifice him as a burnt offering (ch. 22). Only by means of the promised heir are the separate episodes in the Abraham narrative strung together. This does not necessarily mean that every reference to an heir is original, but the theme itself is of such importance that the story falls apart without it. Then one must go on to look at the promise of land and the promise of numerous descendants. These are also key elements in the story but possessing distinctive marks. Finally, the element of one's descendants being a universal source of blessing must also be included, though not strictly adhering to the form of promise.

What of these promises and their possible combinations? Claus Westermann has tackled the problem recently in a very creative manner.[88] The very fact that he spends so much time on this question is encouraging because it indicates that Westermann is not prepared to ignore the aspect of the promises so often merely accepted as being basic. In more recent years debate has centered on whether it was the promise of land or of numerous seed which served as the basic

---

87 *Die Verheissungen an die drei Erzväter* (Leiden, 1956).
88 'Arten der Erzählung in der Genesis,' *Forschung am Alten Testament* (Munich, 1964), pp. 9–91, especially pp. 11–34.

theme.[89] Westermann has shown the inadequacy of this method of investigation by turning to the literary structure of the various promises. He attempts to isolate those promises which are capable of standing on their own from those which appear in various combinations. He feels that the former are original, whereas the latter have been built up over a period of time.[90] When he comes at the problem this way he discovers that the promise of an heir alone fills the bill. Although he is convinced that the promise of land also stood at one time as an independent tradition, it has been overlaid with other aspects.[91] One might question his view with regard to 12:7, where it would appear as if the land promise stands alone, and where, as we attempted to show, it is an integral part of the opening chapter.[92] Westermann concludes that if there was an original promise of numerous descendants which stood independently it too is no longer discernible. Instead, various combinations have resulted: an heir together with numerous seed; numerous descendants with their becoming a blessing; numerous descendants and the land; more involved combinations of promises.[93] Since all of these combinations are possible in pre-P material the manner of combination must be studied together with the process of growth. That is, it ought to be possible to see how these key promises developed and how the Patriarchal tradition itself was reinterpreted in Israel's history. This is a task which will require at least another full paper in itself. Only the most general observations can be offered here.

With some doubt having been cast on the connection between Abraham and David, it surely is required that other possibilities be examined. A little-used control in recent years is the role played by Abraham in non-Pentateuchal sections of the Old Testament. Hoftijzer has advanced the original work of W. Staerk on this point,[94] but as has been suggested above, his conclusions are not entirely sat-

---

89 Alt, for example, spoke of numerous seed as the basic need of the wandering nomad, while von Rad defended the promise of land.

90 'Arten der Erzählung,' p. 32.

91 *Ibid.*

92 *Ibid.*, p. 28; cf. also Hoftijzer, *Die Verheissungen*, p. 15, who argued that 12:7 was secondary because it is really based on the Jacob story since it was Jacob who built the altar at Shechem (33:20). Cf. also Jan Dus, 'Der Jakobbund Gen. 15:8ff.,' ZAW, 80 (1968), 35–7.

93 'Arten der Erzählung,' pp. 32–3.

94 Staerk suggested that the promises to the patriarchs are found only in exilic and post-exilic literature. Abraham may well have been known prior to this time but he was not regarded as important in tradition. See Willy Staerk, *Studien zur Religions- und Sprachgeschichte des alten Testaments* (2 vols.; Berlin, 1899).

isfactory. G. Fohrer has recently come to an interesting conclusion concerning a post-exilic setting for Abraham's growth in fame.[95] The present writer has reached the same conclusion on the basis of a literary study of the story of Abraham, where the evidence clearly suggests an exilic or post-exilic setting for the pre-P patriarchal traditions.[96]

Although this study has been aimed chiefly at destroying the over-simplified reliance on shaky evidence connecting Abraham with David's time, it is hoped that it will also intrigue or anger others into devoting much-needed work to the exploration of countless questions which beg solution.

95 'Zum Text von Jes. xl:8–13,' vt, 5 (1955), 239–49, esp. 240–2.
96 *A Literary Analysis of Genesis 12–36* (Toronto, 1965).

Studies in Relations between Palestine and Egypt during the First Millennium B.C.

I THE TAXATION SYSTEM OF SOLOMON[1]

D. B. REDFORD

The suggestion has often been made that the court functions listed in 2 Sam. 8:16–18, 20:23–26, and 1 Kings 4:2–6 for the reigns of David and Solomon were in part modelled on offices of the royal administration in Egypt.[2] A priori such a suggestion sounds plausi-

---

1 The present paper is part of the author's lecture entitled 'The Miserable Asiatics: Egypt's Relations with Asia, c. 1000–525 B.C.' delivered on 27 March, 1969 as part of the University College Lecture Series, at University College, University of Toronto. The author would like to extend his thanks to Professor J. Holladay and to Dr I. Harari, both of whom discussed the subject with him and offered helpful suggestions. Needless to say, the views expressed are entirely the responsibility of the author, who herewith offers it in honour of the teacher and friend to whom the present volume is dedicated.

2 J. Begrich, zaw, 58 (1940), 1ff.; J. Bright, *A History of Israel* (Philadelphia, 1959), p. 184; R. de Vaux, RB, 48 (1939), 394ff.; *idem, Les institutions de l'Ancien Testament* (Paris, 1961), I, 195ff.; O. Eissfeldt, 'The Hebrew Kingdom,' ch. 34 of vol. II of *The Cambridge Ancient History* (Cambridge, 1965), p. 49; H. Reventlow, *Theologische Zeitschrift*, 15 (1959), 161ff. Elliger's attempt (PJB, 31 [1935], 67) to read Egyptian influence into David's creation of the Thirty Heroes is particularly unconvincing. On the basis of the reference to the m^cb3yt, 'the Thirty,' in the biographical text of Nebwennef (*temp.* Ramses II; K. Sethe, zas, 44 [1907], pl. II, l. 16), Elliger has conjured up a corps of thirty soldiers, attendant upon the Egyptian Pharaoh. Unfortunately he did not consult the many other New Kingdom passages in which this word occurs, otherwise he would not have come to this groundless conclusion. The vizier Nebamun (late Nineteenth Dynasty) calls himself 'a precise judge of the m^cb3yt in administering the laws of his lord' (Cairo 1140, in L. Borchardt, *Statuen und Statuetten*

ble. Yet the titles in question are not technical terms, transliterated from Egyptian,[3] but native Hebrew titles denoting the most common functions, such as those of 'scribe,'[4] 'priest,' 'he who is over the

von Königen und Privatleuten [Cairo, 1911–36], IV, 76); a Middle Kingdom official calls himself 'a judge of the *mᶜbȝyt*' (Cairo 20539, I, 10); at the trial of Horus and Seth both the Ennead of the gods and the *mᶜbȝyt* are present in a judicial capacity (Sir A. H. Gardiner, *Late Egyptian Stories* [Brussells, 1932], p. 40:13); in Amenemope the advice is given, 'do not go into court before the prince and perjure yourself . . . Speak the truth before the prince . . . then he will report your case inside before the *mᶜbȝyt*' (Amenemope, 19, 8ff.); at Medinet Habu, in a spontaneous outburst of joy, the '*mᶜbȝyt* who govern for the king raise aloft their arms in jubilation' (U. Hölscher, *Medinet Habu I. The Earlier Historical Records of Ramses III* [Chicago, 1930], pl. 27–8, ll. 37–8); elsewhere in the same temple (*ibid.* II, pl. 96) the king addresses 'the eldest royal children and the *mᶜbȝyt* who are in attendance,' both of whom are depicted in the accompanying scene as fan-bearing courtiers in long robes! The *mᶜbȝyt* are connected with the scribe's calling, and with Thoth the god of writing: 'skill in (the art of the scribe) is sufficient to make a prince; I have seen many for whom thou (Thoth) hast acted, and they are now in the *mᶜbȝyt*, strong and wealthy through what thou hast done!' (A. H. Gardiner, *Late Egyptian Miscellanies* [Brussells, 1937], p. 60:7–9). In short there is not a single occurrence of the term *mᶜbȝyt* in A. Erman's *Wörterbuch der ägyptischen Sprache* (Leipzig and Berlin, 1926–55), II, 46:16–17, in R. A. Caminos, *Late Egyptian Miscellanies* (Oxford, 1954), p. 234, or in the examples cited above that has not the connotation of a judicial body, a 'grand jury'; and this is clearly the meaning in the passage Elliger cites (Sethe, ZAS, 44 [1907]) where, in response to the words of the king, in the same vein as the assembled court at Medinet Habu (cited above), 'the entourage and the entire *mᶜbȝyt* praised the goodness of His Majesty and kissed the earth.' The 'Leibgarde' which has unfortunately found a place, in the wake of Elliger, in so many popular biblical works is a figment of the imagination; and with this understanding of the situation another of the supposed parallels between Egypt and David's kingdom vanishes.

3   Such technical terms are what one would expect if it were the Egyptian *office* that was being copied. Analogies are forthcoming from the Amarna period, and make the absence of analogous cases from the United Monarchy acutely embarrassing: e.g. *iḥripita* (Egyptian *ḥry-pḏt*, 'battalion commander'; EA 107, 14f.; W. F. Albright, JNES, 5 [1946], 14; T. O. Lambdin, *Egyptian Loanwords and Transcriptions in the Ancient Semitic Languages* [Baltimore, 1952], p. 90); *ruḫi šarri* (possibly *rḫ-nsw*, 'king's acquaintance'; de Vaux, RB, 48, 403ff.; Lambdin, *Egyptian Loanwords*, pp. 90f.; A. Van Selms, JNES, 16 [1957], 122); *weḫu* (Egyptian *wᶜw*, 'infantryman'; EA 150, 6, 9; 152, 47, 50; W. F. Albright, JEA, 23 [1937], 196; Lambdin, *Egyptian Loanwords*, p. 93); *pawūra* (*pȝ wr ᶜȝ*, 'the great prince'; EA 149, 30; 151, 59; Albright, JEA, 23, 196; JNES, 5, 19); *uput(i)* (Egyptian *ipwty*, 'messenger'; EA 151, 20; 152, 56; Albright, JEA, 23, 196; Lambdin, *Egyptian Loanwords*, p. 92); *šaḫšiḫa* (so Albright [JNES, 5, 20], who derives it from *sš-šᶜt*, 'letter scribe'; EA 316, 16; Lambdin, *Egyptian Loanwords*, p. 91).

4   Usually equated with Egyptian *sš-nsw*: de Vaux, RB, 48, 397f.; cf. W. Helck, *Zur Verwaltung des mittleren und neuen Reichs* (Leiden, 1958), pp. 107f. But *sš-nsw*

house,'⁵ 'captain of the host.' If we must postulate a model on which David fashioned his system of court officials, it would seem that the ad hoc nature of the requirements of his kingdom would have dictated the choice of a local example.⁶ Every Canaanite court would

'king's-scribe,' at least under the New Kingdom, is simply a rank title designating the highest offices under the king, such as vizier, chief steward, overseer of the granaries, treasurer, general (cf. Begrich, ZAW, 58, 20f.). The Hebrew title, in contrast, envisages an officer whose title indicates his *function*: he writes for the king. In this regard the *sōpēr* may better be likened to the 'letter-scribe of pharaoh' (Sir A. H. Gardiner, *Ancient Egyptian Onomastica* [Oxford, 1947], I, 21*; Helck, *Zur Verwaltung*, pp. 277f.). The parallels from Canaanite courts render direct recourse to an Egyptian model unnecessary; cf. Zakar-Baal's letter-scribe: Gardiner, *Late Egyptian Stories*, p. 74:4; W. F. Albright, *Archaeology and the Religion of Israel* (4th ed.; Baltimore, 1956), p. 120.

5   Cf. the title in the Joseph story: Gen. 41:40, 43:19, 45:8, or Shebanyah's title in Isa. 22:15; cf. J. König, JBL, 48 (1929), 345; H. Donner, *Bi. Or.* 18 (1961), 45 n. 5. Why the title should be equated with Egyptian *č3ty*, 'vizier' (so de Vaux, RB, 48, 400ff.) and not with *imy-r pr wr*, 'chief steward,' escapes me. The parallel between Rekhmire's task of opening and shutting the doors of the king's house (J. H. Breasted, *Ancient Records of Egypt* [Chicago, 1906], II, secs. 676ff.) and what is said of Shebanyah in Isa. 22:21–22 is surely not to be taken seriously; the Isaiah passage is clearly to be understood metaphorically.

6   A list of functions in the king's administration, together with the names of current incumbents, is known from Babylonia during the reign of Nebuchadrezzar II: cf. J. B. Pritchard, *Ancient Near Eastern Texts Relating to the Old Testament* (2nd ed.; Princeton, 1955), pp. 307f.; cf. pp. 295f. From Egypt we have occasional lists of court and government officials which purport to be complete: e.g. in the Onomasticon of Amenemope, Gardiner, *Onomastica*, III, pl. 7, ll. 12ff.; I, 13*ff.; and the caption over princes and officials in the first court at Luxor in B. Porter and R. Moss, *Topographical Bibliography of Ancient Egyptian Texts, Reliefs and Paintings* (Oxford, 1929), II, 102 (for references). Neither of these, however, lists the offices for their own sake, in order to give a breakdown of the roster of court functionaries. The titles rather occur in a hyperbolic context in which the scribe insists upon the totality of the group in question. Thus the onomasticon, the very design of which was to include *all* creatures and things in the universe, lists 'god, goddess, male and female spirit, king, queen, king's-wife, king's-mother, king's-child, patricians, vizier, courtiers, king's eldest son, overseer of the host, letter-scribe of Horus-Mighty-Bull (the king), chamberlain of the Good God (the king), first herald of the king, fan-bearer on the right of the king, he who performs excellent work for the Lord of the Two Lands, overseer of the court officers of the king, chief of the bureau of his lord, king's-scribe in the palace, vizier and mayor of the city.' At this point a group of military titles appear. The list is redundant, and for all its overtones of completeness, spotty. As a vague reflection of the composition of the Egyptian court around 1100 B.C. it has some value, but it is markedly different in format and purpose from the lists for the reign of David or Solomon. The feeling persists with the present writer that the biblical lists are the product of secondary tabulation of names that the compiler culled from the scattered literary sources available to him, and in no way reflect a genuine document from the time of the United Monarchy.

have contained such officers, not in mimicry of Egyptian ways, but in fulfilment of the ordinary, day-to-day needs of the administration. With the possible exception of the Hebrew *mazkir*, however it is to be translated,[7] there is no need to invoke Egyptian inspiration. A similar doubt must surround the contention, thankfully not often mooted, that Egyptian architecture influenced the style of building under the United Monarchy.[8] Apart from the obvious fact that none of the royal structures has survived from the Jerusalem acropolis, the word pictures of them provided in the Bible conjure up purely Levantine archetypes.[9]

It seems more likely that David and Solomon were impressed by the practical aspects of Egyptian administration, rather than by its superficial manifestation in terms of hierarchy. In this respect attention naturally turns to what was perhaps the most striking innovation of the United Monarchy, usually ascribed to Solomon, viz. the taxation system.

Words denoting tax and taxation in Egyptian are many and varied, and reveal a complex means of collecting the annual dues and imposts. All units of production in the Egyptian economy, be they arable fields, staffs of priests, artisans' workshops, bodies of hunters and fishermen, or municipal officials and the towns they supervised, were obliged to render part of their produce or manufactured articles

---

7 *Mazkir* is usually derived from the Egyptian *wḥmw*, 'reporter, herald'; cf. de Vaux, RB, 48, 396f.; Begrich, ZAW, 58, 11ff.; Reventlow, *Theologische Zeitschrift*, 15, 161ff. Apart from a vague similarity in some translations of the two terms, the offices are not markedly similar. Admittedly we know next to nothing about the duties of the *mazkir*, and there is little point in insisting that what individual *mazkirs* are doing in 2 Kings 18:18, 36 and 2 Chron. 34:8 is part of their duties *as mazkir*. For the *wḥmw* it may be said that his function during the New Kingdom seems more in keeping with that of a private secretary who keeps the king informed, organizes the life of the court, and in general facilitates the king's movements and activities. If it can be shown that the *mazkir* was involved in the same tasks, a case may be made. But the sobering fact is, and it has been taken into account upon occasion by those who maintain the identity of the two, that the hey-day of the *wḥmw* in the royal administration was during the New Kingdom before 1100 B.C. Thereafter references peter out until, in the late Twenty-first Dynasty and under the Libyans, the *wḥmw* is conspicuous by his absence. If David were looking for models, would he not be more liable to copy from contemporary Egyptian titles than to choose an obsolescent function over a century out of date?

8 E.g. de Vaux, RB, 48, 395; M. Noth, *The History of Israel* (London, 1958), p. 207.

9 See most recently for the palace D. Ussishkin, IEJ, 16 (1966), 174ff.; for the temple Th. A. Busink, JEOL, VI (1967), 165ff. (both with full references to earlier literature).

in the form of a tax. In theory the tax was due the king, since he owned the land of Egypt; but in practice he apportioned it to the various institutions (temples, palaces, estates, garrisons, etc.) which were dependent upon him for their upkeep. And it was this prior allotment of the taxes, ever changing as land changed hands and new institutions came into being, and not the procedure for collection, that posed the complex problems for the Egyptian administration. The terms vary and overlap, depending upon their terms of references. When the tax consisted of grain, it could be called *šmw*, which simply means 'harvest,' but in many contexts it has to be rendered 'harvest tax.'[10] When the nuance of legal obligation predominated, the word *š3yt*, 'dues,' could be used, derived from the root *š3*, 'to command, ordain.'[11] A tax required from municipal officials might be called *ipw*, 'assessment.'[12] The impost on an individual could be termed his 'work' (*b3kw*), but when interest centered upon the actual levying of the tax, one might encounter his 'exaction' (*šdyt*).

When referring to the specific needs of an institution in victuals and materials which could be estimated with some exactitude beforehand, the Egyptians often used the noun *ḥtr*. This noun comes from a root meaning 'to bind' or 'to yoke (cattle or horses),[13] and hence the nuance of obligation to serve inherent in the term. The ad hoc nature of the tax, necessitating as it did a prior estimate, probably explains why the root came also to mean 'reckon, estimate';[14] and when followed by the direct object of the person taxed it could as easily be translated 'estimate the amount of tax due from.'[15] The ever-present qualifying phrase 'of every year' (*n tnw rnpt*) suggests 'annual levy' as the closest approximation in English to the noun *ḥtr*.[16]

The projects and institutions which our sources list as benefitting from the annual levy fall in the main under four heads: (1) temples

---

10 Sir A. H. Gardiner, *The Wilbour Papyrus* (Oxford, 1948), II, 24; for comment on
    Gardiner's translation, see K. Baer, JARCE, I (1962), 30 n. 43.
11 Erman, *Wörterbuch*, IV, 402f.
12 K. Sethe, *Urkunden des ägyptischen Altertums, IV Urkunden der 18. Dynastie*
    (Berlin, 1905–61), 1119:16, 1128:16 (hereinafter abbreviated *Urk.* IV).
13 Erman, *Wörterbuch*, III, 202:2–3.
14 Cf. *Urk.* IV, 1669:1, 1821:4–7; Berlin papyrus 9785, line 14 (published by A. H.
    Gardiner, ZAS, 43 [1906], 27ff.); Rhind Pap., 82:1 (published by A. B. Chase,
    L. Bull, and T. E. Peet, *The Rhind Mathematical Papyrus, British Museum
    10057 and 10058* [Oberlin, 1929]).
15 E.g. *Urk.* IV, 1442:8.
16 R. O. Faulkner, *A Concise Dictionary of Middle Egyptian* (Oxford, 1962), p. 181.

(which account for by far the majority of passages), (2) garrison posts and foreign settlements under royal authority, (3) workers in the quarries or on construction sites, and (4) royal residences and harems.

A temple might require a levy for the stocking of its altars with produce, or for the provision of livestock for sacrifice. Thus Thutmose III states, 'lo, My Majesty has given him (Amun) two *rȝ*-geese in the course of every day, as a permanent and eternal levy for my father Amun.'[17] In instructing the priests as to how they were to go about performing the cult for a statue of himself set up in the temple of Amun, the same king says, 'clothe my statue with linen, inasmuch as I have filled the treasury with fine linen [   ], offer to me all kinds of vegetables ... You shall give me roasts and choice cuts in accordance with the levy for me at the beginning of the seasons, (which) consists of cattle.'[18] In the Nauri decree Sety I describes how his Abydene temple was provided with cattle of various kinds, 'properly(?) levied at their several times, in accordance with the regulation of the divine book.'[19] Besides the victims for meat offerings grain was also requisitioned as a levy: Duwa-eneheh describes the fields of Amun which fell under his jurisdiction as 'reckoned in barley, calculated with respect to emmer, in the annual levy (destined) for the temple of [Amun].'[20] By extension the term *ḥtr* could be applied to any manufactured product or produce that was earmarked for a temple treasury. Thutmose III again states with respect to three cities in Galilee that they were 'assigned a levy of work throughout the year, (destined) for the offering endowment of my father Amun.'[21] In a letter dating from the Twentieth Dynasty the 'dues' (*šȝyt*) of the 'herdsmen of the offering table of Amun' are described as consisting of a wide range of items, some edible and some not, and all are qualified by the phrase 'a levy of everything which is required for the treasury of Amunrasonther.'[22] One of the important objects

17 *Urk.* IV, 745:11ff.; cf. H. Gauthier, *La grande Inscription dédicatoire d'Abydos* (Cairo, 1912), l. 86.

18 *Urk.* IV, 753:3ff.; cf. *Urk.* IV, 1395:1, and W. Erichsen, *Papyrus Harris I* (Brussells, 1933), p. 8 (l. 7, 4).

19 Nauri, 19–20 (C. E. Sander-Hansen, *Historische Inschriften der 19. Dynastie* [Brussells, 1933], p. 16); cf. Anastasi VI, 65–6 (Gardiner, *Late Egyptian Miscellanies*, p. 77).

20 *Urk.* IV, 1379:18–19.

21 *Urk.* IV, 744:7–8; cf. Urk. IV, 186:2–3; Erichsen, *Papyrus Harris I*, p. 33 (l. 28, 5).

22 P. Chester Beatty V, recto 7, 12–8, 6 (Gardiner, *The Wilbour Papyrus*, II, 57).

in the temple paraphernalia was the lamp which burned constantly before the shrine; and this along with its fuel of sesame oil was supplied by annual levy: 'established as an annual levy, one lamp in the presence of this god, throughout the course of every day.'[23] Even the income from the god's own estate could be termed 'a levy.' In the Harris papyrus a recurrent heading lists the 'property, dues (*š3yt*) and labour (*b3kw*) of the people of every staff of (temple name) whom the king (Ramses III) gave ... to their treasuries, storehouses and granaries, consisting of their annual levy.'[24] What follows is in fact the quotas of work of the sharecroppers, herdsmen, artisans belonging to, or found upon the lands of, that temple estate.

The offerings at special feasts a ruler might set up for a particular god were usually provided for by imposing an annual levy on somebody. Thus for one of the many feasts Thutmose III established in honour of his military victories, the offerings are listed as 'bread, long- and short-horned cattle, geese, incense, wine, fruit, and all fine things (acquired) by annual levy.'[25] In the Elephantine stela of Amenhotpe II the author tells us: 'His Majesty commanded that one day should be added for his mother (the goddess) Anukit, to her feast of Nubia when she rows upon the river, (and that it should be) provided with bread, beef, fowl, wine, incense, fruit, and all fine and pure things, by annual levy.'[26] Ramses III, according to the Harris papyrus, established 'festival offerings at the beginning of the seasons ... supplied with bread, beer, cattle, fowl, wine, incense, and fruit without number, (provided for) by a new levy ...';[27] and the same monarch endowed newly established feasts of Ptah by 'levying heavily against(?) the treasuries, storehouses, granaries and barns ... each year.'[28]

The Canaanite princes who were brought back to Egypt during the New Kingdom to be educated, and later sent back to their homes,

23 *Urk.* IV, 770:17–771:1; cf. R. A. Caminos, *The Chronicle of Prince Osorkon* (Rome, 1958), secs. 79, 84.

24 Erichsen, *Papyrus Harris I*, 14 (12a, 1–5), 37 (32a, 7–33), 58 (51b, 3ff.); a levy on unguent for the temple of Amun, *Urk.* IV, 641, nos. 24–6; the wine jars, whose dockets are so familiar from Malqata and Tell el-Amarna, and the wine they contained were part of the levy due the temple to which they were sent: cf. J. D. S. Pendlebury and others, *The City of Akhenaten*, III (London, 1951), pl. 87:67 ('chief vintager, responsible for (?) the levy').

25 *Urk.* IV, 746:12–14; cf. 196:7–8.

26 *Urk.* IV, 1299:6–9.

27 Erichsen, *Papyrus Harris I*, 8 (7, 4).

28 *Ibid.*, 54 (48, 10); cf. also Anastasi IV, 1a, 2 (Gardiner, *Late Egyptian Miscellanies*, p. 34).

were kept in Egypt at the king's expense;[29] but this expense was
covered by an annual levy. In the tomb of Rekhmire the owner is
shown watching the distribution of clothing to Syrian captives, and
the accompanying text refers to the captives as those 'brought by the
king as prisoners, their children being provided for by a levy of work,
and given linen, unguent, and clothing in accordance with the year[ly]
custom.'[30] And again we hear of prisoners of war, 'brought as his
Majesty's plunder, provided for by a levy on much food, and large
amounts of meat, cakes, clothing and unguent.'[31] In the great Dedi-
catory Inscription at Abydos Ramses II speaks of the temple of his
father as 'filled with servants and serfs, provided by levy with linen.'[32]
The settlements of the captured Sea Peoples inside Egypt were naturally under the close supervision of the king, and it is not surprising
to find them similarly provisioned. Ramses III says: 'I settled them
in fortresses and bound them with my name. Numerous were their
young recruits, in the hundreds of thousands, and for all of them I
established a levy of clothing and victuals, (reckoned) against the
treasuries and granaries each year.'[33]

Enclaves of hostages, settlements of captives, and garrisons of foreign auxiliaries were institutions not able to provide for themselves
within the existing framework of the Egyptian state, and therefore
the diversion of taxes to accomplish their upkeep was perfectly natural. In respect of provisioning, quarry work and construction work
manifested a similar need. The food and clothing of the necropolis
workmen at Thebes, for example, were provided by a levy raised by
the king;[34] and reference in a Twentieth Dynasty ostracon to 'the
offering cattle(?)[35] of Syria and Kush which are levied for the great

29 Egyptian texts of the New Kingdom often speak of the children of foreign chiefs
  being assigned to various temples, and this assignment is part of the levy for
  that temple; for example Amenhotpe III's temple to Montu at Thebes was 'filled
  with serfs and provided by levy with servants consisting of the children of the
  chiefs of all foreign lands' (*Urk.* IV, 1669:1); cf. also Sander-Hansen, *Historische
  Inschriften*, 7, 9ff.; 9, 17ff.; 11, 18ff.; 16, 1ff.; and *Urk.* IV, 1649:8ff.
30 *Urk.* IV, 1147:8–11.
31 *Urk.* IV, 1921:13–16.
32 *Mḥ.ti m tpw mrw ḥtrw ḥr sšrw*, which latter phrase could as easily be rendered
  'taxed in linen.' But on the close parallel of *Urk.* IV, 1921:14–16, and the similar
  sense of Harris 76, 8–9, I believe Ramses is telling how he provided for these
  serfs.
33 Erichsen, *Papyrus Harris I*,93 (76, 8–9).
34 Cf. P. Turin 557 (quoted in A. Erman and H. Grapow, *Belegstellen zu Wörterbuch* [Leipzig and Berlin, 1926–55], III, 201:17): 'they are not giving us the
  levies that Pharaoh, L.P.H., gave us!'
35 *Ḥrpyw*; "Abgaberinder" (Helck, *Zur Verwaltung*, 177 n. 4).

and august tomb of millions of years of Pharaoh, l.p.h.,'[36] suggests
that part of the workers' meat diet came from foreign sources.[37] The
workers at the Silsileh quarries under Sety I were provided with supplies at least in part through a levy on the local temple of Sobek:
'beef, wine, moringa-oil, *nḥḥ*-oil, ..., honey, figs, milk, fish and vegetables daily, likewise the large garlands of His Majesty, l.p.h., provided for him by the House of Sobek, lord of *Ḥni* (modern Silsileh),
(as?) a daily levy.'[38]

The same procedure in obtaining daily provisions for a body of
people not otherwise supplied is found in texts relating to the vict-
ualling of royal residences and harems. This illumines the purport of
Peftjauibast's promise to Piankhy: 'I shall labour with my subjects,
and Herakleopolis will be taxed for your house (*ᶜryt.k*).'[39] The vassal
king is here binding himself and his entire city to supply Piankhy's
palace by levy. Similarly, under the short-lived Levantine empire of
the Saite Twenty-sixth Dynasty, the produce of the Lebanons were
requisitioned by the residence. The Louvre stela of Psammetichus I's
fifty-second year informs us that 'their[40] chiefs were serfs of the palace with a royal courtier set over them, and their labour was levied
for the residence like the Land of Egypt.'[41] Although much broken,
two passages in the Haremhab decree refer to the levy on goods and
services due the harems and refectories of Pharaoh's residences,[42]
and the Gurob fragments from the close of the Nineteenth Dynasty
list quantities of fish levied upon a local dignitary, apparently for
the harem at Mi-wer.[43]

In generalizing texts, native Egyptians and foreigners within the
empire are placed on the same footing when it comes to the payment
of the levy. Thus Ramses III tells how, for his mortuary temple at
Medinet Habu, he 'imposed a levy on Upper and Lower Egypt alike,

---

36 G. Daressy, ASAE, 22 (1922), 75; J. Černý, *Ostraca Hiératiques* (Cairo Museum
    Catalogue; Cairo, 1930–5), no. 25764.
37 It is also possible that the cattle were intended for sacrifice at the time of the
    interment of the king.
38 Sander-Hansen, *Historische Inschriften*, 3:6. It is not clear whether the last
    phrase, *ḥtr m mnt*, refers to the entire menu-list, or simply to the garlands alone.
39 Piankhi Stela, 74–5; H. Schäfer, *Urkunden der älteren Äthiopenkönige* (Leipzig,
    1905), p. 50.
40 The antecedent seems to be 'terraces' (*ḥtiw*).
41 For bibliography of this well-known text see Porter and Moss, *Topographical
    Bibliography*, III (Oxford, 1931), 211.
42 *Urk.* IV, 2144:10–11, 2146:5–10.
43 P. Gurob, rt. 2, 11–13 (A. H. Gardiner, *Ramesside Administrative Documents*
    [London, 1948], p. 15), vs. 1b, 1–2 (*ibid.*, p. 17).

the Southland and Syria with their labours.'[44] Admittedly, references to the imposition of the ḥtr on foreigners seem to predominate. Ineni, the architect of Thutmose I, speaks of the 'tribute of all foreign lands which His Majesty gave to the temple of Amun as an annual levy';[45] and Hatshepsut states that 'every foreign land was a serf of Her Majesty and [their labour] was reckoned [for the temple of Amun], Lord of Karnak, as an annual levy.'[46] Minmose under Amenhotpe II informs us regarding the computation of the amounts: '[I trod Up]-per [Retenu], following my lord, and I reckoned the levy on [Upper] Retenu, consisting of silver, gold, lapis, all precious stones, chariots and horses without number, cattle and small game in their multi-tudes. I informed the chiefs of Retenu (about) [their] yearly labour. I reckoned the levy on the chiefs of Nubia, consisting of electrum ore(?), of gold, ivory, ebony and numerous vessels of mꜣmꜣ-wood, as an annual levy, like (that of) the serfs of his palace.'[47] But the im-balance is illusory, and should not be taken to mean that the levy was in any way a burdensome indemnity placed on conquered peo-ples. Inasmuch as the aggrandizement of empire had resulted in the 'widening of the boundaries of Egypt,' foreign lands had now become part of Egypt, and foreign town-rulers could be treated like Egyp-tian mayors.[48] Egyptian forms of taxation could now be extended to the provinces.

And it was mainly on mayors and other officials of roughly the same rank that the burden of the levy fell; for it was they who were held responsible for the exaction of the tax from the district under their authority. Normally the institution to which they sent in their levies would be in their own neighbourhood. When Thutmose III

44 Erichsen, *Papyrus Harris I*, 4 (4, 4–5).

45 *Urk.* IV, 70:4–6.

46 *Urk.* IV, 331:14–16; similarly *Urk.* IV, 186:2–3, 436:4–5, 503:8, 744:7–8, 931:8–10, 1236:17ff.; Koller, 4, 7 (Gardiner, *Late Egyptian Miscellanies*, p. 119).

47 *Urk.* IV, 1442:2–11.

48 This is clearly implied in the Haremhab decree where, among those elligible for service on the bench, 'mayors of the interior' (ḥꜣtyw-ꜥ nw ḥnw always signifies Egypt proper, the phrase envisages a kind of mayor (ḥꜣty-ꜥ) who is not 'of the interior.' And these are precisely the town-rulers of Palestine and Syria who, in the Amarna Letters, are termed ḥazannu (see A. L. Oppenheim and others, *The Chicago Assyrian Dictionary*, VI (Chicago, 1956), 163ff.). When this kind of official is referred to in a hieroglyphic inscription, it is ḥꜣty-ꜥ that ought to be found. And, in fact, in the Thirteenth Dynasty the ruler of Byblos does bear this title, which shows that at this period the nascent Egyptian empire included this city, and was already construed as an extension of the Egyptian borders; see J. von Beckerath, *Untersuchungen zur politischen Geschichte der zweiten Zwischenzeit in Ägypten* (Glückstadt and New York, 1965), pp. 107f.

instituted new offerings in the temple of Dedwen in Nubia he provided for them by 'authorizing an annual levy from the mayors and
reeves (*ḥkȝw-ḥwwt*) of Elephantine district in the Deep South.'[49] In
the Gurob fragments the fish consumed by the harem at Mi-wer were
levied from the mayors of the Fayum; thus we have records of 'the
receipt from the levy of fish which is (charged) against mayor [   ]
of the Southern Lake;[50] 300 buri-fish; to be made up(?),[51] 700; total,
1000'[52] and 'the receipt from the levy of fish which is (charged)
against mayor Paser of Mi-wer.'[53] Ramses III, in a passage translated
above,[54] imposed a levy for his new festal offerings on a group of un-
specified 'princes and controllers';[55] and in Haremhab's decree it is
stated that the ships destined to transport certain commodities to
the royal kitchens and harems, as well as divine offerings to the temples, were requisitioned as a *ḥtr* from the lieutenant-general of the
army.[56] The texts on the verso of the Turin Canon of kings, documents long neglected in studies touching on Egyptian methods of
taxation, constitute a series of tax lists of primary importance.[57]
Although in a woefully fragmentary state at present, these tables of
names and amounts, to judge from the wide range of places mentioned, probably once gave a complete list of individuals and institutions upon whom the levy for a particular purpose was placed.[58]
The beneficiary of the levy is not referred to in any way, but it is a
good guess that it was a royal residence, or perhaps the temple of
Amun.[59] The officials included among those obligated to pay the levy

---

49 Urk. IV, 196:7.
50 On this locality see Gardiner, *The Wilbour Papyrus*, II, 46; H. Gauthier, *Dictionnaire géographique* (Cairo, 1929), V, 123.
51 *Tm dmd*.
52 P. Gurob, rt. 2, 11–13 (Gardiner, *Ramesside Administrative Documents*, p. 15).
53 P. Gurob, vs. 1b, 1–2 (Gardiner, *ibid.*, p. 17).
54 Above, p. 147, n. 27.
55 *Srw rwǧw*; on the latter see Gardiner, *Onomastica*, I, 32*; *idem*, *Papyrus
Wilbour*, II, 21.
56 *Urk.* IV, 2144:10–11, 2146:5–10.
57 A. H. Gardiner, *The Royal Canon of Turin* (Oxford, 1959), pls. 5–9.
58 *Ḥtr* occurs in the document in the following places: iii, 10 (pl. 6, 'exact levy'
[*ḥtr mtr*]), v, 23 (pl. 7, 'the levy which is upon them' [*ḥtr wn ḥr.sn*]), viii, x 8, 9
(pl. 8, 'detail? of the levy on the southern and northern oases' [*tp n ḥtr wḥȝt rsyt
mḥtyt*]). Elsewhere the tax is also called 'his work' (*bȝkw.f*, iii, 1), 'the exact dues'
(*šȝyt mtrt*, iii, 4; iv, 20), 'dues of the staff' (*šȝyt n smdt*, iii, 22), 'the precise exaction' (*šdyt mtrt*, iii, 5), and 'his yearly dues: 1 cow' (*šȝy.f n rnpt kȝ l*, v, 25; vii, 1).
59 The provenance of the papyrus is not certainly known; but if it were Memphis
as some think (e.g. H. E. Winlock, *The Rise and Fall of the Middle Kingdom in
Thebes* [New York, 1947], p. 94), this might militate in favour of the palace.

were mayors,[60] lieutenant-[generals(?)],[61] scribes,[62] overseers of fortresses,[63] and controllers,[64] as well as such obscure officials as 'the
keeper of the brazier,'[65] and 'the keeper of natron.'[66] Groups of persons are listed as well as individuals. Thus 'the fishermen of the Lake
of Sobek,'[67] and the 'Medjay'[68] appear, while general entries such as
'every staff of the harbour'[69] and 'every town in the Southern District'[70] suggest that every settlement and guild had to bear an impost collectively, probably via the intermediary of their leader or
headman.

The fact that the levy was exacted mainly for the purpose of supplying provisions on a regular basis accounts for the ubiquitous occurrence of the phrase 'of every year,' for victuals had to be made
available without cessation when the time for their delivery fell due.
Those few texts which supply us with more details about how the
ḥtr was assessed indicate that, at least where daily provisions are in
question, the foodstuffs were reckoned on a day-to-day basis, and
requisitioned by the month. Supplies for annual or monthly feasts
would, of course, be demanded at their appointed times. Thus in one
of the decrees issued by the high-priest Osorkon for the temple of
Amun, ca. 834 B.C., the daily supply of castor oil for a lamp set in
the temple was requisitioned from three sources, each presumably
being responsible for four months of the year.[71] The 'Gold House of
Amun' and the 'Gateway of Alabaster' (or those responsible for their
upkeep) were to give 365 hin of castor oil each, and the Hour-priests
of Amun 485 hin per year, yielding approximately 3⅓ hin per day
for the lamp. In a second decree issued at the same time[72] Osorkon
makes provision for the incense and honey offerings of the god by
levying quantities of silver from six specified sources annually. By
implication each contributed for two months of the year. The reck-

---

60 Turin Canon, iii, 6, 13; vi, x 13.
61 *Ibid.*, i, 2; iii, 7; vi, x 14; in each case there is a break after *idnw*, so that the
   presence of *mš^c* cannot be verified.
62 *Ibid.*, iii, 8.
63 *Ibid.*, iv, 20; v, 16.
64 Charged with the supervision of frontier wells and forts: *ibid.*, iv, 3; vi, x 19;
   viii, x 1–6.
65 *S3w ꜥḥ*; a priestly title? *Ibid.*, iii, 1 (assessed at 5,000 fish).
66 *S3w ḥsmn*, *ibid.*, iii, 2 (assessed at 1,000 deben of gold). On this and the preceding title, see J. A. Wilson, JNES, 19 (1960), 299.
67 Turin Canon, iii, 5; iv, 18. The Fayum is intended.
68 *Ibid.*, vi, x 15.   69 *Ibid.*, iii, 22.
70 *Ibid.*, iii, 22.   71 Caminos, *Chronicle*, sec. 85.
72 *Ibid.*, sec. 79.

oning of the levy on the basis of daily needs is made plain time and again by the recurrence of the figure '365,' or multiples thereof, in yearly totals of offerings or exactions.[73]

The most detailed description extant of the imposition of an annual levy comes, interestingly enough, from the reign of Sheshonq I, a later contemporary of Solomon. On a stela found at Herakleopolis in 1907 and now in the Cairo Museum,[74] the king tells how he restored the daily sacrifice in the temple of Arsaphes in Herakleopolis, and specifies in detail the source of the levy. After the king's titulary (partly preserved), and a statement that he was already devising ways and means to benefit the cult of Arsaphes, the text continues:

> The king's son, the general Namlot, came into His Majesty's presence and said, 'the House of Arsaphes, the King of the Two Lands, has ceased (making) the daily ox-offering. I found it (the temple) fallen to ruin (from) what (it) had formerly been in the times of the ancestors. It would be well to have it resumed.'[75] Said His Majesty, 'may my *ku* praise thee, my son, who hath come forth from me! Thy heart is like the heart of him who begat thee, my body made young again! It is my father Arsaphes, the King of the Two Lands, the Lord of Herakleopolis, that makes sound every utterance of thine in his house, for ever!' A decree was issued in the Palace, L.P.H., to supply the House of Arsaphes, the King of the Two Lands, the Lord of Herakleopolis, and to restore to it this daily ox-offering, as it had been in the times of the ancestors. In proportion to his needs the decree placed a levy for the daily ox-offering on the towns and villages of the Herakleopolite (nome), without exception(?).[76] It shall not be discontinued for him for ever and ever. The King of Upper and Lower Egypt, the Lord of the Two Lands, *Ḥǧ-ḫpr-rᶜ Stp.n-rᶜ*, Lord of Diadems, *mry-Imn* Sheshonq, given life like Re for ever.

There follows the 'quota(?)[77] of the levy which consists of 365 oxen throughout the year, (now) and for ever more.' The remainder of

---

73 Besides the passages just cited, see *ibid.*, sec. 93 (730 geese to two Theban temples yearly), and cf. A. Badawy, ZÄS, 87 (1962), 82f., as well as the 365 bulls of the yearly quota due the temple of Arsaphes (see below).

74 See Porter and Moss, *Topographical Bibliography*, IV (Oxford, 1934), 121 for literature, to which add P. Tresson, *Mélanges Maspero*, I (Cairo, 1934–8), 817ff.

75 Lit. 'cause that it go forth.'

76 Text doubtful; perhaps lit. 'without the occurrence of an erasure(?) among them.'

77 *Tp n ḫtr*; cf. above, n. 58.

the text is arranged in twelve monthly sections with a final section for the five epagomenal days, and under each are listed the officials and towns responsible for supplying the temple during that month, together with the amount of their levy.[78]

The parallel between Sheshonq's and Solomon's provisioning systems is striking. Like Sheshonq, Solomon too divided a specified territory into twelve districts,[79] requiring each to furnish victuals and materials for one month of the year. As in the case of the Egyptian $ḥtr$, the levy on the Israelites was for the purpose of provisioning: (1 Kings 4:7f.) 'Solomon had twelve officials over all Israel to supply food for the king and his household, each man being responsible for the supply during one month of the year,' (1 Kings 5:7) 'These officials, one per month, supplied food to king Solomon, and to all those who had access to king Solomon's table, so that they lacked nothing.' The figures for grain and cattle transmitted in 1 Kings 5:2 as daily quotas look much more like *monthly* require-

---

78 The twelve sections are not based ostensibly on geographical divisions, save for the first three months of *shmu* (where towns alone are listed); rather the sections comprise the titles of certain officials, or groups of artisans (fourth month of *shmu*), who are responsible for a certain number of cattle. Nevertheless, a closer examination will reveal a geographical grouping of officials (e.g. for the fourth month of *akhet* the titles indicate a connection with the temple estate of Arsaphes, for the first month of *proyet* three functionaries in the temple of Khnum are named, and for the second month of *proyet* the four titles apparently connect their bearers with the chapel of the commandant); and a moment's reflection will disclose that in the quasi-feudal system of the Libyans behind each title lay an estate or a parcel of land of some size. This was probably not true for the artisans, or for the lowly officials; but these may well have been allowed to discharge their obligation in some other form. The discrepancy between the number of cattle mentioned in the text translated, viz. 365, and the actual total of the thirteen sections (243, with some lacunae) does not concern us here.

79 On the twelve districts see A. Alt, AFO, 18 (1950), 21f.; *idem*, *Kleine Schriften zur Geschichte Israels*, II (Munich, 1964), 76ff.; Noth, *The History of Israel*, pp. 211f.; Bright, *A History of Israel*, pp. 200f.; de Vaux, *Institutions* I, 206f.; Eissfeldt, 'The Hebrew Kingdom,' 55f.; G. E. Wright, *Eretz Israel*, 8 (1967), 58*ff.; Albright, *Archaeology and the Religion of Israel*, pp. 121f., 140. It is dangerous and misleading to interpret the system as an arrangement of provinces, since this term to us moderns has a different connotation. Significantly the text of 1 Kings 4:7ff. refers to the officials, not to their bailiwicks, which were wholly artificial and were set up solely for taxation purposes. If we had a document from the United Monarchy similar in intent to the stela of Sheshonq, we should probably find that it was a group of officials and towns that was listed by month, and that it was by inference that we extracted the underlying framework of districts.

ments: 'Solomon's daily provision was as follows: 30 *kor* of fine flour, 60 *kor* of meal, 10 fat oxen, and 20 pasture oxen ...'[80] One wonders whether what has been preserved with a clear aura of the gargantuan about it,[81] as the fare of the king's table, was not originally the daily offering list of the House of Yahweh under the United Monarchy. One head of cattle, on this hypothesis, would have constituted the morning holocaust, exactly as in the Egyptian temples.[82] Again, like the Egyptians, Solomon employed the levy to stock his garrison posts with supplies: (1 Kings 5:8) 'and each man according to his assignment had barley and straw brought for the horses and chariots, to the place where they were stationed.' The stocking of garrison posts by means of the annual *ḥtr* was well known in Palestine under the Egyptian empire. The upkeep of the garrisons in the Egyptian port cities was, under Thutmose III, the responsibility of the Canaanite kinglets of the Lebanon region;[83] and without a doubt the maintenance of such Egyptian strong-points as Gaza[84] and Beth-shean[85] was assigned as a levy to the cities of Palestine. In northern Galilee three cities and their environs were annexed by Thutmose III to the estate of Amun, and their produce taken to Egypt as an annual levy.[86]

It is highly likely that Solomon was consciously using this common

80 The text continues with sheep and a fantastic variety of wild animals.
81 The passage occurs after the reasonably reliable 'Succession Document' has abruptly come to an end (1 Kings 2:46), in that part of the account of Solomon's reign which is folkloristic in tone, and has little interest in specific historical events recounted chronologically; M. Noth, *Überlieferungsgeschichtliche Studien* (Tübingen, 1957), pp. 66f.
82 De Vaux, *Institutions*, II, 468f.
83 *Urk.* IV, 700:6–9: 'Lo, the harbours were provided with everything in accordance with their levy, pursuant to the yearly practice for them, together with the produce of Lebanon . . .'
84 For Gaza as an Egyptian strong-point and administrative centre for southern and central Palestine, see W. Helck, MDOG, 92 (June 1960), 6f., 12; E. Edel and W. F. Albright, *Geschichte und altes Testament* (Tübingen, 1953), pp. 50f.; W. F. Albright, 'The Amarna letters from Palestine,' ch. 20 of vol. II of the *Cambridge Ancient History* (Cambridge, 1966), 7; for explicit reference to the garrison resident there, cf. H. Goedicke and E. F. Wente, *Ostraka Michaelides* (Wiesbaden, 1962), no. 85 (pl. 93), in which the scribe of the garrison *Ypwy* writes to a colleague about, inter alia, 'the feast of Anath of Gaza,' preparation for which he was responsible. For the suggestion that Gaza was the site of a royal residence under the Ramessides, see E. Edel, MDOG, 92 (June 1960), 18.
85 On Beth-shean see most recently H. O. Thompson, BA, 30 (1967), 110ff.
86 *Urk.* IV, 186, 744; see above, p. 146.

Egyptian means of taxation for supplying the organs of a central government with sustenance.[87] Whether he was directly inspired by contemporary Egyptian practice, or whether he derived it indirectly through the practice of the former Egyptian empire in Canaan, is a moot point. Certainly, while it may have been well known to the Canaanites under the Hebrew empire, it proved new and intolerable to the rustic Israelites.

---

87 Babylonian parallels to Solomon's provisioning system have been suggested (cf. R. P. Dougherty, AASOR, 5 [1923–4], 23ff.), but these provide only the vaguest analogy: cf. de Vaux, *Institutions*, I, 207.

Cylinder C of
Sîn-šarra-iškun, a New Text
from Baghdad

A. K. GRAYSON

It is appropriate that in a volume dedicated to Professor F. V. Winnett who has spent so much time in the Near East gathering text material an article containing a new cuneiform inscription from Iraq should appear.[1] As it turns out, the new text forms the missing link in the so-called Cylinder C of Sîn-šarra-iškun, one of the last kings of Assyria (?–612 B.C.),[2] and with the additional material a reasonably coherent narrative is now available. I have, therefore, edited the whole cylinder in this article. The text, IM 3209 + 3249, is in the Iraq Museum, Baghdad. A copy, prepared by J. J. A. van Dijk, is scheduled to appear in TIM 7. Since van Dijk's time in Iraq I have collated and recopied the inscription. I am grateful to Professor van Dijk for first bringing the text to my attention. For permission to collate the tablet and prepare a new copy and for their helpful and friendly hospitality I am indebted to Dr Isa Salman el-Hamid, Director General of Antiquities, to Dr Fauzi Rachid, director of the Iraq Museum, and to the museum staff.

The reign of Sîn-šarra-iškun is a crucial one in Assyrian history for during the short time he was on the throne the empire, the name of which only a few years before had struck terror into the hearts of Babylonians, Elamites, Hebrews, and Egyptians, was on its death-

1 I am grateful to the Canada Council for providing the funds for my trip to the Near East in the spring of 1969. The abbreviations used in this article are according to the list given in the *Chicago Assyrian Dictionary* [CAD], 1/2 (A) (Chicago, 1968), with the following addition: TIM = *Texts in the Iraq Museum* (Baghdad, 1964–).
2 Cf. J. A. Brinkman in A. Leo Oppenheim, *Ancient Mesopotamia* (Chicago and London, 1964), p. 347.

bed. At the end of Sîn-šarra-iškun's reign Nineveh fell to the Medo-
Babylonian coalition (612 B.C.) and within a few years Assyria had
completely disappeared as a political entity. It is a dark period for
the modern historian. There are few sources and many problems as a
perusal of recent literature will show.[3] Any new document from this
time is a welcome addition, and thus the importance of the text from
Baghdad far exceeds its modest size.

A bibliography of the inscriptions of Sîn-šarra-iškun will be found
in M. Falkner, AfO, 16 (1952–3), 305–7, and in R. Borger, JCS, 19
(1965), 68 and 76–8. Also note the prayer (šu-íl-la) of Sîn-šarra-iškun
to Marduk, BM 123395, mentioned in W. G. Lambert and A. R.
Millard, *Catalogue of the Cuneiform Tablets in the Kouyunjik Collection of the British Museum, Second Supplement* (London, 1968), p. 22.
Of special significance for Cylinder C are: Cylinder A (abbreviation:
Cyl. A): bibliography in Falkner, AfO, 16 (1952–3), 305; and Cylinder B (abbreviation: Cyl. B): bibliography and edition (without
translation!) in Borger, JCS, 19 (1965), 76–8. As will be seen, many
restorations can be made in Cylinder C on the basis of parallel passages in Cylinders A and B.

The major contribution of the new text is coherency. For the first
time the various fragments of Cylinder C can be accurately placed
and most of the narrative can be reconstructed. Only one significant
lacuna is left, in the middle of the text, and even here only a few lines
at the most are lacking. In addition to being able to properly place
pieces already known to belong to Cylinder C, two previously uniden-
tified fragments (DT 64+ and K 8541 – see the source list below) are
now recognized to be part of this cylinder.[4] In addition, the Baghdad
text provides some new words and phrases and a whole new section
at the end (lines 21'–27'), consisting of curses, which does not appear
in the other exemplars.

The typology and content of Cylinder C are normal for a Neo-
Assyrian royal inscription. Typologically, there are four main divisions: subject (1–2'), temporal clause (3'–11'), predicate (12'–15'),
blessings and curses (16'–27'). Basically the inscription reads: 'I,

---

3   For the fall of Assyria and the reign of Sîn-šarra-iškun in particular, the most
important of the recent studies are: M. Falkner, AfO, 16 (1952–3), 305–10;
R. Borger, JCS, 19 (1965), 59–78; J. Oates, *Iraq*, 27 (1965), 135–59; W. von
Soden, ZA, 58 (1967), 241–55.
4   Borger's suggestion in JCS, 19 (1965), 68, to call these two fragments 'Cylinder
D' is thereby automatically invalid. The two cylinder fragments 80-7-19, 13 and
K 8540 + 82-5-22, 28 (King, CT 34, 3f.) are hardly part of Cylinders A to C and
therefore represent yet another or other cylinders.

Sîn-šarra-iškun, when the gods did certain things for me, rebuilt a certain structure. May a later prince who respects my inscription be blessed, but he who mistreats it, may he be cursed.' The section I call 'subject' is by far the longest (over twenty-five lines) and contains numerous royal epithets. The predicate, which theoretically is the whole reason for the inscription, is the shortest (four lines). Cylinder C is in the first person throughout whereas both Cylinders A and B waver between first and third person. The content concerns restoration work upon a structure which is called 'the building of alabaster, the western entrance which [*leads*] to *the p*[*alace* ...], [(the structure) which] Sennacherib ... [had built].' Falkner, AfO, 16 (1952–3), 306, has suggested that this structure is the west wing of the southwest palace of Sennacherib at Nineveh. Since all references to a building adorned with alabaster (*gišnugallu*) in Sennacherib's inscriptions are to his palace,[5] I believe Falkner is probably right.

A serious attempt to sort out the various cylinder fragments of Sîn-šarra-iškun was made as early as 1916 by M. Streck, Asb., pp. CCVII–CCXVI, CDXCIVf., 382–9, and 838–43. A bibliography of publications earlier than 1916 is given by Streck. Copies of the fragments of Cylinder C which were in the British Museum were published in 1914 by L. W. King, CT 34, 2f. and 5–7. A translation of the cylinder fragments published by King appeared in 1927 in D. D. Luckenbill's *Ancient Records of Assyria and Babylonia*, vol. 2 (Chicago, 1927), pp. 409–13. A bibliography of and comments upon Cylinder C will also be found in Falkner, AfO, 16 (1952–3), 306. For Cylinder C we actually have five fragments (a bibliography and explanation of symbols appears below), which represent a maximum of five or a minimum of three exemplars.[6] All but one of the exemplars are cylinder fragments. The exception, which is the text (*e*) from Baghdad, is on a tablet but was copied from a cylinder as a scribal note on the tablet indicates: '(Inscribed) cylinder from the wall of Nineveh.' Apart from one major and several minor variations, the exemplars are exact duplicates.[7] The major variation is the omission

---

5 D. D. Luckenbill, OIP 2, 106:16, 110:41, 123:36. The source of *gišnugallu* is mentioned in the same work on 107:54 and 121:43. Objects of *gišnugallu* are mentioned on 62:90 and 106–8:32, 65, 69. In all these references note that Luckenbill has read *parûtu*, not *gišnugallu*.

6 *a*, *b*, and *e* represent three distinct exemplars. *c* and *d* are distinct from one another. *c* could not belong to *a* if my suggested reconstruction for lines 17′f. (see subvariants) is correct, but it could belong to *b*. *d* could belong to either *a* or *b*.

7 In a few cases some exemplars (*a* and *c*) appear to omit certain lines (*a* omits 8′ and 11′, and *c* omits 6 and 11) but it may be, in at least some instances, that the scribes simply squeezed the signs closer together. Cf. the commentary to line 12.

from *a* and *c* (*b* and *d* are not sufficiently preserved to be relevant to this discussion) of the curses. These appear only in *e* (ll. 21′–27′). I have no explanation for this. All of the fragments come from Nineveh.[8] Dates are preserved on two of the exemplars, *a* and *e*. The dates are different and, on the basis of Falkner's study of post-canonical eponyms in AfO, 17 (1954–6), pp. 100–20, *a* was written in 617 B.C. (*līmu* of Nabû-tappūti-ālik) and *e* was written two years earlier in 619 B.C. (*līmu* of Bēl-aḫa-uṣur).[9] It is worth noting that copies of Cylinder A have the same date as *e*, viz. 619 B.C. (*līmu* of Bēl-aḫa-uṣur).[10] There are three scribal errors in *e*.[11]

SOURCES FOR CYLINDER C

		Lines
a	Ki 1904-10-9, 352 + Ki 1904-10-9, 353	
	King, CT 34, 2f.	1–6, 6′–20′
b	81-7-27, 8 + 82-5-22, 26	
	King, CT 34, 7	1′–12′
c	DT 64 + 82-5-22, 27	
	King, CT 34, 5f.	1–17, 17′–20′
d	K 8541	
	King, CT 34, 5	12–23
e	IM 3209 + 3249	
	van Dijk, TIM 7	1–21, 16′–27′

TRANSLITERATION

In the following transliteration ideograms are distinguished according to the system of W. von Soden and W. Röllig, *Das Akkadische Syllabar* (AnOr 42; 2nd ed., Rome, 1967), pp. 75f. In the translation square brackets are used sparingly since the reader can always check the transliteration to see exactly what is preserved and what is restored.

8 The provenance of *e*, the Baghdad tablet, itself is unknown but the scribal note quoted above leaves no doubt as to the original location of the cylinder from which it was copied.
9 That two duplicate inscriptions recording the same building operation were written two years apart is not a unique phenomenon. Cf. the Oriental Institute Prism and the Taylor Prism of Sennacherib (A. K. Grayson, AfO, 20 [1963], 83) where exactly the same time interval is attested.
10 See Falkner, AfO, 16 (1952–3), 305.
11 All three errors are in sign forms. ŠAR and RU (lines 22′ and 26′ respectively) are badly inscribed. BALA in line 27′ must be an error (see the commentary).

1   *a-na-ku* ^{md}*Sîn*(en.zu)*-šarra-iškun*^{un} *šarru rabû šarru dan-nu*
    šàr kiššati(šú) *š*[*àr* ^{kur}] ^d*A ššur*^{ki}

2   *ni-iš īnē*^{II} ^d*A ššur* ^d*En-líl* ^d*Nin-líl šakkanakku*(gìr.nitá) *mut-nin-nu-ú* ^{lú}[x]x *É-šár-ra*

3   *ma-al-ku šuk-nu-šu i-tu-ut kun lìb-bi* ^d*Sîn*(XXX) ^d*Nin-gal*
    ^d*Šamaš u* ^d*A-a na-ram* ⌜^d⌝ [*Marduk* ^d*Zēr-bān*]*i-tum* ^d*Nabû*
    ^d*Tašmētu*(lál)

4   *tab-šu-ut* ^d*Iš-tar a-ši-bat Ninua*^{ki} ^d*Iš-tar a-ši-bat Arba-ìl*^{ki}
    mi-gir [^d*Nergal*] ⌜*ù*⌝ ^d*Nusku*

5   [*šá* ^d*A ššur* ^d*Ni*]*n-líl ù ilāni*^{meš} *rabûti*^{meš} *bēlī*^{meš}*-ia ina bi-rit*
    maš-ši-ia ki-niš i[*p-pal-su-ni-ma is-su-qu-n*]*i a-na šarru-u-ti*

6   *za-n*[*i-nu*]*-*⌜*ú*⌝*-ti kiš-šat ma-ḫa-zi šangu*(é.bar)*-ú-t*[*i gi-mir*
    eš]*-re-e-*[*t*]*i*

7   *re-ᵓ-ú-u*[*t*] *nap-ḫar ṣal-mat qaqqadi e-pe-šu iq-bu-u-ni*

8   *ki-m*[*a*] *abi u* [*ummi i*]*t-ta-*[*n*]*ar-ru-in-ni-ma i-na-r*[*u a-a-bi-ia*
    ú-šam-qí-tú] *ga-ri-ia*

9   *ṭ*[*a*]*-biš ú-še-šib-u-in-ni ina* ^{giš}[*kussê šarru-u-ti abi*] *bāni-ia*

10 ^d*É-a an* x *ilāni*^{meš} *a-na e-nu-ti kiš-šá-ti ib-nu-i*[*n-ni ina nap-ḫar*]
    x ru *nab-ni-ti*

11 ^d*Sîn*(XXX) *šàr a-ge-e a-na kun-ni išdē māti šu-*[*te-šur ba-ᵓ-ú-la-a-ti a-ge-e bēlu-u*]*-ti e-pir-an-*[*ni*]

12 ^{giš}*ḫaṭṭi šarru-u-ti ú-šat-me-eḫ rit-tu-u-a*

13 ^d*Nin-líl a-ši-bat Ninua*^{ki} *An-tum* x [... ... *ul-l*]*i*(?) *rēšī*^{meš}*-ia*

14 *eṭ-lu šu-pu-ú a-a-ru šu-t*[*u-ru*(?) (*a-ḫi-iz ṭè-e-me u mil-ki*)
    mu-ta]*-mu-ú dam-qa-a-ti*

15 [*lìb-b*]*u rap-šú ka-raš ta-šim-t*[*i šá at-mu-šú eli* ...] *ar-ma-niš*
    ṭābū

16 [*šá*(?)] ⌜*ú*⌝*-sa-a-ti u ta-ḫa-zu* [... ...]*-ru du-un-qu-šu*

17 [...] x [... ...] x *zik-ri-šú-un*

18 [... ...] x [... ...] *ma*(?) *šu*(?) bi

19 [... ...] lu x [...] *rēšī*^{meš}*-šú*

20 [*mār* ^m*A ššur-bāni-apli šarru rabû šarru dan-nu šàr kiššati*(šú)
    šàr ^{kur} ^d*A ššur*^{ki}] *šar₄ Šumeri*^{ki} *ù* [*Akkadî*^{ki} *šar₄*] ⌜*kib-rat*⌝
    erbettim^{tim}

21 [*mār* ^{md}*A ššur-aḫa-iddina*^{na} *šarru rabû šarru dan-nu šàr*
    kiššati(šú) *šàr* ^{kur} ^d*A ššur*^{ki} *šakkanak*(gìr.nitá) *Bābili*^{ki} *šàr*
    Šumeri^{ki}] ⌜*ù*⌝ *Akkadî*^{ki}

22 [*mār* ^{md}*Sîn-aḫḫē*^{meš}*-erība šarru rabû šarru dan-nu šàr kiššati*(šú)
    šàr ^{kur} ^d*A ššur*^{ki} *rubû la šá-n*]*a*(?)*-an*

23 [... ...] x
Lacuna

1′   [... ...] x DÙG.GA *iḫ-ti-*x x [x] x [...] *ban*(?) *ni k*[*i*(?) ... ...]

2′ [... ...]-ú-tu ilāni^meš rabûti^meš pit-lu-ḫa-ku áš-ra-te-šú-nu
   áš-te-ɔ-ú ú-sal-lu-ú bēlu-u[t-su-nu (...)]

3′ [ul-tu ^dAššur ^dBēl ^dNabû ^dSîn ^dŠamaš] ⌈^d⌉ A-a i-zi-zu-ma
   ú-sa-at dum-qí e-pu-šu-ú-ni ki-mu-ú-a i-tap-pa-lu i-na-ru
   a-a-bi-i[a ...]

4′ [... ... na]krī^meš-ia ik-mu-ú a-a-ab ^kur Aš-šur^ki la ma-gi-ru-ti
   šarru-ti-ia iṣ-bu-t[u₄ ...]

5′ [... ...] x x im meš ti-bu-ti-ia ú-šab-bi-ru kab-[...]

6′ [ina rē]š šarru-ú-ti-ia ina maḫ-re-e palê-ia ša ina ^giškussê
   šarru-ú-ti [ūšibū]

7′ [šá za-na-a]n ma-ḫa-zi šuk-lul eš-re-e-ti dūrāni^meš da-ád-me ^kur
   Aš-šur^ki [šu-te-šur]

8′ [(par-ṣi ki-du-de-e)] x-e-ri ka-a-a-an uš-ta-da-na [kar-šú-u-a]

9′ [... il]āni^meš šá ap-tal-la-ḫu-šú-nu-ti ilu-us-su-nu [...]

10′ [bēl/ēpiš e]n-ni-ti-ia de-e-ni i-pu-šu-ma eli ṣēri ⌈ú(?)⌉-[...]

11′ [... ...]-x-in-ni [...]

12′ [ina ūm]e^me-šú bīt ^na4gišnugalli ni-rib amurri(im.mar.tu) ša a-na
   ē[kalli(?) ...]

13′ [... ^md]Sîn(XXX)-áḫḫē^meš-erība šàr ^kur[Aš]-šur^ki abi abi
   bāni-i[a ēpušū]

14′ [ēnaḫma an-ḫu-u]s-su ad-ki ul-t[u uššē-šú]

15′ [a-di gaba-dib-bi-šú ...]-x-im-ma ši-kit-ta-šú ú-[rab-bi(?) (...)]

16′ [rubû] arkû^ú i-na šarrāni^meš ^ni mārī^m[eš-ia e-nu-ma bītu šú-a-tú
   in-n]a(?)-ḫu(?)-m[a(?)]

17′ [il-la-ku la-ba-riš an]-ḫu-us-su lu-ud-diš [mu-ša]r-ú [ši]-ṭir
   šumi-ia

18′ ([...]) ⌈ù mu-šar-ú ši-ṭir⌉ šu-me ša ^mdSîn(XXX)-[áḫḫē^meš-erība
   šàr ^kur Aš-šur]^k[i] ⌈abi abi⌉ bāni-ia li-mur-ma

19′ ⌈šamna⌉ lip-šu-uš niqâ liqqi^qí it-ti mu-šar-e ši-ṭir šumi-šú
   liš-kun

20′ ^dAššur ^dNin-líl ik-ri-bi-šú i-šim-mu-u

21′ ša mu-šar-u ši-ṭi[r šumi-ia u]l-tú áš-ri-šú ú-nak-ka-ru

22′ it-ti mu-šar-e ši-[ṭir] šumi-šú la i-šak-ka-⌈nu⌉

23′ ^dAššur ^dNin-líl ^dSîn(XXX) ^dŠamaš ^dM[ardu]k ^dZēr-bāni-tum
   ^dNábû ^dTašmētu(lál) ^dIštàr šá Ninua^ki

24′ ^dŠar-rat kid-mu-ri ^dIštàr šá ⌈Arba-ìl⌉^ki ilāni^meš rabûti^meš šá
   šamê u erṣetim^tim

25′ ^giškussâ-šú li-šá-bal-ki-tú li-ru-ru palâ-šú

26′ ^gišḫaṭṭa-šú li-ṭi-ru idē^II-šú lik-su-u ina šapal(ki.ta) ^lúnakri-šú
   li-še-ši-bu-uš ka-me-iš

27′ ag-giš li-ru-ru-šú-ma šum-šú zēra-šú pirḫa(! text: BALA)-šú
   na-a[n-n]ab-šú ina nap-ḫa[r māt]āti([kur].kur) li-ḫal-li-q[u]

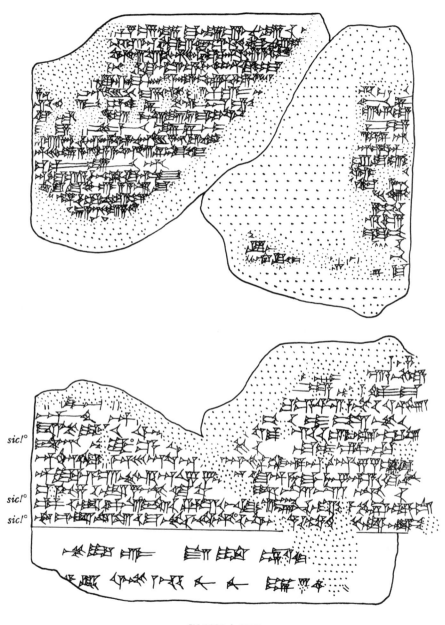

sic!°

sic!°
sic!°

IM 3209 + 3249

TOP: obverse; BOTTOM: reverse

Scribal Note on e

mu-šar-ú ša dūr Ninua^{ki} ([...])
(Inscribed) cylinder from the wall of Nineveh.

Date on a

^{iti}*Duʾūzu*(šu.gar.numun.na) *li-mu* ^{md}*Nabû-tap-pu-ti-*⌜*a*⌝*-[lik]*
Month of Tammuz, eponym of Nabû-tappūti-ālik.

Date on e

[ⁱ]^{ti} *Ulūlu*(kin) *lim-mu* ^m*Bēl-áha-úṣur* ^{lú}*šākin pān* [*ēkal*]*li*([k]ur)
Month of Elul, eponym of Bēl-aha-uṣur, palace overseer.

TRANSLATION

Subject

1   I, Sîn-šarra-iškun, great king, mighty king, king of the universe, king of Assyria, favourite of Aššur, Enlil, (and) Ninlil; pious governor, [...] of Ešarra, devout prince, chosen of the steadfast Sîn, Ningal, Šamaš, and Aia; beloved of [Marduk, Ṣarpan]ītu, Nabû, (and) Tašmētu; ... *of* Ištar who dwells in
5   Nineveh (and) Ištar who dwells in Arbail; chosen of [Nergal] and Nusku; *the twin* [whom Aššur,] Ninlil, and the great gods my lords [gazed upon] steadfastly [and selected] for sovereignty; they charged me with the task of providing for all the cult centres, with the priesthood [of every] shrine, with the shepherding of the entire black-headed (people); as father and [mother] they have always cared for me, slain [my enemies (and) felled] my opponents; graciously they had me ascend the
10 [royal throne of the father,] my begetter; Ea, ... of the gods, created [me, of all] creatures, for lordship of the universe; Sîn, king of the crown, placed upon me [the lordly crown] (and) put in my hand the royal sceptre to hold steadfast the foundations of the land (and) to [properly direct the population]; Ninlil who dwells in Nineveh, Antu [... ...] exalted me; famous man, [*exceptional*] male, [(endowed with insight and counsel), one who
15 speaks] well, magnanimous, perceptive, [whose speech] pleases [...] like the (aromatic) *armannu* (tree); [*whose*] help and battle [... ...] his good fortune, [... ...] their words, [... ...] his head;

20   [son of Aššurbanipal, great king, mighty king, king of the uni-
      verse, king of Assyria,] king of Sumer and [Akkad, king of] the
      Four Quarters;

21   [son of Esarhaddon, great king, mighty king, king of the uni-
      verse, king of Assyria, governor of Babylon, king of Sumer] and
      Akkad;

22   [son of Sennacherib, great king, mighty king, king of the uni-
      verse, king of Assyria,] unrivalled [prince];

Lacuna

2'   [... ...] I ever revere the great gods, I seek (oracles in) their
      dwellings, I pray to [their] lordship:

Temporal Clause

3'   [When Aššur, Bēl, Nabû, Sîn, Šamaš,] (and) Aia aided me by
      doing me a kind favour, they always acted (lit. answered) in
      my stead, they slew my enemies, [... ...] they bound my adver-
      saries, they captured the enemies of Assyria who would not ac-
      cept my sovereignty [... ...] ... of the attack against me they

5'   shattered [...]; [in] my accession year, at the beginning of my
      reign when I [ascended] the royal throne, [when] I constantly
      deliberated upon [providing] for the cult centres, perfecting the
      regions, fortresses, (and) settlements of Assyria, (and) [prop-
      erly directing the (ordinances, rites, and)] *offerings*; [when] the

10'   gods, whose divinity I ever revere, [...] pronounced judgment
      upon [those who] sinned against me and over the open country
      they [... ...]:

Predicate

12'   [At] that [time] the building of alabaster, the western entrance
      which [*leads*] to *the p*[*alace* ...], [(the structure) which] Senna-
      cherib, king of Assyria, grandfather of my begetter, [had built,
      had become dilapidated and] I removed its [rubble]. [I] *rebuilt it*

15'   from [top to bottom] and [*enlarged*] its size.

Blessings and Curses

16'   May a later [prince] among the kings, my offspring, [when that
      building] becomes dilapidated [and goes to ruin]: may he re-
      store the damage; may he see my inscribed cylinder and the in-
      scribed cylinder of Sennacherib, [king of Assyria,] grandfather

of my begetter; may he anoint (them) with oil; may he make
sacrifices; may he place (them) with his (own) inscribed cylin-
20' der; then will Aššur (and) Ninlil heed his prayers.
21' But he who removes my inscribed cylinder from its place (and)
does not replace (it) together with his (own) inscribed cylinder:
may Aššur, Ninlil, Sîn, Šamaš, Marduk, Ṣarpanītu, Nabû,
Tašmētu, Ištar of Nineveh, Šarrat-kidmuri, Ištar of Arbail, the
great gods of heaven and underworld, overturn his throne,
curse his reign, take from him the sceptre, bind his arms, (and)
make him sit in bonds at the feet of his enemy; angrily may
27' they curse him and eradicate from all lands his name, his seed,
his offspring, (and) his progeny.

VARIANTS

4	*a* has *a-ši-bat* ᵘʳᵘ*Ninua*
6	*c* appears to omit the line
7	*c* has *iq-bu-ni*
11	*c* appears to omit the line
12	*e* has *rit-tu-um*(?)-*ma*(?)
16	*e* has -*šú*
18	*d* appears to omit the line
20	*e* seems to have [*erbetti*ⁱ]ⁱ
6'	*a* has *i-na maḫ-re-e*
7'	*a* has *eš-rit dūrāni* ᵐᵉˢ ⁿⁱ
8'	*a* appears to omit the line
9'	*a* has *ša*
10'	*a* has *e-pu-šu-ma*
11'	*a* appears to omit the line but (since widely spaced in *b*) it could have been squeezed in at the end of 10' or beginning of 12'
17'f.	Traces of the end of two lines in *c* could be read: [... ... *lu-ud*]-*diš* [... ... *šu*]-*mu* (*ša Sîn-aḫḫē-erība*)
20'	*a* has *ik-ri-bi-š*[*u*]; *c* has [*i-šim-mu*]-*ú*

RESTORATIONS

Following is a list of parallel passages in Cylinders A and B on which
restorations in Cylinder C are based. Parallel passages for preserved
portions in Cylinder C are not normally cited.

4	Cyl. B 4	6	Cyl. B 6
5	Cyl. B 4f.	8	Cyl. A 18, Cyl. B 7

9	Cyl. A 19, Cyl. B 21	6′	Cyl. A 16 and 19, Cyl. B 27
10	Cyl. B 8	7′	Cyl. A 20, Cyl. B 25
11	Cyl. A 3–5, Cyl. B 9	8′	Cyl. A 20, Cyl. B 25f.
13	Cf. Cyl. B 12	14′f.	Cyl. A 30
14	Cyl. B 13	16′	Cyl. A 36, Cyl. B 39
15	Cyl. A 7, Cyl. B 14	17′	Cyl. A 37, Cyl. B 39f.
20	Cyl. A 12f., Cyl. B 17f.	19′	Cyl. A 38, Cyl. B 40
21	Cyl. A 13f.	21′	Cyl. A 40, Cyl. B 42
22	Cyl. A 14f.	22′	Cyl. A 41, Cyl. B 42
3′	Cyl. A 16f.		

COMMENTARY

2 $^{1\acute{u}}$[x] x *É-šár-ra*. This epithet does not otherwise appear in the inscriptions of Sîn-šarra-iškun, Aššurbanipal, Esarhaddon, or Sennacherib.

4 *tab-šu-ut*. Difficult. The obvious interpretation is as an epithet of the king: '... of (Ištar).' In such a case, it is a hapex legomenon. If it is an epithet of Ištar it could be connected with *t/sabsūtu*, 'midwife,' on which see W. von Soden, AfO, 18 (1957–8), 119–21, and cf. *sa-ab-su-ut*(!)-*ta-ka ra-bi-tu a-na-ku mu-še-niq*(!)-*ta-ka* (of Ištar of Arbail) 4R 68 iii 23–25 (reference and reading courtesy R. D. Biggs). But the lack of epithets for any other god in this passage and the position of the word in the sentence render this interpretation dubious.

5 *maš-ši-ia*. Without fuller knowledge of the exact relationship between Sîn-šarra-iškun and Aššur-etel-ilāni one cannot be certain whether this word should be translated literally 'my twins' (see W. von Soden, AHw, p. 631) or figuratively 'my real brother(s).' Cf. von Soden, ZA, 58 (1967), 252, and Borger, WZKM, 55 (1959), 73, n. 41.

6 é.bar = *šangu* ŠL 324, 270 and cf. Cyl. B 6.

10 x ru. Can one take this as the end of *nap-ḫ]a-ru*? For a similar form cf. *nap-ḫa-ri kaspi* TMH 2, 257:8.

12 This line is widely spaced in *e* and I doubt that anything more than *ušatmiḫ* is missing in the break (cf. Cyl. A 6f. and Cyl. B 10). If this is correct, then there may have been room in *c* for both lines 11 and 12 on one line (note that line 12 is relatively crowded in *c*).

14 *a-a-ru*. Cf. AHw sub *ajjaru* III and CAD sub *ajaru* D. Until now the word was attested only in synonym lists and PN s.

20–22 I have restored exactly the way the phrases appear in Cyl. A
        although there may not have been room for the full titulary of
        each king and variant sign forms may have been used.

2'   Streck, Asb., p. CCXI restores [bēlu]-ú-tu but this is redundant
        in connection with the end of the line. In any case, the parallels
        cited by Streck are not in the same context.

3'   The DN s here are obviously somewhat different than those in
        Cyl. A. I have made a guess as to which deities were men-
        tioned.
        ki-mu-ú-a i-tap-pa-lu. Cf. CAD I/2 (A), p. 161b.

15'   ši-kit-ta-šú ú-[rab-bi(?)]. Cf. Streck, Asb., pp. 272–4:13f. and
        276:13f.

17'ff. mušarû, 'cylinder.' See R. S. Ellis, Foundation Deposits in An-
        cient Mesopotamia (Yale Near Eastern Researches, 2; New
        Haven and London, 1968), p. 151, to which add these examples.

26'   ina šapal ... kamêš. Cf. Borger, Esarh., p. 99:56.

27'   pirḫa(! text: BALA)-šú. Cf. Cyl. A 44 and OIP 2, p. 139:71f.

ADDENDA

Possibly another inscription of Sîn-šarra-iškun is represented by YOS
9, 80. Borger and Stephens independently (cf. Borger, Einleitung I,
p. 100) suggested this was an inscription of Ninurta-tukulti-Ashur.
But it is more likely that it is an inscription of Sîn-šarra-iškun as
Landsberger suggested in a private communication to Borger (I am
indebted to Professor Borger for this information). Cf. CAD I/2 (A),
p. 171 sub apītu, last reference. W. W. Hallo and his assistant Mr C.
Hoffman kindly collated line 5 but they concluded that there are
difficulties with reading either royal name.

Another duplicate of Cylinder B is BM 123414 published by A. R.
Millard, Iraq, 30 (1968), pl. XXVI. I am indebted to Professor Borger
for drawing this identification to my attention.

To ina bi-rit maš-ši-ia in line 5 compare i-na bi-ri-it a-aḫ-ḫe-ia, Kraus
and Frankena, AbB 2, 86:25. This reference was kindly provided by
Professor R. F. G. Sweet.

To the bibliography in n. 3 add: R. Borger, Or., N.S., 38 (1969),
237–9.

To n. 6 add: Dr E. Sollberger has examined the fragments and kindly
informed me that c probably belongs to b. If so, d could not belong
to b but could belong to a. I wish to thank Dr Sollberger for this
information.

Bibliography of
Professor Winnett's
Publications

AASOR *Annual of the American Schools of Oriental Research*
BASOR *Bulletin of the American Schools of Oriental Research*
BCSBS *Bulletin of the Canadian Society of Biblical Studies*
IDB *The Interpreter's Dictionary of the Bible*
JAOS *Journal of the American Oriental Society*
MW *The Moslem World*

The Paradise of Eden (Toronto, 1929)

A Study of the Lihyanite and Thamudic Inscriptions (Toronto, 1937)

'The Founding of Hebron,' BCSBS 3 (1937), 21–9

'Allah before Islam,' MW 28 (1938), 239–48

'Notes on the Lihyanite and Thamudic Inscriptions,' *Le Muséon* 51 (1938), 299–310

'The Place of the Minaeans in the History of Pre-Islamic Arabia,' BASOR 73 (1939), 3–9

'The Daughters of Allah,' MW 30 (1940), 113–30

'Primitive Arabian and Semitic Religion,' *The Review of Religion* 4 (1940), 282–5

'A Monotheistic Himyarite Inscription,' BASOR 83 (1941), 22–5

'References to Jesus in Pre-Islamic Arabic Inscriptions,' MW 31 (1941), 341–53

'The Prophet as Poet,' BCSBS 7 (1943), 8–9

'A Himyaritic Inscription from the Persian Gulf Region, BASOR 102 (1946), 4–6

'A Brief Comment on Genesis 37:22, BCSBS 12 (1947), 13

'A Himyarite Bronze Tablet,' BASOR 110 (1948), 23–5

The Mosaic Tradition (Toronto, 1949)

'Abraham, the Friend of God,' BCSBS 15 (1950), 1–14

'An Epigraphical Expedition to

North-eastern Transjordan,'
BASOR 122 (1951), 49–52
'Report of the Director of the
School in Jerusalem,' BASOR
124 (1951), 4–7
'Excavations at Dibon in Moab,
1950–1951,' BASOR 125 (1952),
7–20
Review of G. Ryckmans, *Les
religions arabes préislamiques*
(2nd ed., Louvain, 1951), in
JAOS 72 (1952), 178
Review of *Corpus inscriptionum
semiticarum*, Pars quinta, In-
scriptiones saracenicas con-
tiens, Tomus I, fasciculus I:
Inscriptiones safaiticae (Paris,
1951), in JAOS 73 (1953), 40–3
'Minaean Records,' in *Twentieth
Century Encyclopedia of Reli-
gious Knowledge*, edited by
L. A. Loetscher, vol. 2 (Grand
Rapids, 1955), 740
'Phoenicia, Phoenicians,' in
*Twentieth Century Encyclope-
dia of Religious Knowledge*,
edited by L. A. Loetscher, vol.
2 (Grand Rapids, 1955), 878
Editor (with W. F. Albright) of
AASOR 29–30 (1955)
Editor of AASOR 31 (1956)
Safaitic Inscriptions from Jordan
(Toronto, 1957)
'*Ketuvot tamudiyot min ha-negev*,'
ᶜ*Atiqot* 2 (1958), 130–3
'Why the West Should Stop Sup-
porting Israel,' *Maclean's*
(January 18, 1958), 8, 47–8
Editor of AASOR 32–33 (1958)
'Report of the Director of the
School in Jerusalem,' BASOR
156 (1959), 4–7

'Thamudic Inscriptions from the
Negev,' ᶜ*Atiqot* 2 (1959), 146–9
Review of R. L. Bowen, Jr., and
F. P. Albright, *Archaeological
Discoveries in South Arabia*
(Baltimore, 1958), in *Amer-
ican Journal of Archaeology* 63
(1959), 318–20
'Nord-est de la Transjordane,' in
'Chronique archéologique,'
Revue biblique 67 (1960), 244–5
Annotated Bibliography on Pre-
Islamic Arabia in *The Amer-
ican Historical Association's
Guide to Historical Literature*,
edited by G. F. Howe (New
York, 1961), section F, nos.
11–16, 31, 40, 65–70, 125–9,
166–70, 189, 199, 200, 234–9,
249, 250, 264, 265
Review of K. Cragg, *Sandals at
the Mosque: Christian Presence
amid Islam* (New York, 1959),
in *Canadian Journal of The-
ology* 7 (1961), 139–40
'Bronze,' in IDB, edited by G. A.
Buttrick, vol. 1 (New York
and Nashville, 1962), 467
'Copper,' in IDB, edited by G. A.
Buttrick, vol. 1 (New York
and Nashville, 1962), 680
'Iron,' in IDB, edited by G. A.
Buttrick, vol. 2 (New York
and Nashville, 1962), 725–6
'Metallurgy,' in IDB, edited by
G. A. Buttrick, vol. 3 (New
York and Nashville, 1962),
366–8
'Mining,' in IDB, edited by G. A.
Buttrick, vol. 3 (New York
and Nashville, 1962), 384–5
'A Fragment of an Early Moabite

Inscription from Kerak,' with W. L. Reed, BASOR 172 (1963), 1–9

'The Excavations at Dibon (Dhībân) in Moab: Part 1: The First Campaign, 1950–1951,' AASOR 36–37 (1964), 1–30, plates 1–25

'Re-examining the Foundations,' *Journal of Biblical Literature* 84 (1965), 1–19

Ancient Records from North Arabia, with W. L. Reed (Toronto, 1970)